New Mexico

Nancy Harbert

Photography by Michael Freeman, Paul Chesley,
and Kerrick James

COMPASS AMERICAN GUIDES
An Imprint of Fodor's Travel Publications

New Mexico
Fourth Edition

Compass American Guides, Inc., 5332 College Ave., Suite 201, Oakland, CA 94618, USA
ISBN 0-679-00438-6

Managing Editor: Kit Duane
Editors: Kit Duane, Julia Dillon
      Cheryl Koehler
Designers: Christopher Burt, David Hurst
Map Design: Mark Stroud, Moon Street Cartography
First published in 1992 by Compass American Guides, Inc.
5332 College Avenue, Suite 201, Oakland, CA 94618, USA

Production house: Twin Age Ltd., Hong Kong   Manufactured in China
Cover: Acoma Pueblo, New Mexico

10 9 8 7 6 5 4 3 2 1

ACKNOWLEDGMENTS

GRATEFUL APPRECIATION IS DUE to Fritz Thompson, a Wagon Mound native son, for his editorial comments and boundless knowledge of New Mexico's hidden treasures shared over numerous green chile enchilada lunches. Thanks also goes to Phoebe Latimer for her unwavering support, to Martin Frentzel for his professional guidance, and to Judge Tibo Chavez for sharing his knowledge of herbal medicines.

Recognition also goes to Kit Duane, my editor, for her patience and encouragement.

COMPASS AMERICAN GUIDES wishes to acknowledge the Museum of Fine Arts, Boston for the photo on p. 83; the Museum of New Mexico for photos on pp. 21, 29, 37, 60, 66, 92, 96, 115, 119, 163, 167, 182, 187, 193, 205, 206, 207, 242-243, 244, 251, 253, 273; the Albuquerque Museum for the photo on p. 41; and the U.S. Forest Service for the photo on p. 229. The publisher also wishes to thank the following photographers for the use of their work: Paul Chesley, pp. 3, 14, 72, 73, 84, 161, 171, 191, 194, 198, 199, 202, 214, 215, 247, 260, 264, 265, 283, 292, 298; Mark Downey p. 42; Kerrick James, cover, pp. 44, 54, 55, 68-69, 77, 85, 93, 102, 104, 105, 113, 120, 140, 141, 151, 153, 156, 213, 223, 238-239, 256; Eduardo Fuss, pp. 51, 158-159, 274-277; Mark Middlebrook, p. 71; Jack Olson, p. 26.

To Jessica and Jack Harbert.
I hope this book brings you both to New Mexico.

C O N T E N T S

Literary Excerpts

Topical Essays

Maps

NEW MEXICO GUIDEBOOK
SECTION DIVISIONS

NORTH-CENTRAL

SANTA FE-TAOS

NORTHWEST

NORTHEAST

ALBUQUERQUE

ALBUQUERQUE ENVIRONS

SOUTHWEST

SOUTHEAST

Aztec
Farmington
Chama
Raton
Cimarron
Clayton
Taos
Los Alamos
SANTA FE
Las Vegas
Gallup
Tucumcari
Grants
Albuquerque
Santa Rosa
Clovis
Portales
Socorro
Roswell
Ruidoso
Truth or Consequences
Cloudcroft
Silver City
Alamogordo
Lordsburg
Carlsbad
Deming
Las Cruces
El Paso
Ciudad Juárez

N
W   E
S

0   50   100 Miles
0   50   100   150 Kilometers

(following pages) Artist Ernest Blumenschein's studio in Taos is a perfect representation of the now popular "Santa Fe Style."

OVERVIEW

ALBUQUERQUE

New Mexico's largest city, **Albuquerque,** flanks the Rio Grande, stretching between the petroglyph-etched boulders of the **Seven Sisters** and the red-tawny slopes of the **Sandia Mountains.** Museums and galleries reflect the city's rich history and its long-established ethnic mix of Native American, Anglo, and Hispanic. In historic **Old Town,** 300-

year-old adobe buildings line the narrow streets, and the smell of hot tortillas wafts from restaurants on the old Plaza. *Pages 34-78.*

NORTH-CENTRAL & SANTA FE

Edged by the rugged **Sangre de Cristo** and **San Juan mountains** and the softer **Jemez range,** north-central New Mexico contains much that has made the state famous. **Santa Fe,** capital city and birthplace of Southwestern style and cuisine attracted painter Georgia O'Keeffe, who admired the brilliant light. She later immortalized the purply brown sandstone cliffs at **Abiquiu,** as well as **Taos Pueblo,** a multi-storied adobe structure occupied since 1350. The low-key, high-altitude **town of Taos** draws artists and skiers. *Pages 80-147.*

NORTHWESTERN NEW MEXICO

American Indian influence is greater here than anywhere in the state. About 1,000 years ago, Anasazi built massive rock and mortar buildings like **Pueblo Bonito** in **Chaco Canyon.** Today, much of the land belongs to the Navajo, Apache, and Pueblo, and **Gallup** is known as the Heart of American Indian Country. The region's landscape of sandstone bluffs and meadows is punctuated by the **Bisti Badlands**, a surreal dreamscape of mushroom-shaped stone; and **Shiprock**, a jagged, vertical shaft towering 7,000 feet above the desert. *Pages 148-177.*

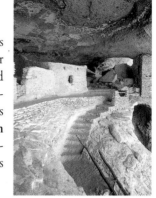

SOUTHWESTERN NEW MEXICO
This wild and beautiful corner of the state offers cactus prairie, forested mountains, and, further south, vast stretches of desolate desert basins. Old railroad towns like **Deming** line what is today Interstate 10; further north, historic mining towns like **Silver City** lie in the foothills of the **Mogollon Mountains**, where Indians built cliff dwellings centuries ago. The **Rio Grande** divides the state's southwest and southeast regions. *Pages 178-216*

SOUTHEASTERN NEW MEXICO
Most of the southeastern region comprises vast prairies, even sandy desert, as at **White Sands National Monument**. **Lincoln National Forest**, with its pine-covered mountains and resort towns—many clustered around the **Rio Ruidoso**—stands out here. No doubt the area's major attraction, **Carlsbad Caverns** is a three-mile maze of vaulted rooms furnished with grand obelisks and icicles of stone. *Pages 218-247.*

NORTHEASTERN NEW MEXICO
Here in the high plains, windmills and ranch houses dot these grama grasslands, where cattle outnumber people. The otherwise flat landscape is interrupted by a few ancient cinder cones such as **Capulin Volcano,** not far from the Colorado border. At the foot of the **Sangre de Cristo Mountains, Las Vegas** is a treasure trove of Victorian architectural styles, thanks to a wave of high-minded 19th-century settlers. *Pages 248-273.*

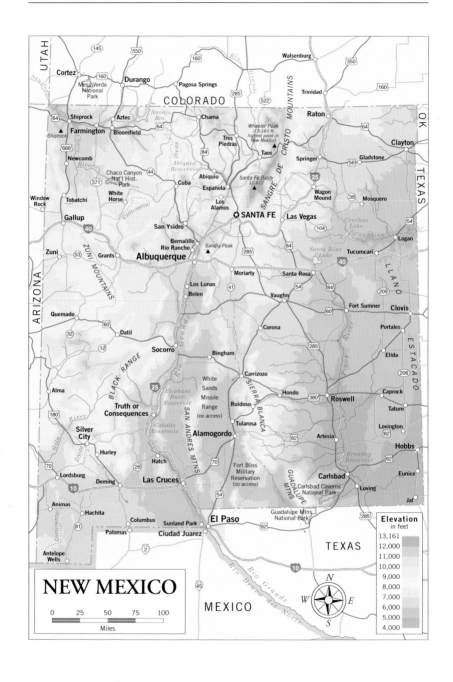

UTAH

COLORADO

ARIZONA

TEXAS

OK

TEXAS

MEXICO

Cortez
Mesa Verde National Park
Durango
Pagosa Springs
Walsenburg
Trinidad
Shiprock
Aztec
Bloomfield
Chama
Raton
Clayton
Farmington
Shiprock
Newcomb
Tres Piedras
Wheeler Peak (13,161 ft. highest point in New Mexico)
Gladstone
Springer
Taos
Chaco Canyon Nat'l Hist. Park
Cuba
Abiquiu
Santa Fe Baldy 12,622
Wagon Mound
Mosquero
Window Rock
Tohatchi
White Horse
Espanola
Los Alamos
SANTA FE
Las Vegas
Logan
Gallup
San Ysidro
Conchas Lake
Zuni
Grants
Bernalillo
Rio Rancho
Sandia Peak
Tucumcari
Albuquerque
Santa Rosa Lake
Moriarty
Santa Rosa
Los Lunas
Belen
Vaughn
Fort Sumner
Clovis
Quemado
Datil
Corona
Portales
Socorro
Bingham
Elida
Alma
White Sands Missile Range (no access)
Carrizozo
Caprock
Truth or Consequences
Elephant Butte Reservoir
Ruidoso
Hondo
Roswell
Tatum
Silver City
Caballo Reservoir
Tularosa
Alamogordo
Artesia
Lovington
Hobbs
Hurley
Hatch
Fort Bliss Military Reservation (no access)
Brantley Reservoir
Lordsburg
Deming
Las Cruces
Carlsbad
Carlsbad Caverns National Park
Eunice
Loving
Jal
Animas
Hachita
Columbus
Sunland Park
El Paso
Guadalupe Mtns National Park
Palomas
Ciudad Juarez
Antelope Wells
TEXAS

NEW MEXICO

0   25   50   75   100
Miles

Elevation
in feet
13,161
12,000
11,000
10,000
9,000
8,000
7,000
6,000
5,000
4,000

N
W   E
S

SANGRE DE CRISTO MOUNTAINS
ZUNI MOUNTAINS
BLACK RANGE
SAN ANDRES MTNS
SIERRA BLANCA
GUADALUPE MTNS
LLANO ESTACADO
Navajo Res.
Abiquiu Reservoir
Rio Grande
Continental
Gila River
Rio Grande del Norte

INTRODUCTION

NEW MEXICO'S MAGIC HAS BEEN INTRIGUING VISITORS FOR CENTURIES. Its natural beauty immediately captivates those who see it, and its elusive, indefinable character enriches all those who let it in. Spacious skies and vistas, magical light, and the sense of this place's *purity* have all been named as the latent quality that has attracted travelers and settlers, artists and scientists, who've come in search of treasure, tangible and intangible.

In prehistoric times, Native Americans hunted game in New Mexico's mountains and farmed along its river banks. Pueblo Indians expressed their reverential relationship with the land through flat-roofed earthen architecture, drawings on rock faces, and rhythmic chants and dances. Spanish explorers followed, first in search of gold, then souls. The two cultures clashed, often violently. But eventually they came to tolerate each other and even to share their traditions. Pueblo Indians passed on their innovative uses for chile, beans, and corn, the main ingredients of what ironically has come to be known as Mexican food. The Spanish passed on their skill at metal work, which the Indians incorporated into intricate jewelry.

In the later half of the 19th century, determined groups of "Anglo" settlers began arriving via the Santa Fe Trail, bringing to New Mexico a third culture— Victorian, technologically emerging. In the early twentieth century, a new wave of immigrants of Italian, Lebanese, German, Irish, and Russian descent—also "Anglos" in New Mexican parlance—came to set up shops or work in coal, silver, and gold mines across the state. The Anglos may have been the last of the three main cultural groups to arrive, but they became the most influential. They mined the mountains for gold and precious metals, and uncovered vast deposits of coal, oil, and natural gas. They brought the railroad, the highway, and the atomic bomb. They came to capture the state's magic—on canvas, in photographs, in their souls.

The state's Spanish community, once comprised mainly of descendants of the original settlers who came via Mexico, has expanded to include thousands of new Hispanic, or Spanish-speaking, immigrants from Central and South America. Today's Hispanics are responsible for a vitality and sensuality that has become part of New Mexico's mystique. Religion still permeates this culture and nearly every town honors its patron saint once a year in an exuberant fiesta. This sensitivity carries through in the imperfect sloping walls of adobe buildings, hand-punched tin-work, and strains of melodic *corridas* (love songs) that waft from open doorways. Carved *bultos* and intricately painted *retablos* once adorned only church altars and walls, but now are found in gift shops and galleries.

Today, New Mexico's Indians often straddle two worlds: teaching math to fifth graders or arguing the First Amendment before a federal judge during the week, then returning to the reservation on weekends to participate in traditional dances where they exchange their button-down clothes for feathered headdresses and moccasins.

The state's landscape is as varied as its cultures. The Rio Grande is the lifeblood for much of this arid land, and serves as the natural east-west dividing line as it snakes through the mountainous north, skirting Albuquerque and providing the lifeline for the agricultural southwest before flowing into Texas at El Paso. Away from the river, pine and spruce forests blanket much of northern New Mexico. There you'll find pristine trout streams, bountiful hunting grounds, and world-class ski slopes. A small section of the vast Navajo Reservation covers the northwestern corner of the state, and continues into neighboring Arizona. In the southwest is the 3.3-million-acre Gila National Forest, once home to the Mimbres Indians, known for their distinctive black-on-white pottery. East of the mountains lies the irrigated Mesilla Valley, with acres of green chile, cotton, and onions.

On the vast plains of eastern New Mexico, lumbering herds of cattle and bands of sheep share windswept grasslands. Dryland farming has prospered in pockets of the Llano Estacado (Staked Plain), a western extension of the Great Plains that covers much of eastern New Mexico. To the west rise the Sacramento Mountains, home to the Mescalero Apaches. One of the world's greatest natural wonders spreads out in massive rooms beneath a limestone ridge at Carlsbad Caverns.

New Mexico's cities are small, with the exception of Albuquerque, which holds one-third of the state's people and serves as its economic and education center. A cursory glance might fail to distinguish it from any other spread-out Western metropolis, but most residents agree it's an unusually congenial place to live: traffic jams are few, winters are mild and summers dry, and friendly smiles abound.

Sixty miles north of Albuquerque, the state capital of Santa Fe huddles in the shelter of the Sangre de Cristo Mountains. Here, narrow streets wind among centuries-old adobe buildings, and dirt roads are considered assets in the city's nicer neighborhoods. Students of acupuncture, massage, and natural healing live among long-time Hispanic residents and Indian artisans.

It's not a coincidence that New Mexico is known as the Land of Enchantment. The spells it casts are many and varied. For those who haven't yet experienced it, all it takes is to cross its borders to enter New Mexico's magical embrace.

El Malpais National Monument region. (Paul Chesley)

H I S T O R Y

SHALLOW SEAS COVERED THE AREA NOW KNOWN as New Mexico for most of the Paleozoic Era, from 570 million to 245 million years ago. When they dried up they left behind brachiopods, trilobites, corals, and crinoid stems fossilized in limestone and shale. In southeastern New Mexico, the Capitan Reef grew to surround the Delaware Basin, a 10,000-square-mile sea. Vast deposits of oil and gas remain where the basin once was, along with gypsum, potash, and salt. During this time, volcanic explosions created mountain ranges and coated the earth with layers of lava that hardened into a jagged black landscape.

Eighty-million years ago, the Rocky Mountains jutted into existence, the southern end spilling into northern New Mexico. The seas dried up, camels, bears, large cats, and wild dogs replaced dinosaurs, and some of the state took on a lunar appearance of rugged mountains and vast plains covered with boulders and gravel.

Two fault zones cut across New Mexico from north to south. About 25 million years ago, the tension between the faults caused a long sliver of the Earth's crust to drop down in between them. This trough, known as the Rio Grande Rift, would eventually carry the waters of the Rio Grande from its headwaters in the Colorado Rockies 1,885 miles to the Gulf of Mexico. The west side of the rift, where the crust had been stretched thin, erupted with violent volcanic explosions. One created the Jemez Mountains, centered by the 12-mile-diameter Valle Grande caldera. Another fracture extended from present-day Quemado almost to Clayton, which produced Capulin, a volcanic mountain in northeast New Mexico, and El Malpais (the Badlands) lava flow south of Grants. Such widespread volcanic activity left behind rich mineral deposits scattered throughout the region, such as copper, lead, and zinc, as well as numerous geothermal pockets, some of which bubble to the surface as hot springs.

Beginning two million years ago during the ice ages, glaciers covered the state's highest mountains, and spread as far south as present-day Sierra Blanca. Later, large lakes filled basins in closed valleys in southern and central New Mexico. One of these bodies of water, Lake Lucero, evaporated, and winds blew its gypsum sediments into 50-foot drifts, now known as White Sands. Glaciers probably still hung down from mountaintops and a few remaining volcanoes were still blowing their tops when the state's first human visitors arrived as early as 20,000 years ago.

■ EARLY INHABITANTS

Grasslands and forests covered much of New Mexico when big-game hunters followed mammoth, mastodon, sloth, bison, antelope, camel, and horse driven south by ice age glaciers that moved across much of North America. These early hunters chipped scrapers and spear points from flint, obsidian, jasper, and chert, then staked out their prey at watering holes.

About 12,000 years ago, the Clovis people regularly pursued the giant bison throughout southeastern New Mexico. Hundreds of miles away in the Sandia Mountains, the Sandia people, whom historians say were unrelated to the Clovis, hunted the same animals. Spear points up to three inches long and more finely honed than those of the Clovis or Sandia cultures were crafted in northeastern New Mexico by the Folsom people, appearing 1,000 years later than the earlier hunters. Mysteriously, no bones of these early people have been found, only the skeletons of prey pierced with their spear points.

As the glaciers melted, New Mexico warmed up and dried out. Piñon and juniper forests thinned, drought-resistant grama grass replaced lush grasslands, and cactus, mesquite, and creosote bush prospered. Large lakes near present-day Estancia and Lordsburg evaporated. Mastodons and mammoths disappeared, perhaps due to lack of food, disease, and over-zealous hunters.

■ THE INDIANS

The big-game hunters moved on, most likely to the Great Plains where they pursued smaller animals. They were replaced in New Mexico, beginning in A.D. 900, by the Desert Culture, whose hunters spread across western New Mexico in pursuit of elk, deer, antelope, turkey, and rodents. They fished in streams and gathered nuts, berries, the thirst-quenching fruit of cactus, and seeds. Noticing that seeds left in place grew into plants, these people soon added farming to their hunting and gathering. Later, because it was easier to care for crops by staying in one place, they established permanent settlements.

Two primary groups grew from the initial Desert Culture. In southwestern New Mexico, the Mogollon learned from their southern neighbors in present-day Mexico how to cultivate corn, squash, and beans, and how to fashion pottery. One branch, the Mimbres Indians, developed exquisitely stylized black-on-white designs based on birds and animals, as well as meticulous geometric patterns. The Mogollon's first homes were oval pits dug four feet into the earth, covered with timber and dirt roofs. Built close together, these pit houses formed villages. In northwestern New Mexico, the Anasazi culture borrowed agricultural and pottery techniques from the Mogollon, but developed more slowly. At their peak, however, the Anasazi displayed a sophistication far beyond that of their predecessors. By A.D. 900-1000, the Anasazi were living in stone dwellings built into the sides of high cliffs, and in free-standing multi-storied apartment buildings of finely fitting rock slabs held together with mud mortar. At Chaco Canyon, they designed a system of dams and ditches that directed the flow of water into fields. Roads connected far-flung pueblos. Men wore ornamental jewelry made of shell, turquoise, and other gemstones, and women wove textiles from cotton they grew in their fields. These ingenious people were the ancestors of today's Pueblo Indians.

Between A.D. 1000 and 1500, Athabascan-speaking tribes, including the Navajo and Apache, began making their way down from Canada into the Southwest. Decidedly different from the sedentary, agrarian Anasazi, the nomadic Navajo were adept traders, exchanging baskets, animal hides, and jerky with Pueblo Indians for corn, cotton cloth, and turquoise. Eventually, the Navajo built hogans, circular mud-plastered dwellings, and learned from the Pueblo Indians how to grow corn, beans, squash, and melons. They never completely gave up their wandering ways, even as they herded across the countryside small bands of sheep and goats, which were introduced by the Spanish. Families lived in clustered hogans, but villages as we think of them did not develop.

When the Apaches arrived in New Mexico, they separated into bands and never considered themselves a single tribe. The bands staked out their territory: the Jicarilla Apaches wandered across northern New Mexico and southern Colorado and learned how to cultivate corn from the pueblos; the Mescaleros stayed within southeastern New Mexico, and the Chiricahuas, who later became known for their fighting skills, roamed throughout southwestern New Mexico and southeastern Arizona. Like the Navajo, the Apache hunted bison and deer and gathered roots, nuts, and berries. Broad-faced with high cheekbones and a muscular physique, Apaches lived in thatched *wickiups* and animal-skin tepees. The women in the Mescalero bands roasted the meat of the mescal plant (an agave cactus also known as a century plant), wove baskets from its fibers, and tanned buckskin and buffalo hides into silky smooth shirts and knee-high boots for the men and straight shifts decorated with beads for themselves.

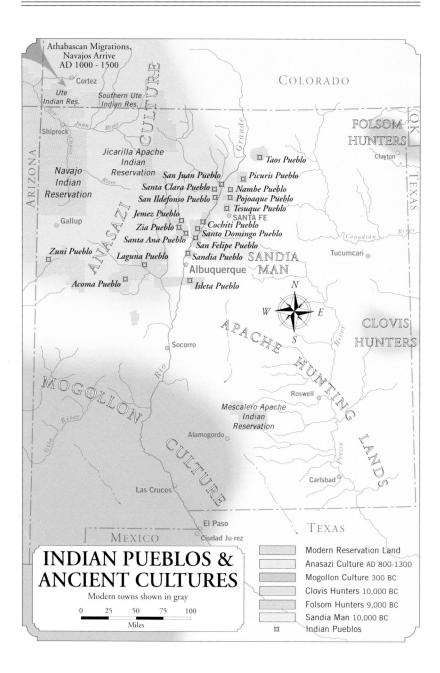

Athabascan Migrations,
Navajos Arrive
AD 1000 - 1500

Cortez

Ute
Indian Res.

Southern Ute
Indian Res.

COLORADO

Shiprock

FOLSOM
HUNTERS

Clayton

ARIZONA

Navajo
Indian
Reservation

Jicarilla Apache
Indian
Reservation

San Juan Pueblo
Santa Clara Pueblo
San Ildefonso Pueblo
Jemez Pueblo
Zia Pueblo
Santa Ana Pueblo
Laguna Pueblo

Gallup

Zuni Pueblo

Acoma Pueblo

Taos Pueblo

Picuris Pueblo

Nambe Pueblo
Pojoaque Pueblo
Tesuque Pueblo
SANTA FE
Cochiti Pueblo
Santo Domingo Pueblo
San Felipe Pueblo
Sandia Pueblo
Albuquerque

Isleta Pueblo

SANDIA
MAN

Canadian

River

Tucumcari

N

W   E

S

APACHE

HUNTING

LANDS

CLOVIS
HUNTERS

Socorro

MOGOLLON

River

Gila

Roswell

Mescalero Apache
Indian
Reservation

Alamogordo

CULTURE

Pecos

Las Cruces

Carlsbad

El Paso

MEXICO   Ciudad Juárez

TEXAS

INDIAN PUEBLOS &
ANCIENT CULTURES

Modern towns shown in gray

0   25   50   75   100
Miles

Modern Reservation Land
Anasazi Culture AD 800-1300
Mogollon Culture 300 BC
Clovis Hunters 10,000 BC
Folsom Hunters 9,000 BC
Sandia Man 10,000 BC
Indian Pueblos

At the same time a settled and sophisticated Pueblo culture thrived. When Spanish explorers arrived in the 1500s they found nearly 80 pueblos (many of these multi-storied) scattered along the Rio Grande and along adjacent streams to the west.

■ SPANISH EXPLORERS

The lure of gold and silver initially drew Spanish explorers to New Mexico. In 1521, after conquering the great Aztec Empire of Mexico, Spanish officials heard from the Aztecs rumors of seven cities in the uncharted lands to the north, laden with gold and other riches. The story wasn't too different from a Spanish legend dating to the eighth century, in which seven bishops, fleeing Spain after it was conquered by the Moors, sailed westward until they reached a land where each set up a church, and each church became fabulously wealthy. The legend told of streets paved in gold, houses bedecked with sapphires and turquoise, and natives so weighed down in diamonds and other valuable minerals they could barely walk. The similarities between the Spanish and Aztec myths propelled the conquistadors northward.

In 1539, a party of adventurers went looking for the seven cities. The group was led by Fray Marcos de Niza and by an extraordinary Moorish slave by the name of Estevanico (who had survived the wreck of a Spanish ship off the coast of Florida and made his way to Mexico through uncharted territory by convincing hostile Indians he was a God). Estevanico went ahead of the Niza party as an advance scout and was instructed to send back crosses to signal his discoveries: small ones representing insignificant finds and large ones for something of value. Before the main party had entered New Mexico, a cross "as high as a man" came back to the friar. The expedition hurried ahead, only to be told that Estevanico had been killed after entering Hawikuh, a Zuni village. Undaunted, de Niza proceeded, but was refused entry to the pueblo, forcing him to view it from afar. His account to Antonio de Mendoza, viceroy of New Spain, as Mexico then was called, told of terraced, stone houses in a settlement comprised of seven villages, the total larger than Mexico City.

Within a year, Francisco Vásquez de Coronado was traveling north, leading a slow-moving caravan of 336 horsemen equipped with 559 horses, some of their wives and families, a few priests, and 100 Indians who tended small herds of cattle and sheep. They left Compostela, New Spain, on February 22, 1540, exactly 192 years before George Washington was born. Six months later, the entourage arrived at Hawikuh only to find small villages of mud huts.

Disappointed but not discouraged, Coronado headed east where he wintered at Alcanfor, known later as Kuaua, a pueblo on the Rio Grande near present-day Bernalillo. The following spring, he continued his eastward drive, this time in search of Quivira, described—by a Pawnee slave whom the Spaniards named El Turco because he looked like a Turk—as another rich land with gold-paved streets and golden water jugs. Coronado's journey ended near Lyons, Kansas, at the grass huts of the Wichita Indians. A copper plate hung around the neck of the tribe's chief, and no gold was in sight. Furious with El Turco's deception, Coronado ordered the Indian's death, then returned to Alcanfor across the plains of eastern New Mexico. After another cold winter at the pueblo, the expedition returned empty-handed to New Spain, where Coronado stood trial for defrauding his country of immeasurable wealth and of abusing the natives. He was cleared, but never recovered his pride or his status. Coronado died in 1556 a broken man.

Coronado party arrives in New Mexico. Mural by Gerald Cassidy, 1921. (Museum of New Mexico)

■ SPANISH SETTLERS

Despite their curiosity about the land to the north of Mexico, the Spaniards' first attempt to settle New Mexico wasn't until the Juan de Oñate Expedition in 1598. Oñate, the son of a wealthy Zacatecas miner, led a caravan consisting of 83 *carretas* hauled by oxen, 129 soldiers, 7,000 head of cattle, a handful of clergy, and 400 settlers, some with families. Following the Rio Grande northward, the weary travelers encountered one pueblo after another, receiving the wide-eyed stares and forced hospitality of Indians whose lives would forever be changed by these newcomers.

Six months after they left Mexico, the thirsty, ragged, and demoralized colonists came to an arable river valley near the confluence of the Rio Grande and Chama River. With the slate-blue Sangre de Cristo Mountains as a distant backdrop, construction began on San Gabriel, New Mexico's first capital. Nearby, residents of San Juan Pueblo guardedly observed the Spaniards, many of whom were disappointed to find no gold jewelry accenting the simple clothing of the Indians.

After establishing the colony, Oñate continued to explore and claim the far reaches of the state for Spain, leaving behind the settlers. But instead of working the soil and planning for a future, they spent their time searching for precious metals. Having failed both as farmers and as miners, the colonists returned to New Spain. Even Oñate admitted defeat and on October 7, 1604, left San Gabriel.

Six years later, Pedro de Peralta led a second group of settlers into the area. With dreams of riches carefully tempered, he chose a high valley tucked into the shadows of the Sangre de Cristo Mountains alongside a narrow stream. De Peralta named the new capital La Villa Real de la Santa Fe de San Francisco de Asis, ultimately shortened to Santa Fe (Holy Faith). An able administrator, De Peralta marked municipal boundaries, assigned house and garden lots to colonists, and supervised construction of government offices, which he forced the Indians to help erect.

As the capital was being established, church officials wasted no time in reciting the virtues of God and the Catholic church to their new neighbors. For the next 70 years, 250 Franciscan friars circulated among the state's pueblos, converting the Indians and forcing them to adopt a Spanish lifestyle. The Spanish required Indian men to wear pants and shirts and Indian women to wear skirts and blouses. Indian

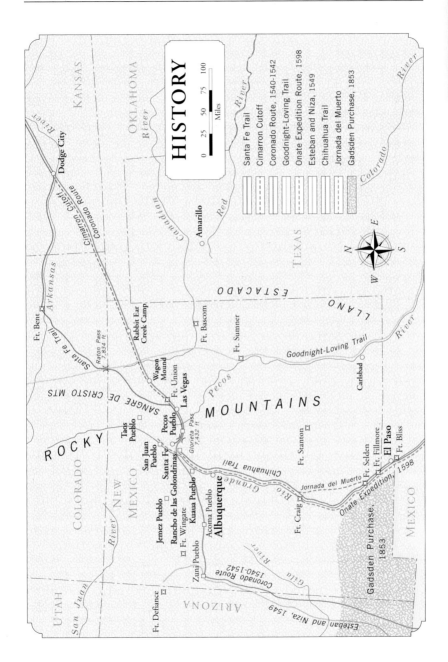

HISTORY

Miles
0 25 50 75 100

Santa Fe Trail
Cimarron Cutoff
Coronado Route, 1540-1542
Goodnight-Loving Trail
Onate Expedition Route, 1598
Esteban and Niza, 1549
Chihuahua Trail
Jornada del Muerto
Gadsden Purchase, 1853

marriages became monogamous, and weddings followed Christian rituals. Indians also were forced to construct large mission churches. Men cut and hauled huge logs for roof beams, while women and children laid adobe bricks, which they plastered with mud and whitewashed with gypsum. The Indians also labored in the workshops, barns, vegetable gardens, and orchards.

By 1680, fed up with the destruction of their culture, the Pueblo Indians prepared to remove the Spanish intruders from their land. On August 10, they attacked settlers, burned mission churches, destroyed holy statues, and killed priests at their altars. Led by Popé, a medicine man from San Juan Pueblo, the angry Indians proved too much for the surprised Spanish, who surrendered the capital 12 days later and marched—frightened and defeated, south to El Paso.

For the next 11 years, the Spanish stayed away from New Mexico, reevaluating their position on the unruly province—was it worth the cost? By 1691, they decided it was and chose Diego de Vargas to recapture the battered land. After two trips, the capital was his and would never again fall into Indian hands.

To ensure harmony, the Spanish made concessions to the Indians. They no longer destroyed sacred objects or punished those who did not attend church. Throughout the eighteenth century, the Spanish and Pueblo Indians settled into a cooperative existence, accepting their differences and even sharing farming, weaving, jewelry-making, and carving techniques. With the province secure, more colonists traveled in caravans north on the Camino Real, also known as the Chihuahua Trail, a 533-mile trade route that connected the Mexican city of Chihuahua with Santa Fe. This was the only trade route that led out of New Mexico, since the Spanish Crown prohibited Santa Fe from trading with the United States.

Lured by vast tracts of land, these homesteaders lived in small settlements and grew corn, wheat, beans, chile, and cotton, and grazed cattle and sheep. Life was basic and hard, made even more challenging by unannounced attacks of Apache, Comanche, Navajo, and Ute Indians who usually made off with livestock and occasionally captured or killed settlers.

JORNADA DEL MUERTO

There's a stretch of desert in southwestern New Mexico that most early explorers would have preferred they'd never seen. This 90-mile expanse of sandy prairie strewn with spiny mesquite trees, black grama grass, and creosote bush starts north of Las Cruces and ends south of Socorro. It has earned the name *Jornada del Muerto*, or Journey of Death. Luckily today no one will double dare you to cross it, because a portion of it is within the confines of White Sands Missile Range, and therefore off limits to adventuresome travelers seeking to relive the horrors of the past.

But in the 17th century, Spanish expeditions regularly crossed this near-waterless portion of El Camino Real. They had the option of taking a more circuitous route, thick with deep arroyos and dense vegetation, along the Rio Grande. Most opted for the direct Jornada because it was easier on their wagons and could save a few days' travel time. In addition to the absence of water, weather extremes ranged from 100 degrees F on summer days to nighttime temperatures of 20 degrees F below 0 in winter. Then there were the bands of Apaches who seldom failed to miss a move of the noisy caravans. Unlike the European travelers, the Apaches knew the location of every water hole and where to hunt jackrabbits, antelope, deer, and bighorn sheep. They also knew when the travelers would be at their weariest and most susceptible to attack.

The first Spaniard to cross the Jornada was Juan de Oñate, who set out in 1598 to colonize New Mexico and cash in on the riches Francisco Vásquez de Coronado failed to find 50 years earlier.

The day before Oñate headed into the unknown desert, a foreboding incident occurred—one of his men, Pedro Robledo, died and was buried at the base of a mountain that today bears his name. Undaunted, the explorer and his entourage left behind the Rio Grande Valley as scheduled. Oñate was hoping the route would curve back to the Rio Grande. Instead, the Jornada passed in between the Caballo and Fra Cristóbal mountain ranges on the west and the San Andrés range to the east, and access to the river was severed.

Within one day, water ran short and animals began to die. The party crept along, spread out for miles. On the evening of the second day, a resourceful dog returned to camp with mud on its paws and muzzle, and probably saved the expedition. One of the soldiers followed pawprints in the sand to a nearby spring, which he named *Los Charcos del Perrillo* (the Pools of the Little Dog). This site became a regular stop on the trail for future travelers, and its name was shortened to Perrillo.

Refreshed, the settlers continued, and Oñate and a few horsemen pushed on ahead. A few days later, they arrived at present-day Socorro, exhausted, dehydrated, and certainly dispirited. Oñate spied the sun-dried adobe walls of Pilabo, a Piro pueblo where he found long-haired men and women planting fields of corn, beans, and squash. They were probably startled at his unkempt appearance, but he nevertheless convinced them to provide corn and water for himself and the other hungry travelers who were behind him.

After Santa Fe was settled in 1610, the Chihuahua Trail became a major trade route between Chihuahua, Mexico, and the New Mexico capital. The Jornada remained the most dreaded portion of the trip. Apaches, increasingly upset by the invasion of their territory and realizing the vulnerability of the wagon trains, increased their attacks. Countless Spaniards died in this God-forsaken expanse. Even Oñate's family wasn't spared. During a return trip to Chihuahua, the governor fought in vain to protect his son, who was killed in an Indian ambush.

After the Pueblo Revolt of 1680, an estimated 2,500 colonists fled the Indians, assembling at present-day El Paso. On their trek across the Jornada del Muerto, as many as 573 Spaniards died before help reached them a few miles north of Perrillo.

Indian raids continued to be the major hazard along the Jornada. In 1854, Fort Craig was built at the northern end of the trail and in 1865 Fort Selden at the southern end. After the railroad arrived in the early 1880s, paralleling the trail, horses and wagons no longer crossed the feared Jornada. Cattle replaced the early travelers, finding plenty to eat in patches of desert grasses.

On July 16, 1945, the Jornada once again became a topic of conversation when the world's first atomic bomb was detonated at its far northeastern edge. Today only military trucks and jeeps travel a network of gravel roads that crisscross the desolate range.

*Tombstone at Ponil Park Cemetery
in Carson National Forest. (Jack Olson)*

■ UNDER MEXICAN RULE

In 1821, Mexico gained its independence from Spain, taking New Mexico along with it. Little changed, except that Mexican leaders allowed Santa Fe to trade with the United States. This new situation proved fortuitous for William Becknell, a famed Indian fighter who arrived in New Mexico amid independence celebrations, laden with brightly colored cloth, kettles, knives, and looking glasses he hoped to exchange with Indians. Instead, the Missouri trader sold his wares to Spanish settlers in Santa Fe and quickly returned to Missouri for more. Thus, the Santa Fe Trail was born.

At first, the trail was used by daring tradesmen, who hauled tools, cloth, shoes, and nails across the prairie. Soon, mountain men were dropping down to trap beaver and hunt deer in New Mexico's mountains. Once word spread of a new frontier, settlers from the United States (Anglos) headed for New Mexico.

For 25 years, Mexico ruled the state from afar; while officials there regarded the Anglos suspiciously, they mostly took a hands-off approach to the province, permitting the New Mexico governor to run the show. In 1846, war broke out between Mexico and the United States, the culmination of a disagreement over the U.S. annexation of Texas the year before, which Mexico refused to recognize. The two countries also disputed Texas' southern boundary—the U.S. claimed it was the Rio Grande, but Mexico deemed it to be the Nueces River. Added to the situation was a growing expansionist movement in the U.S. led by President James Polk, who wished to acquire New Mexico and California.

General Stephen Watts Kearny was given the task of seizing the Southwest, but was warned not to frighten its residents. With the support of 1,600 troops, he crossed the Mountain Branch of the Santa Fe Trail that wound into Colorado before dropping into New Mexico. Kearny met no resistance at Las Vegas, where he announced from a rooftop that New Mexico was now part of the U.S. On August 18, the general peaceably claimed the capital of Santa Fe for his homeland, promising its citizens that their property rights and religion would be respected and that their new country would protect them from hostile Indians.

A month later, Kearny moved on to California, leaving a portion of his Army of the West to manage the transition to the government of the Americans. He appointed trader Charles Bent as New Mexico's first U.S. governor. Another segment of Kearny's troops, led by Col. Alexander Doniphan, marched across the state, signing a peace treaty with Navajo Chief Zarcillos Largos and defeating a Mexican force on the Rio Grande south of Las Cruces at the Battle of Brazito. The troops captured the city of Chihuahua the following February.

Back in New Mexico, however, not everyone wanted to be an American. In mid-January, on a visit to his home in Taos, Governor Bent was scalped and killed by an angry mob of colonists and Indians. The insurgents were swiftly trapped inside a mission church at Taos Pueblo. A bloody battle ended with the capture of the rebels, followed by speedy trials and executions of their leaders. Thus ended opposition to the new government. For the next year, New Mexicans lived by American rules, but did not officially become part of the U.S. until the signing in 1848 of the Treaty of Guadalupe-Hidalgo, which ended the war. Even then, the southwestern corner of the state remained part of Mexico until the Gadsden Purchase in 1853 brought into the U.S. the fertile fields of the Mesilla Valley and the cactus-pocked desert west of the Rio Grande.

■ THE ANGLOS

Across the Santa Fe Trail they came—German-Jewish merchants eager to tap a wide-open market; a French bishop, Jean Baptiste Lamy, prepared to lead the territory's Catholic church; and lawyers seeking to snatch up New Mexico's valuable land and gain a foothold in its fledgling political arena.

Military officials honored Kearny's promise and erected forts across the state. In addition to providing a refuge from marauding Apaches, Comanches, Navajos, and Utes, these army posts also helped to secure stagecoach routes through the Southwest.

When the Civil War broke out in 1861, New Mexico found itself in the middle of the conflict: Mesilla Valley settlers identified with the Confederates, but northern residents sided with the Yankees. Officially, the state remained part of the Union.

In February 1862, Brig. Gen. Henry Sibley led a small Confederate army of 2,600 men up the Rio Grande. Sitting proudly astride their range-raised Texas horses, the soldiers met little resistance until they reached Valverde, a tree-shaded ford on the Rio Grande. Here, on February 21, Sibley was greeted by 3,800 Union troops led by the West Point pal who had served as the best man at his wedding:

Col. Edward Canby, commander of federal forces in New Mexico. Brandishing squirrel rifles, double-barrel shotguns, pistols, and Bowie knives, the Rebels charged across the river, overrunning the inexperienced Union troops. By day's end, Canby's troops were retreating south toward Fort Craig. Sibley led his men northward where they hoisted the Confederate flag above defenseless Albuquerque and Santa Fe. Both cities were devoid of troops, which had shifted north to join forces with Fort Union soldiers and a group of Colorado Volunteers.

A month later, at Glorieta Pass, a wide swath of grassland bordered at either end by steep cliffs, Sibley's army was outsmarted. Major John Chivington and a group of Colorado Volunteers crept behind Confederate lines, destroyed ammunition supplies, burned 73 wagons, and killed 600 horses and mules. Often referred to as the Gettysburg of the West, this battle marked the beginning of New Mexico's expulsion of Confederate troops. Sibley retreated, pursued by Canby and his regrouped army, until Sibley slipped out of the territory.

While U.S. soldiers were preoccupied with the Civil War, New Mexico's Apache and Navajo stepped up their raids on settlers, driving off sheep and cattle. The Indians met little resistance until Gen. James Carlton and his California Column arrived in 1862, following the withdrawal of Confederate troops. After enlisting the help of Col. Kit Carson in negotiating with the Navajo, the general rounded up 400 Mescalero Apache in southern New Mexico and moved them to the new Bosque Redondo Reservation. The reservation spread alongside the cottonwood-shaded banks of the Pecos River near Fort Sumner, a new installation built to supervise the Indians' relocation. Carlton's idea was for the Apaches—warriors and hunters whose nomadic way of life was a part of their self definition—to settle down as farmers.

Kit Carson. (Museum of New Mexico)

Over in western New Mexico and eastern Arizona, Kit Carson was unable to make peace with the semi-nomadic Navajos. Thus, a campaign began in which Carson's men relentlessly burned hogans and butchered sheep, chopped down peach trees, and destroyed fields of corn. Weakened and demoralized, the Indians finally acquiesced in 1864 and agreed to relocate to Bosque Redondo. What followed was the "Long Walk," in which thousands of Navajos trudged across 300 miles of desert covered with yucca, cholla cactus, and hardened lava beds. This brutal march so affected the Indians that they date historical events by referring to whether the events occurred before or after the Long Walk.

At the reservation, 8,500 Navajos failed to mix with their historic enemies, the Apache. Both tribes resented their imprisonment. Disease ravaged their ranks, and the crops were destroyed by parasites. A few years later, Carlton admitted failure. In 1868, the Navajos were given 3.5 million acres amid the red-rock canyons and piñon mesas of their homeland. In 1873, the Mescaleros received 460,177 acres among the forested slopes of the Sacramento Mountains.

To reward the Pueblo Indians for remaining neutral throughout the Civil War, President Abraham Lincoln in 1863 presented each of the 19 pueblos with a black ebony cane crowned with silver and inscribed with his signature. These symbols of

Kitchen of Martínez Hacienda near Taos.

the pueblos' sovereignty, along with silver-tipped staffs given to the pueblos in 1620 by the Spanish government, are brought out every January and ceremoniously conferred upon a new governor as he takes office.

Comanches and Kiowas remained a threat on the eastern plains, raiding caravans and sometimes brutally murdering travelers on the Santa Fe Trail. Chiricahua Apaches, led by Victorio, his son-in-law Nana, and Geronimo, attacked soldiers and looted settlements along the southern Rio Grande and in Arizona. The raids of these nomadic Indians came to an end when the final rails of the Santa Fe Railroad were laid, connecting the territory to the rest of the country. Their horses couldn't keep up with the moving cars, and travelers were safe inside the metal cocoons.

Once the Indian threat was removed, settlers crowded onto trains bound for the vast Southwest territory, where they expanded railroad camps into thriving towns, established enormous sheep and cattle ranches on the eastern plains, and irrigated acres of farmland with annual snowmelt and the water from small streams. Drovers escorted thousands of longhorn cattle up from Texas through the Pecos River Valley on into Colorado, establishing the Goodnight-Loving Trail. Miners arrived to search for gold and to work in the coal mines near Gallup, Raton, and Madrid, as well as the silver and copper mines near Silver City.

Many of New Mexico's immigrants during the late 1800s were the sort who took the law into their hands. Saloons outnumbered churches in many towns, and the law of the smoking gun often prevailed over that of men with badges. Range wars erupted, along with violent struggles for power. Cattle rustlers operated freely, and Anglo lawyers who received their fees in property benefited most in disputes over land-grant boundaries.

■ STATEHOOD

Soon after Stephen Kearny raised the stars and stripes above Santa Fe in 1846, debate began over whether or not New Mexico would be better off as a state or as a territory. But every time the statehood issue reached the halls of Congress, it was defeated. Eastern politicians feared the strong Hispanic influence and uncivilized character of the Southwestern frontier.

That attitude changed after the 1898 Spanish-American War. Determined to demonstrate New Mexico's dedication to the Union, Gov. Miguel Otero called for 340 cowboys to ride with the Rough Riders cavalry unit led by Theodore

Roosevelt. Never did these men, many of Spanish ancestry, hesitate as they sweated and struggled up San Juan Hill on foot after their horses failed to receive a transport to Cuba.

Still it took another 14 years for statehood to finally arrive in 1912. Immediately, New Mexico's powerful politicos jockeyed for seats in the new state legislature and vied for positions in Congress. But most of its nearly 300,000 citizens held onto their own well-rooted ways of life: Pueblo Indians maintained their intimate relationship with Mother Earth, dancing in thanks for bountiful crops and their health, while learning the language and customs that would help them get along in the Anglo world. Hispanics devotedly filled Catholic churches and danced whenever they had a reason to schedule a fiesta—for a wedding or a saint's day.

In the 1920s, New Mexico's clear air and uncluttered landscape attracted a new wave of eastern Anglos, some of whom were sent by their doctors to recover from tuberculosis, and others by the military to establish air bases on the expansive prairie. Another group of Anglo immigrants worked tirelessly to capture the soft red glow of the desert sunsets and the square jaws of New Mexico's native citizens in photographs, on canvas, and in the written word. Once exposed to the state's ever-changing skies, these artists rarely looked elsewhere for their subjects.

An isolated plateau at the edge of the Jemez Mountains, blanketed in volcanic ash and tall pines, in 1943 lured a small group of scientists who worked in secrecy for two years. Families lived in near-seclusion at what had been the Los Alamos Ranch School, a private boys' institution. In the early-morning hours of July 16, 1945, before the parched earth heated up for the day, the result of the scientists' efforts was unearthed amid the cholla and yucca cactus of the Tularosa Basin in central New Mexico: the detonation of the world's first atomic bomb. This event set the state on a direct path toward a nuclear future. Los Alamos National Laboratory, Sandia National Laboratories, and White Sands Missile Range were later created to fabricate and test this potent technology.

Scientists have since mixed with the state's other residents, who continue to alter its makeup. Regardless of the numerous influences wrought by history, New Mexico remains rooted to tradition and the Earth: adobe construction first used by the Pueblo Indians remains a status symbol; Spanish rolls off tongues in offices, fields, and schools; and brilliant sunsets that bathe mountain slopes and tall-grass prairies in a rosy light still evoke a sense of wonder.

ALBUQUERQUE

A L B U Q U E R Q U E

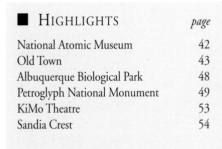

Food & Lodging on pages 281-285.

ALBUQUERQUE IS A STUDY IN CONTRASTS. Long ago it was no more than a dusty frontier outpost of the Spanish colonial empire, an isolated enclave of rudimentary adobe homes along the banks of the Rio Grande. Today, it is the most vital city in New Mexico, spreading 12 miles east of the river to the foothills of the Sandia Mountains and 3.5 miles west to a rugged volcanic escarpment. A major scientific and high technology center, Albuquerque serves as the state's economic, education, and transportation core. With a population approaching 500,000, it is also a melting pot for the state's three primary cultures: Native American, Hispanic, and Anglo. In recent years, a vital Asian community has sprung up as well, adding to the ethnic mix.

The Rio Grande, shaded by leafy cottonwoods, cuts a north-south swath through the city. Five dormant volcanic cones, the Sleeping Sisters, mark the city's western edge, and a shrub-covered mesa spreads out under their shadow. Between this mesa and the cactus-covered foothills of the Sandia and Manzano mountains, Albuquerque stretches forth in a shimmering sea of asphalt and flat rooftops.

To early Spaniards, the Sandia (Watermelon) Mountains resembled a wedge of watermelon—especially at sunset, when they glowed a pinkish red. The Manzano (Apple) Mountains received their label not because they resemble the fruit, but because an apple orchard was planted on their eastern flank in the 19th century.

Sandia Crest rises 10,678 feet from the valley floor, and its cool summit is within easy reach via an 18-minute tram-car ride. From it you can see a breathtaking panorama of the city, river, and mesas that extend toward 11,000-foot snow-capped Mt. Taylor, 70 miles away. In the skies overhead you may see red-tail hawks, golden eagles, hot-air balloons, hang gliders, or fighter jets from Kirtland Air Force Base.

To someone driving through (or flying over), the city might seem just one more homogeneous, sprawling, western metropolis, with streets set out in a grid pattern and shopping centers at nearly every major intersection. But those with a little more time will find there's much to discover. Because Albuquerque is not a congested city, it's easy to take a leisurely drive through its neighborhoods. In the mostly Hispanic, rural **South Valley**, which follows the river south of Old Town, billboards advertising cigarettes read "El Sabor Rico y Suave" ("A Mild, Rich

Flavor"), and in autumn newly harvested green chiles roasting outside fruit and vegetable stands saturate the air with a nose-tingling aroma. **Northeast Heights** and **Southeast Heights** are made up of new developments and contain a heavy proportion of the city's businesses. In the **North Valley** tall grass grows along Rio Grande Boulevard as it winds beside horse farms and orchards. At the original Albuquerque townsite, restored as **Old Town,** you can still enjoy a horse-and-buggy ride through the narrow streets.

Even though the city contains one-third of the state's residents and is New Mexico's largest contribution to urban America, Albuquerque retains the informality of a small town. Among shopkeepers and folks on the street, friendly smiles are the norm. Albuquerque doesn't tolerate pretensions, and its citizens don't concern themselves much with desert visions or astral planes. Residents are down to earth and readily accept, and even thrive on, their city's normalcy.

■ HISTORY

The first people to scale the granite outcroppings of the Sandia Mountains and look out over the future site of Albuquerque probably arrived at the end of the last Ice Age, about 12,000 years ago. Hunters, they came in pursuit of mammoths, mastodons, bison, and antelope. Over the course of their sojourn in the valley they left behind spear points and scrapers in Sandia Cave, a deep cave on the northeastern flank of the mountains. The people who used it for protection were therefore referred to as Sandia Man.

Thousands of years after these primitive hunters moved on, ancestors of today's Pueblo Indians began living along the Rio Grande in settlements which date from A.D. 500. By about A.D. 1300, these Indians were cultivating beans, maize, and squash, coiling pottery, and living in four-story pueblos they built of *terrones*—sod squares made with twigs, grass, dirt, and water. Men wore deerskin shirts, and when they wished to marry, they wove a blanket and placed it in front of the woman of their choice. A woman accepted by wrapping the blanket around herself, thereby becoming a wife.

This was the world that Spanish conquistador Francisco Vásquez de Coronado stumbled upon when he arrived in the autumn of 1540 at the pueblo of Kuaua, 17 miles north of present-day Albuquerque. (The Spanish referred to the pueblo as Alcanfor.) He was looking for a place to winter his entourage of 336 soldiers, 100 Indians, and slaves from Mexico, and thousands of horses and mules. During the two winters and one summer he based himself at the pueblo, Coronado searched tirelessly for gold around the state and as far north as Kansas. In 1542, he returned empty-handed to the city of Mexico in the Spanish colony of New Spain.

Despite a few subsequent Spanish expeditions into New Mexico and a settlement in Santa Fe to the north, the area around Albuquerque remained largely free of European influence until the last years of the 16th century. By that time the Pueblo Indians (if not the Apaches) were more or less subdued, and with increasing numbers of Spanish settlers arriving in the New World, the Spanish Crown began issuing land grants at the far northern perimeter of its empire.

Typically, a land grant was a small plot near a water supply. On it, settlers built a rustic home and grew corn, wheat, beans, chile, and fruits. They cultivated cotton for cloth and sewed their own clothes. Cattle and sheep were grazed on *ejidos* — larger parcels of common land shared by grant recipients. While life was grueling and very basic, the Spaniards believed they were investing in a provident future: then, as today, land represented freedom and independence.

These individuals were a hardy lot. Women helped with planting, spent long hours grinding corn on well-worn *metates,* fashioned their own brooms from meadow grass, and of course bore and raised many children. Men braved blinding windstorms and cold winters to herd their cattle and sheep, and felled tall ponderosa pine trees to fabricate furniture. Because metal was scarce, they

The carreta *was the most common vehicle of transport in Spanish colonial New Mexico. This one was photographed at Tesuque Pueblo in 1890. (Museum of New Mexico)*

designed wooden plows, hoes, and shovels. They also built the only vehicles used in the state during the 1700s and early 1800s—two-wheeled, wooden, oxen-drawn carts known as carretas.

The entire family worked in the fields, breaking the soil, planting seeds, pulling weeds, and harvesting crops. The men dug and maintained irrigation ditches called *acequias.* Transferring water from the Rio Grande to fields in the Albuquerque area, these acequias were so wide that small bridges were built across them. Homes were constructed of five-inch-thick, handmade, adobe bricks that weighed 50 pounds each. For insulation, thick mud was plastered in between the bricks. At the more isolated ranchos, often targeted by Apache attacks, defensive *torreones* were built—round, rock-walled towers equipped with a few small windows.

In 1706, Francisco Cuervo y Valdés, provisional governor of New Mexico, moved 30 families from the trading center of Bernalillo (where a number of haciendas flourished adjacent to Kuaua) to a spot 17 miles south in the middle Rio Grande Valley, which boasted steady water, good soil, grassland, and timber. To flatter the Duke of Alburquerque, then viceroy of New Spain, Valdés named the new community after him, and it later became known as the "Duke City." (The first "r" was later dropped.) Settlers cleared the land, cut the timber, and baked bricks, building their squat mud houses and small adobe church around a central plaza, today known as Old Town. Ten soldiers were assigned to protect the new villa from Indian attacks. No walls or fortification were constructed at the new settlement of Albuquerque, but as Indian raids increased, homes were built closer together and closer to the plaza. Some original family *ranchos* were incorporated into the city as neighborhoods, such as Duranes, Los Poblanos, and Los Griegos.

These early residences weren't much to look at, but their adobe construction provided natural insulation: warmth in the winter and relief from a glaring summer sun. By day, they looked dreary. But as the sun set on the West Mesa, a rosy-red and golden glow that bathed the nearby mountains also fell across the townsite, giving it the appearance, albeit fleeting, of a prosperous village.

◆ ARRIVAL OF THE RAILROAD

The town of Albuquerque remained huddled for protection around its plaza for more than 170 years—until the arrival in April 1880 of the Santa Fe Railroad. Built across the desert two miles east of the original villa, the railroad soon sprouted a second settlement—New Albuquerque—which rose up along the tracks. Because many of the new residents came from east of the Mississippi River, their homes reflected the Victorian architecture of the Midwest—gabled wooden houses. These two-story, pitched-roof homes were far less amenable to life in the desert than those of naturally insulating adobe bricks built low to the ground.

This period also brought to Albuquerque its first African-American residents, who came to work for the Santa Fe Railroad. Today, their South Broadway neighborhood remains a center of black cultural life, and a broad selection of African American topics can be found at its public library branch.

With the arrival of the railroad, Albuquerque's population skyrocketed and so did its vitality. The city's first entrepreneur was Peter "Shorty" Parker, who opened a saloon by staking out space in a vacant lot and erecting a bar that consisted of a board placed across two upended barrels. Soon 14 new saloons (with roofs) and gambling houses sprang up between First and Third Streets on Railroad (now Central) Avenue. Men stood along the wooden bars, paying 15 cents for a shot of whiskey. Respectable women listened from afar to songs played on a honky-tonk piano or accordion. The White Elephant, whose solid mahogany bar could accommodate 50 men at one time and whose glassware was imported from Belgium, served the town nabobs. One block away, the no-frills Bucket of Blood catered to the railroad workers; when a man drank away his paycheck during the weekend, owners John and Mary Boyle made sure he was sobered up in time to report to work on Monday morning. Another of these early taverns, the Silver Dollar, embedded its namesake in the floor.

Street fights, murders, and hangings were commonplace, as were stories like this one: In 1881 someone fired a shot into the air at the same time a railroad carpenter by the name of Charles Campbell was crossing First Street. A bystander said it was the carpenter who fired the shot, so the town's marshal, Milt Yarberry, and his friend, Monte Frank Boyd, pumped 12 bullets into Campbell to teach him a lesson. Two years later, Marshal Yarberry was hanged for murder in front of 100 people, some of whom had paid a dollar to witness the event. One newspaper related that the marshal had been "Jerked to Jesus."

The era's showpiece was the Huning Castle, with its five-foot-thick wood-veneered sod walls dug from a nearby meadow. A flat roof trimmed with ornamental grille work and a tower decorated with balconies gave the two-story home the feeling of a castle, which is what owner Franz Huning called it. Huning, one of Albuquerque's prominent Anglo merchants, was a German immigrant. (By 1955, the architectural novelty was considered an embarrassment by its neighbors and was torn down.)

Along with the debauchery brought by the railroad came education, first in the form of public schools in 1884, followed by parochial schools the next year. In 1889, the University of New Mexico was founded a mile east of the railroad tracks on a sandy yucca-filled tableland. The university's third president, William Tight, was responsible for transforming the desert into a shady oasis. He transplanted hundreds of trees and native plants from nearby mountains, dug a well so they could be watered, and imported squirrels from his previous home in Ohio. Presumably, it is the descendants of these squirrels who still romp in the trees today.

President Tight was so impressed by the surviving Pueblo Indian culture that he envisioned a campus that would reflect the Indians' unique architecture. He quickly saw to the construction of flat-roofed adobe buildings with portals and *vigas*, and went so far as to remove the gables and to plaster adobe over Victorian-style Hodgin Hall. Soon, public outcry over Tight's attachment to "primitive" architecture grew so loud that he was removed from office. (In later years, however, Tight's vision was resurrected and much is seen today in the work of famed Santa Fe architect John Gaw Meem, a major proponent of the Spanish-Pueblo style. As university architect for 25 years, Meem designed many of the campus' finest examples of that style, including Zimmerman Library and Scholes Hall.)

By the turn of the century, the high desert city of Albuquerque was becoming a haven for tuberculosis patients. Seventeen tuberculosis centers were built, including Lovelace Clinic, founded by tuberculosis patient William Randolph Lovelace. Today the full-service medical facility carries out state-of-the-art medical research.

In 1926, Route 66, the much ballyhooed national highway that linked Chicago with the West Coast, passed through Albuquerque's central business district. As a result, Central Avenue blossomed with a highway culture of tourist courts, diners, and storefronts. Many of these establishments retain a down-home ambiance in hospitality and architecture, as well as dazzling vintage neon signs.

In 1939, up-and-coming financier Conrad Hilton turned his attention to his home state. A native of San Antonio, a rural hamlet 86 miles south of Albuquerque, Hilton was convinced Albuquerque was destined for growth and designated the lot of the former Trimble Livery Stable as the site for his next project. He set about building a 10-story Hilton Hotel, with an airy two-story lobby accented with carved corbels, a Mexican tiled floor, and white-washed arches. In 1942, Hilton married Georgia Gabor (better known by her nickname Zsa Zsa) in Santa Fe, and they spent a few nights at the Albuquerque Hilton. The hotel escaped the ravages of 1960s urban renewal and was restored in the 1980s. Today, no longer a Hilton hotel, it operates as La Posada de Albuquerque.

(top) Original Victorian-style Hodgin Hall at the University of New Mexico, and Hodgin Hall redone in the Pueblo Revival style (bottom). (Albuquerque Museum)

ALBUQUERQUE

■ MILITARY, AVIATION, AND BALLOONING

Nothing better suits an airplane pilot than clear sky, and since Albuquerque enjoys an abundance of it, the United States Army Air Corps designated the city as a service station for military planes in 1940. The following year, as the U.S. seemed about to become embroiled in World War II, the Air Corps Advance Flying School was established on land adjacent to the municipal airport. This school was expanded, and in 1942 became Kirtland Field, a major defense installation.

You can catch a glimpse of **Kirtland Air Force Base** if you drive to the **National Atomic Museum** set inside its borders. This museum traces the history of the top-secret Manhattan Project, centered in the isolated mountain hideaway of Los Alamos. On display is a copy of a letter written by Albert Einstein to President Franklin D. Roosevelt encouraging him to develop the atomic bomb. The museum has detailed exhibits on the development of nuclear weapons and the peaceful uses of nuclear energy. *Wyoming Blvd.; 505-284-3243.*

At the end of World War II (but paradoxically the beginning of the Cold War), the nuclear research begun at nearby Los Alamos continued unabated, and

The Albuquerque International Balloon Fiesta is the largest such event to take place annually in the world. (Mark Downey)

expanded to **Sandia National Laboratories**, created during the war for munitions development. Together, Kirtland Air Force Base and the labs are Albuquerque's largest employers, with more than 19,000 workers between them. Among their employees are some of the world's foremost experts in the science of destruction, as well as in those aspects of high technology that may significantly enhance life. At Sandia, scientists developed a non-invasive infrared technology that is used to test glucose levels in the bloodstream. The initial technology was created to assess how chemical explosives in nuclear warheads age. Thanks to the secondary application, diabetics don't have to prick their fingers: they can use a painless beam of infrared light to measure with great accuracy their blood glucose levels.

Another aspect of flight that has captured the imagination of Albuquerqueans is hot-air ballooning. In the early 1970s, pioneer balloonists Sid Cutter, Maxie Anderson, and Ben Abruzzo first fired up propane burners and injected heat into 60-foot-high nylon balloons attached to wicker baskets. Soon they were gracefully lifted upward, flying thousands of feet above a silent sweep of desert. In 1972, Cutter established the **Albuquerque International Balloon Fiesta**, which today is one of the largest balloon gatherings in the world, attracting more than 800 balloons for nine days every October. *Call 888-422-7277 for more information.*

Anderson and Abruzzo, meanwhile, chose adventure. The two pilots, along with Larry Newman of Phoenix, Arizona, won worldwide fame in 1978 when they completed the first trans-Atlantic helium balloon flight. By using helium instead of propane, they were able to fly at higher elevations and for longer periods. Abruzzo and Anderson also participated in the first trans-Pacific helium balloon flight. Both Anderson and Abruzzo died in flight accidents: Anderson at a 1983 West German balloon race and Abruzzo in a private plane crash two years later.

■ OLD TOWN *map page 35, E-4 & 5*

Old Town offers a refuge from the encroaching monotony of Albuquerque's modern-day malls and suburbs. All it takes is a few steps inside to become immersed in the flavor of the past. A well-used, jet-black stagecoach carries you through the narrow streets of the city's original townsite, passing by adobe buildings whitewashed or tinted in colors from beige to chocolate brown. Wooden doorways and windowsills are livelier—painted in magenta, turquoise, and navy blue.

Luminarias (candle lanterns) decorate the plaze in front of San Felipe de Neri Church during Christmastime. (Kerrick James)

San Felipe de Neri Church

The original church was begun in 1706, but disintegrated after years of weathering and neglect. Its replacement (1793) is impeccably cared for. Outside, its flower beds are tidy and bright; inside, a pressed-tin ceiling rises above wooden arches and dark wooden paneling and pews. No stained glass graces San Felipe's windows, but flickering lights from votive candles reflect an atmosphere of reverence. San Felipe Church overlooks the central plaza.

Central Plaza

The plaza was once a dirt-covered square well known to settlers and adventurers, and soldiers preparing to fight the Indians. Later, Confederate and Union armies alternated possession of the outpost, and today two Civil War cannons still sit in the plaza.

A whitewashed wooden and cement gazebo now serves as a bandstand for musicians and dancers, and tall, broad-leafed cottonwood trees provide welcome shade for picnickers and shoppers resting on cast-iron benches.

La Placita Dining Rooms

All of the original homesites that face the plaza have been transformed into shops, galleries, and restaurants. An example is La Placita Dining Rooms, originally built in 1706 as the Armijo family home. Today the smell of hot *sopaipillas* (deep-fried bread dough) and tortillas frying in oil wafts from the old home, whose rooms meander throughout the restaurant. Out front, local artisans line the brick sidewalk with blankets upon which they display handmade jewelry and weavings.

Romero Street Fights

If you happen to be wandering the streets on Sunday afternoon, you might suddenly find yourself diving for cover when gunshots ring out, signifying the beginning of the weekly Romero Street fight. Gunslingers wrangle over women and money, and before long prone bodies are spread around the street. Then everyone gets up and walks away.

Albuquerque Christmas Eve

While Old Town receives most of its visitors during the warm summer months, those willing to brave the brisk temperatures of a chill Christmas Eve will find the neighborhood transformed into a world of shimmering light. On that evening, in traditional Hispanic style, Old Town's citizens set out more than 500,000 *luminarias* (votive candles nestled in a handful of dirt in a small brown paper bag— called *farolitos* in other parts). These are set along sidewalks, adobe walls, and rooftops as a sign of rejoicing and festivity. Some people say the twinkling brilliance represents illuminating the way for Mary and Joseph when they were in search of a bed for the night.

Walking Tours

Away from the plaza, narrow backstreets weave among adobe buildings nearly 300 years old. If time is limited and you want to know where to find authentic Navajo rugs, Acoma pottery, and hot-air-balloon cookie cutters, pick up a map at the visitor center at the northwest corner of the plaza. For those who'd like some insider knowledge of the district, guided walking tours leave the Albuquerque Museum Tuesday through Sunday at 11 A.M. Tours are free. *2000 Mountain NW; 505-242-4600*

San Felipe de Neri church, Albuquerque.

But if you already have been bitten by the mañana bug and aren't in a hurry, stroll among the 200 shops, restaurants, and galleries. Find out for yourself which shop sells jalapeño jelly beans, green and red chile pasta, and tortilla-shaped potholders. You might find a cottonwood tree with a Madonna carved into the trunk. Some stores have remodeled interiors, while others retain solid oak display cases and creaky wooden floors.

■ MUSEUMS AND GALLERIES

Albuquerque's museums reflect the region's unique heritage and rich history, natural or not. Several are in or near Old Town.

New Mexico Museum of Natural History
Spike the *Pentaceratops* and Alberta the *Albertosaurus* stand guard at the entrance. A *Quetzalcoatlus* soars over a *Camarasaurus,* an *Allosaurus,* and a life-size model of *Coelophysis*—the New Mexico state fossil, so small you can look him straight in the eye. There are educational as well as entertaining exhibits—many were designed by artists who worked at Disneyland.

A walk through 4.6 billion years of New Mexico's geologically tumultuous past immerses you in a tropical seacoast environment complete with sharks and sea anemones, takes you inside a simulated active volcano, and leads you through the grassy plains of eastern New Mexico when primitive hunters roamed the region, about 12,000 years ago. An "evolator," which looks suspiciously like an elevator, whisks you through 38 million years in time. *1801 Mountain NW; 505-841-2800.*

Also in the museum is the Lodestar Astronomy Center, offering visitors an unequaled celestial experience. Virtual Voyages will take you on a virtual science mission, with your seat moving in six directions, and a highly sophisticated planetarium will reveal real-time research from the dark side of the earth. *505-841-5960.*

Albuquerque Museum of Art and History
Documenting 400 years of the state's history, this huge museum offers a wealth of artifactual information on the culture of the Spanish settlers. The museum's gem theater regularly shows films on Albuquerque's history. Prominent works from the museum's collection and a broad variety of acclaimed traveling exhibits are regularly displayed as well. *2000 Mountain NW; 505-242-4600*

In 1997, the museum acquired Casa San Ysidro, a reconstructed 18th Century Hispanic home in Corrales. The rancho brims with a vast collection of Spanish Colonial, Mexican, and New Mexican furniture and crafts amassed by the former owners. Guided tours are offered. *505-898-3915.*

American International Rattlesnake Museum
Dedicated to conservation and preservation, the museum houses the world's largest collection of poisonous snakes. They slither

in natural settings, behind glass, of course, and can most often be seen resting peacefully, coiled beneath a piece of petrified wood. *202 San Felipe NW; 505-242-6569.*

Explora Science Center and Children's Museum of Albuquerque

Children of all ages can blow giant bubbles, paint, weave and create paper sculptures, and conduct all manner of science experiments. There is a discovery trail for toddlers. *The museum is temporarily housed at Winrock Mall, but will relocate near the Natural History Museum; 505-842-1537.*

University Museums

If you're curious about early *Homo sapiens* and ancient cultures in the Southwest the **Maxwell Museum of Anthropology** invites you to walk through four million years of human evolution. You'll see a life-size (3-foot 7-inch reconstruction of your average three-million-year-old woman. In a glass case facing her, primate jawbones (complete with teeth), start with a chimpanzee and progress to modern man. The artwork of our more recent ancestors is reproduced in a cave whose walls are decorated with horses, bison, and wolves painted red and black and resembling those found at Lascaux, France. A two-story gallery shows off items from the museum's permanent collection of Mimbres and Pueblo pottery, Navajo weavings and textiles, American Indian basketry, *kachina* dolls, and jewelry. You can try your skill at grinding corn the Indian way by using a *mano* (hand stone) in a *metate* (stone bowl). *505-277-4404*

Also on campus: the **Geology and Meteoritic Museum** with meteorites and a variety of regional rocks, the **University Art Museum** with regional contemporary exhibits, and the **Jonson Gallery**, housing a collection of the late modernist painter Raymond Jonson, and changing contemporary shows.

Dartmouth Street Gallery

Contemporary works by some of New Mexico's best artists *Just east of the univeristy in the Nob Hill District, 3011 Monte Vista NE; 505-266-7751.*

Tamarind Lithography Institute and Gallery

Some of the world's foremost modern artists, including Sam Francis, Jasper Johns, Robert Motherwell, Frank Stella, Claes Oldenburg, and Roy Lichtenstein, have processed prints of their work in this institute, founded in 1970. Tours are offered the first Friday of every month. *108-110 Cornell SE; 505-277-3901.*

Ernie Pyle Memorial Branch Library

Okay, this is not an official museum, but this bungalow was Pyle's last home and in addition to library books, it contains memorabilia from the war correspondent's life. *900 Girard SE; 505-256-2065.*

Indian Pueblo Cultural Center

An inside look at the creative, social, and historical aspects of New Mexico's Pueblo Indians can be found at this center, operated by the All-Indian Pueblo Council, a coalition of the governors of the state's 19 pueblos. Most weekends and holidays Indians wear traditional dress, and dance to the beat of animal-skin drums in a central courtyard. Its walls are covered with murals of eagle and buffalo dancers and of horses roaming atop mesas.

Don't miss the museum on the lower level, with exhibits on Native languages and lifestyles. For example, in the warm months, men and children wore little except for sandals woven from yucca fibers, and women wore a mini-skirt made of string. In the winter, they all donned soft robes of tanned deerskin or rabbit fur. Men kept their hair long, but women cut theirs to make cords and ropes. Also of interest are instructions on how to bake bread in an *horno* and a video in which famed San Il defonso Pueblo potter Maria Martinez demonstrates, step by step, the process by which she achieved her distinct black-on-black glaze. Each pueblo has its own display case. Sandia Pueblo exhibits red clay pots and buckskin moccasins; San Felipe its Heishi necklaces made from semi-precious and precious stones; and Isleta its clay storyteller sculptures. Upstairs, Indian pottery, jewelry, and rugs are for sale, and a restaurant serves a selection of Indian cuisine, from frybread to tamales to buffalo burgers. *At the corner of 12th Street and Indian School Road NW; 505-843-7270*

■ ALBUQUERQUE PARKS

Albuquerque has grown out instead of up, and now encompasses 163 square miles of high desert. More than 145 city parks help break up the urban sprawl.

Albuquerque Biological Park
This complex includes a zoo, an aquarium, and a botanic garden. The **Rio Grande Zoological Park** is set in a grove of ancient cottonwood trees about a mile south of downtown. It is home to more than 1,200 exotic animals from around the world: a bleach-white polar bear splashes in a giant pool that only he can make appear small, and a lanky cheetah wanders silently amid sandstone cliffs and outcroppings. In the reptile house, iguanas, skinks, and crocodiles enjoy their own natural environment thanks to special controls that vary ambient temperatures and seasonal day-lengths for each species. *505-764-6200.*

At the **Albuquerque Aquarium,** located along the river about two miles north of the zoo, visitors can trace a drop of water from the headwaters of the Rio Grande to the Gulf of Mexico. A 285,000-gallon shark tank is home to a variety of the sleek predators, as well as rays and colorful reef fish. Even seasoned divers will be amazed to walk through a cave filled with eels, many of which strike full-length poses. Next door, at the **Botanic Garden**, visitors can learn about native plants. *505-764-6200.*

Rio Grande Nature Center
Two miles of trails lead through a riparian environment or bosque (woodlands) that attracts pheasants, roadrunners, toads, skunks, and beavers. The visitor center is built partially underground, and the unobtrusive design enables visitors to watch bird life both above and below the surface of a three-acre pond. During the migration months of May and October, Canada and snow geese, sandhill cranes, and the occasional whooping crane stop at the center to rest. Free guided walks along the park's trails are conducted every weekend. *Candelaria Road near Rio Grande Boulevard.*

Petroglyph National Monument

Across the river on the West Mesa, along a boulder-strewn volcanic escarpment beneath the five Sleeping Sisters, are at least 15,000 petroglyphs, which date as far back as A.D. 1300. A walk among the craggy boulders takes you past drawings of long-legged birds, animated dancers, snakes, and shields etched in dark basalt. Standing in front of any one of them, it's hard not to wonder about the world of these artists. What were they thinking and what were they trying to say? Most scholars agree the designs were symbolic and not meant to represent actual events. "It is not a language. You can't read them," says Polly Schaafsma, author of *Indian Rock Art of the Southwest.* "They are a graphic expression of ideas from their world, how they describe and define their world and how they put value on it." The national monument was created to protect the mystical rock art from encroaching housing developments. Start at the visitor center, at Unser Boulevard and Western Trail, and go two miles north to Boca Negra Canyon. Three short paved trails lead to a concentration of petroglyphs. Rangers guide tours during summer months. For the best viewing and to save yourself from an intense summer sun, wander into the park's canyons in the morning or late afternoon hours. *505-899-0205.*

■ ALBUQUERQUE EATING

Because Albuquerqueans are cowboys at heart and expect to get their money's worth, food almost spills over the edges of the plates at most Albuquerque restaurants. But if quantity—and not necessarily originality— has long characterized the city's cooking, today's chefs are experimenting with new versions of the local cuisine. Cooks find countless uses for the state vegetable, chile, using it in soups and sandwiches, as well as in pizza and cornbread. Piñon nuts are popular in ice cream, tarts, and muffins; at **Scalo Northern Italian Grill** (3500 Central NE), local red chiles and piñon nuts (not Italian pignoles) grace the pastas. **Kanome,** an Asian diner, offers gingered shrimp with green onion corn cakes on a menu where nothing is traditional.

Ethnic restaurants have taken this frontier town into the international mainstream. Come to Albuquerque now and you can enjoy Thai, East Indian, Vietnamese, Chinese, and Mediterranean cooking. But Albuquerque hasn't forgotten how to make classic New Mexican food. At **Sadie's,** located at 6132 Fourth NW in the North Valley, try *papitas fritas con frijoles* (fried potatoes with beans) or chicken tacos with guacamole. Just *try* to finish a dinner plate here! At **El Patio** (142 Harvard SE) across from the university, the green chile chicken enchilada plate is a favorite and the honey *sopaipillas* are tops. At the downtown **M&J Sanitary Tortilla Factory** (403 Second SW), lines often stretch out the door at

CHILE V. CHILI

In New Mexico, when folks believe in something, you'd best believe it too. Take, for example, the spelling of 'chile.' A small matter, you might say, but not for New Mexicans, who refuse to accept the way the rest of the country spells it— 'chili.' Chile, the Spanish spelling, is found on menus, in stores, and in newspapers throughout the state. New Mexicans are so adamant about the spelling that in 1983, they directed their senior U.S. legislator, Senator Pete Domenici, to enter into the Congressional Record the state's stand on the spelling.

"New Mexicans consume mass quantities of this magical and life-giving fruit from birth, and labels on chile products, descriptions of dishes at New Mexican restaurants and billboards and advertisements all reinforce the fact that chile is spelled with an 'e' and not an 'i.' A naiveté exists among native New Mexicans who wrongly assume that everyone spells it with an 'e.'

"Even the dictionary makes the error, stating that chili is defined as the pod of any species of capsicum, especially *Capsicum frutescens.* Chili is the preferred spelling and chile is only mentioned as an alternate spelling. Knowing that criticizing the dictionary is akin to criticizing the Bible, I nevertheless stand here before the full Senate and with the backing of my New Mexico constituents state unequivocally that the dictionary is wrong.

"Native New Mexicans are extremely sensitive about this spelling, for the *Capsicum frutescens,* commonly known as green chile, and when dried in the autumn sun in great strings called *ristras,* becoming red chile, is New Mexico's most famous agricultural product. Though the chile can be grown in other parts of the country, it is known worldwide that the New Mexico soil produces a chile pod with a mouth-watering flavor that none can even brag about coming close to.

"New Mexicans know that 'chili' is the inedible mixture of watery tomato soup, dried gristle, half-cooked kidney beans, and a myriad of silly ingredients that is passed off as food in Texas and Oklahoma. The different tabascos and jalapeño sauces added to the mixture do little good and in most cases simply cause a casual visitor to suffer great gastrointestinal distress.

"Contrast this to New Mexico, where ordering a bowl of chile is a delightful experience. Hospitable as we are to all visitors, we have chile that is mild enough to make a baby coo in delight, or hot enough to make even the strongest constitutions perspire in a sensual experience of both pleasure and pain.

"I could go on and on about the wonders of red and green chile, but in reality, all I wanted to do was inform Congress on the correct way to spell the word."

The state's loyalty to chile didn't stop with Sen. Domenici's speech. In 1999, the state Legislature approved an official state question: "Red or Green?" in reference to the standard question asked when placing an order for New Mexican food in restaurants. It refers to whether you prefer red or green chile atop your enchiladas or burritos. Some diners ask for "Christmas", which indicates they want both red and green chile.

Cornucopia of chiles. (Eduardo Fuss)

lunchtime as students, lawyers, and artists (and the occasional visiting Hollywood celebrity) vie for mismatched vinyl booths. The food is excellent, and the atmosphere is even better. The walls are covered with local artwork and letters of appreciation to the friendly owners, who bustle about making sure you have enough fresh salsa and iced tea.

As for breakfast, Albuquerque today has more to offer than cowboy coffee and a pot of mush at daybreak. Good, strong coffee is preferred, and you can easily find *good* cappuccinos, croissants, and bagels. If after a few days in town you find yourself craving chile first thing in the morning, try a breakfast burrito—a flour tortilla wrapped around scrambled eggs, bacon or *chorizo* (spicy sausage), cheese, home-fried potatoes, and chile, then topped with more cheese and chile. That same combination is offered as a "Pileup" at the 66 Diner, a '50s-style eatery serving '90s cuisine on Central Avenue. You won't have to eat the rest of the day. *(Restaurant listings begin on page 282.)*

■ NIGHTLIFE

Albuquerque's nightclub circuit runs the gamut of musical tastes: there's rock and roll, rhythm and blues, jazz, Latin, acoustic, piano bars, and, of course, country and western. Most of the country bars offer free dance lessons on weeknights, and you'll see men with their names engraved into their leather belts and women in full skirts heading toward them, determined to learn the two-step, polka, waltz, jitterbug, and cotton-eyed joe.

If your visit falls on the third Friday of the month, you can join **ArtsCrawl**, a self-guided tour of galleries that concentrates on a different section of the city each month. From 5 to 9 P.M., gallery owners offer beverages and hors d'oeuvres along with a look at their current exhibits.

A leisurely drive along old Route 66, these days known as Central Avenue, takes you past the city's colorful gallery of neon signs, some dating to the 1930s when the highway bustled with transcontinental traffic. Central Avenue is marked by two stainless steel, tile, and neon arches that bookend Nob Hill, with its cluster of stores and cafes. While largely a shopping district by day, at night Nob Hill transforms into one of the city's most active gathering places. Restaurants with outdoor seating fill up with patrons, and coffeehouses featuring powerful java are abuzz with conversation. Window shopping is a great way to walk off the food.

Likewise, Albuquerque's downtown, which centers around Central Avenue, is filled with suit-wearing adults from nine to five, but gives itself over to a younger, less serious set come nightfall. The recent opening of taverns, college hang-outs, and a pool hall has made this one of the city's liveliest nocturnal neighborhoods. At downtown's center sits the ornate KiMo Theatre (see following), where you can catch some kind of live performance nearly every night of the week.

◆ KiMo Theatre   *map page 35, C-2*

Electric eyes beam from garlanded horned buffalo skulls, installed as sconce lights. Plaster-of-Paris Indian shields grace inside and outside walls. Wrought-iron balusters resemble stylized waterfowl on stairways leading to the balcony. Plastered ceiling beams are textured to look like wooden *vigas* and decorated with painted thunderbirds, butterflies, and geometrical designs. Chandeliers are shaped like war drums, and air vents are disguised as Navajo rugs. Everywhere you turn are visions only described by an exotic vocabulary.

This is the KiMo Theatre (the name means "Mountain Lion" in one Pueblo dialect). It reflects the vision of Oreste Bachechi, an Italian-American immigrant who sought to honor the community that had made him a successful liquor and grocery dealer. Desiring to build a premier motion picture palace, he hired Hollywood architect Carl Boller to create a theater that would combine the traditions, arts, and culture of New Mexico and the American Indian. Boller traveled extensively throughout the state, visiting Acoma and Isleta pueblos, and the Navajo Reservation. Back in Albuquerque, he fused traditional Indian designs with Spanish mission styles and certain flamboyant motifs of the day into a new—but short-lived—architectural style called Pueblo Deco. He took months choosing colors, and making sure Native American interpretations were properly represented in minute detail. For example, red portrays the life-giving sun; white, the approaching morning; yellow, the setting sun of the west; and black, the darkening clouds from the north.

Bachechi paid $150,000 to build the magnificent theater, which opened in 1927. He spent an additional $18,000 for the elaborate Wurlitzer organ, which was played by Frances Farney during each silent film showing.

The KiMo also served as a major stepping stone for local talent. Albuquerque resident Vivian Vance, who gained fame as Ethel Mertz of the *I Love Lucy* television series, worked at the theater. Other Hollywood stars to grace its stage were Sally Rand, Gloria Swanson, Tom Mix, and Ginger Rogers.

Through the years, the KiMo has been altered several times to keep up with current theater trends. By 1968, it closed as a movie house. During the next decade, it served as offices for Commonwealth Theatres and occasionally hosted local performing arts groups. The city purchased the theater and reopened it in 1977 as a public performing space. Interior renovation went slowly, with voters consistently rejecting bond issues. In 1989, a non-profit group organized to help preserve the historical theater provided financial assistance to restore the murals, including those in the lobby painted by Albuquerque artist Carl von Hassler. One of the larger ones, however, had been destroyed.

Today, the theater is open almost every night for performances ranging from regional professional productions to traveling shows of all kinds, from Ballet Folklorico to tap dance revues.

■ SANDIA CREST   *map page 35, A-5*

In just 18 minutes, one of two cars at the **Sandia Peak Aerial Tramway** whisks passengers through four of Earth's seven life zones, rising nearly 4,000 feet to the top of the mountain known as Sandia Crest. On its silent 2.7-mile journey, the tram quickly leaves behind clusters of cholla cactus and ascends above jagged granite outcroppings until it reaches the windy pine-covered summit of the Sandia Mountains. From the top, the city and surrounding desert stretch to the horizon,

The Sandias form a backdrop to downtown Albuquerque. (Kerrick James)

Twilight view over the city from Sandia Crest. (Kerrick James)

sliced by the greenbelt of the Rio Grande. Hikers and backpackers can set off along forested trails to enjoy cool relief in the summer. In the winter, skiers glide along cross-country trails or schuss the groomed slopes of **Sandia Peak Ski Area,** *(see page 304)* carved from the forest on the mountain's eastern flank. In summer and fall, one of the ski area's chairlifts carries sightseers and mountain bikers over grassy slopes. Deer and rabbits dart for cover in nearby stands of pines. This ride is especially enjoyable in the fall when the aspen's green leaves turn golden and shimmer in the sunlight. Dusk is the most dramatic time to be atop the 10,600-foot peak. When the sun disappears behind the West Mesa, it casts a rosy glow across the city, which gradually becomes a sea of twinkling lights.

At the summit of Sandia Crest, the High Finance Restaurant serves steaks and hot chocolate, and provides luxurious shelter from gusty winds that often buffet the mountaintop. A one-mile trail along the edge of the ridge leads to Sandia Crest House, a small gift shop and snack bar. *Sandia Peak Aerial Tramway operates daily; hours vary. 505-856-1532.*

HARVEY GIRLS

When the railroad snaked its way into New Mexico in the late 1800s, connecting the southwestern frontier with the eastern United States, little thought was given to the comfort of the passengers who would be riding the iron horse. Towns, if you can call them that, consisted of a few canvas tents and flimsy wooden shacks, one designated as the depot. Another wooden shack served as a very basic dining hall for train passengers. Inside, they ate greasy meat, canned beans, rancid bacon, and eggs preserved in lime and shipped from the East Coast. Worst of all, passengers had 20 minutes to gulp down this unsavory repast before they reboarded, resuming a jolting journey at 20 mph (32 kph) across the dusty desert. To avoid this unpleasant eating ritual, seasoned travelers either headed for a saloon, which was amply supplied and more comfortable than the dining shack, or they brought along apples, bread, and cheese, hoping it would last throughout their trip. Often, it didn't. This mediocrity failed to concern railroad executives, but one young entrepreneur knew customers deserved better and would pay for food they could digest.

Fred Harvey was born in London. After emigrating to New York City at 15, he spent years working in restaurants. He knew the value of quality food and service and he was convinced a network of classy restaurants along a rail line was not just a good idea, but a great one. In 1878, he talked officials at the Atchison, Topeka and Santa Fe Railway into giving him a shot. That was all he needed, for Harvey and his Harvey Houses brought a refinement to the Santa Fe Railroad unsurpassed by other rail lines.

In New Mexico, 16 Harvey Houses graced the tracks. Usually they were two-story brick buildings with dining rooms on the main floor and staff living quarters upstairs. Situated in isolated communities such as Clovis, Deming, Belen, Vaughn, and Raton, these welcome whistlestops also served as social centers for area residents. In addition, five of the railroad's showpiece hotels lined the tracks in New Mexico: the Montezuma and Castañeda in Las Vegas, the Alvarado in Albuquerque, and El Navajo in Gallup. Santa Fe's La Fonda, while not on the railroad tracks, was a Harvey hotel popular with passengers stopping at Lamy. (The Alvarado and El Navajo have since been demolished.)

Unlike the Spanish or Mission Revival style of most of the Harvey Houses, El Navajo opened in 1923 as a tribute to the American Indian. Furniture was upholstered in Navajo weaving designs, and Navajo sand paintings adorned walls of the elegant restaurant and hotel.

Many of the women who worked for the chain received their training at El Navajo. Midwesterners between the ages of 18 and 30, most from poor families, left Missouri towns and Kansas farms and headed West, not so much for the adventure, as for the much-needed job. Although their duties were strictly to serve customers, these women never were referred to as waitresses. They were known proudly as Harvey Girls. Immaculately attired, they served a four-course meal in less than 30 minutes, usually three times a day, to rail passengers.

Rules were rigid: no makeup, no jewelry, hair pulled away from the face atop the head. They wore starched black-and-white skirts, white aprons, high-collared shirts, black shoes and stockings, and hairnets. Introduced in 1883, this uniform changed little during the next 50 years. If they spilled anything on their precisely pressed uniforms, no matter how small a spot it left, they were instructed to change into a fresh outfit. And they were forbidden to marry while under contract with Fred Harvey.

No matter where they were sent—the windswept plains of Vaughn, the heart of Indian country at Gallup, or the bustling state capital of Santa Fe—most of the women loved the West. Many married rail workers or fellow Harvey House employees and raised families in their adopted towns.

ALBUQUERQUE ENVIRONS

Food & Lodging begins on page 280.

IN THE IMMEDIATE AREA AROUND RAPIDLY EXPANDING ALBUQUERQUE lie ancient Indian pueblos, the site of explorer Coronado's first winter encampment in New Mexico, lovely countryside, and the Turquoise Trail. All are worth a day or two of pleasurable meandering.

■ TO BERNALILLO   *map page 59, B-2*

The sleepy village of **Alameda,** north of Albuquerque on Fourth Street, was once a Tiwa Pueblo. After the 1680 Pueblo Revolt, the pueblo was abandoned for 15 years, at which time a small group of Spanish colonists moved in. Today, an adobe church fronts the street, along with copper-brown homes and businesses. North of Alameda, the street becomes NM 313 (old US 85) and slices through the Sandia Indian Reservation, paralleling railroad tracks and irrigation ditches. Fifteen miles north of Albuquerque is **Bernalillo,** one of the oldest European towns in the United States.

Before Francisco Vásquez de Coronado wintered just north of Bernalillo at the Kuaua Pueblo in 1540, the area was home to Tiwa Indians who had drifted down from Chaco Canyon around a.d. 1300. At the 1,200-room pueblo built along the banks of the moody Rio Grande, which flows muddy in the spring and deep-green in the winter, these Indians grew beans, squash, and corn. Women gathered in a

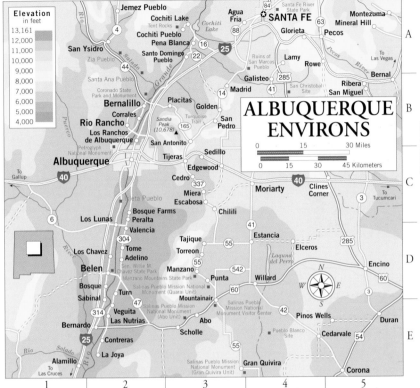

special building to grind corn by rhythmically moving a small stone (mano) across a rectangular stone trough (metate). Once the corn was made into meal, they pounded it into flat bread, a staple of their diet. While they worked, a man would sit at the door, playing a flute carved from an eagle bone, as the women sang to his music.

These people built several underground ceremonial *kivas*, which they entered by ladder through an opening in the roof. On the walls of one kiva they painted black fish, masked kachinas dressed in yellow shirts with black skirts and white sashes, white rabbits, white clouds, seed and corn, and white-tipped red arrows. Near the end of the seventeenth century, the Indians abandoned the pueblo, probably moving south, and sands drifted over Kuaua's mud walls, burying it for the next 250 years.

*Corn Dance photographed by Nathan Kendall in 1913 at
Santo Domingo Pueblo. (Museum of New Mexico)*

◆ CORONADO STATE MONUMENT   *map page 59, B-2*

When archaeologists excavated the pueblo in 1935, they discovered 85 layers of adobe plaster inside the *kiva*, 17 of which contained painted symbols of the Indians' complex relationship with the earth and the heavens. Some of these original murals are encased in glass inside the visitor center at **Coronado State Monument**, which was created in 1940 to preserve the pueblo ruins. Reproductions of the paintings line the walls of a reconstructed *kiva*, which you can enter by climbing down a solid wooden ladder into the cool subterranean interior. *One mile west of towm on NM 44; 505-867-5351.*

Outside, tumbleweeds wedge themselves into corners of the crumbling rock walls of the pueblo. A trail winds among cholla cactus, four-wing saltbush, and clumps of grass alongside the low, eroding walls that divide the pueblo's rooms. In the distance, the craggy ridges of the pale-green Sandia Mountains loom against the eastern sky and, closer in, ducks float atop the gently flowing Rio Grande, which passes by rust-colored reeds and sweet-smelling Russian olive trees in front of the pueblo. Adjacent to the monument is **Coronado Campground,** a collection of picnic shelters and campsites set atop additional ruins, some older and some newer than Kuaua, and the charred remains of a Spanish *hacienda* that was burned during the Pueblo Revolt. *505-980-8256.*

Even though Coronado was unimpressed with the fertile greenbelt of present-day Bernalillo, other Spaniards recognized its value and many made their homes along the river there in the late 16th century. Unlike most pioneers to the north who built simple homes and tended their own small farms or ranches, these upper-class Bernalillo colonists received large land grants. The Montoyas, Bacas, Castillos, and Pereas hired *paisanos* to tend the new crops they introduced to the region, such as grapes, Castillian wheat, plums, and peaches, and to look after their vast herds of cattle and sheep. The Gonzales-Bernal family owned the largest spread, and the town was named for them.

These *hacendados,* or wealthy land barons, lived in 40-room homes and protected their privacy by fencing their immaculately kept grounds with high adobe walls. Inside their houses were finely carved tables and tall cupboards that were hauled up from Mexico over the Chihuahua Trail. They ate with silver knives and forks, sometimes off of silver plates. Men trimmed their clothes with silver buttons, silk sashes, and silver buckles, and women adorned bright skirts with ribbons, silk, lace, and velvet. Their field workers, along with servants and their families, lived in Las Cocinitas (Little Kitchens)—a barrio of squat adobe houses whose ruins may be seen today at the south end of Bernalillo.

Diego de Vargas spent a night at the settlement during his reconquest of New Mexico after the Pueblo Revolt; three years later, in 1695, he founded Bernalillo. Nine years later, while on a campaign against Indians, he died there, probably from wounds received in a skirmish. From the beginning, Bernalillo flourished as a trading center where local hacienda owners exchanged vegetables, wool, and meat for iron tools, shoes, paper, and sugar from caravans heading north on the Chihuahua Trail.

In 1871, Nathan Bibo opened a branch of the Bernalillo Mercantile Company, which already had stores in the lumber town of Porter and the gold-mining settlement of Bland, along with trading posts near Acoma and Laguna pueblos. No item was too large or too unusual for Bibo to stock. He sold coffins, harnesses, overalls, tractors, Studebaker wagons, feathers, spittoons, loggers' hooks, blue cornmeal, and dolls. Customers could rent rooms at the "Merc" while they waited to have their wheat ground or to sell their sheep. Today, the refurbished building sells hardware and groceries.

Bernalillo's decline began in 1878 when five well-tailored men disembarked from a stagecoach to meet with José Leandro Perea, the leading *patron* of the day. The men had selected the town as the site of the main offices and chief division point for the Atchison, Topeka & Santa Fe Railroad, which soon would wend its

SPANISH COLONIAL LIFE:
THE WEDDING FEAST

*A*t last all was ready, and the engaged youth and maiden, who though under the same roof since their betrothal had kept away from one another, now met again and before the altar in the evening, accompanied by their godparents. They were married in candlelight, with the handshaped earthen walls of their family about them, and a burden upon them of solemn commitment. Tensions broke when the vows were done. All gathered in the sala for the wedding feast. Now a river house had put forth another reach of growth and promise of the future, all in proper observance of ways that were as old as memory. In her white silk wedding dress the bride went on the arm of her husband in his rich silver-braided suit and his lace-ruffled shirt. Everyone came past to embrace them, and then the feast began. Roast chickens basted in spiced wine and stuffed with meat; piñons and raisins; baked hams; ribs of beef; fresh bread of blue meal; cookies, cakes, sweets; beakers of chocolate and flasks of wine; bowls of hot chile; platters of tortillas, all stood upon extra tables draped to the floor with lace curtains. All feasted.

Then came music, and dark eyes fired up. The sala was cleared, while the musicians tuned up on two or three violins, a guitar and a guitarron, or bass guitar. Servants came to spread clean wheat straw on the earth floor to keep dust from rising, or stood by with jars of water from which to sprinkle the floor between dances. In the candlelight the faces of the woman, heavily powdered with Mexican white lead, looked an ashen violet, in which their eyes were dark caves deeply harboring the ardent emotion of the occasion. The orchestra struck up . . .

While the dancing went on, the bride had an obligation to fulfill. Retiring from the floor in her wedding dress, she reappeared presently in another gown from her trousseau, and later in another, and another. Everyone was eager to see what she had been given. Politely and proudly she gratified them. They fingered her silks and examined the set of jewels given her by the groom—matching earrings, necklace, bracelets, combs, brooches, and gold inlaid with enamel, or seed pearls, rose diamonds, amethysts or garnets.

Before midnight the bride retired not to reappear. Her maiden friends and her godmother went with her. The groom drank with the men in whose company he now belonged, while boys watched and nudged. The dancing continued, and humor went around. The groom's father calling above the noise in the hot, hard-plastered room, urged everyone to keep right on enjoying themselves. Presently the groom managed to slip away. In the bridal chamber the ladies admitted him and left him with his bride. Across the patio the merriment continued. Voices were singing. Someone shouted a refrain. The violins jigged along in a remote monotonous sing, and the gulping throb of the guitarron was like a pulse of mindless life in the night.

—Paul Horgan, *Great River: The Rio Grande in North American History,* 1954 way into the region. Perea, however, saw no need for the noise and clutter the operation would bring. He over-priced plots requested by the rail line—charging $425 an acre for land that was worth maybe $3 an acre. The men returned to their coach and headed to Albuquerque, where the main offices were constructed, spurring the growth of what went on to become the state's largest city. Bernalillo received a red-painted frame depot, a railroad siding, and a grade crossing. As its southern neighbor grew, Bernalillo remained unchanged. Today, nearly all streets have Spanish names, and single-story, tin-roofed adobe homes are preserved at the north end of town. These are the work of Abenicio Salazar, a local carpenter who built hundreds of adobe buildings in the early 1900s.

Every summer, townsfolk spend many weekends and evenings rehearsing for the annual **Fiesta de San Lorenzo.** During the three-day event (always held August 8, 9, and 10), they share great spreads of chile, tortillas, bread, and desserts, and some of them turn into actors and perform Los Matachines, a dance-drama traced to medieval Europe. The colorful dance reflects Spanish, Moorish, and Aztec influences and has probably been performed every year since the 1600s. *505-867-3311 ext. 133.*

The story pits good against evil as Montezuma, last emperor of the Aztec Empire, is Christianized during the dance. La Malinche, a young girl dressed in white to emphasize her goodness, is said to be Doña Marina, an exiled Aztec princess who spoke both the Mayan and Aztec languages and served as interpreter and later mistress to Hernando Cortez. El Toro is the evil force, and some interpretations have him as Cortez. El Monarca, as the Montezuma figure is known, leads in dance other monarchs dressed like himself in brightly colored shawls draped over street clothes. Red, pink, yellow, and blue ribbons cascade down their backs. They wear tall headgear, known as *coronas,* decorated with silver belt buckles and jewelry, striped brocade, beads, and Christmas ornaments. In one hand these men carry a gourd rattle and in the other a three-pronged wooden ornament known as a *palma.* Plaintive strains from fiddles and guitars create a somber mood. Providing comic relief are the *abuelos* (grandfathers) who act as clowns and threaten the town's children with whips to keep them in line.

■ INTO THE SANDIAS   *map page 59, B-2 & 3*

Across I-25 east of Bernalillo, NM 165 winds its way among gently rolling hills covered with bushy piñon pines and junipers, passing through the tiny village of **Placitas.** Once home to 21 families, recipients of the 1745 San Antonio de las

Huertas Grant, Placitas has evolved from a rural, once-popular hippie haven into an upscale Albuquerque subdivision. Expensive multi-level adobe homes with walls of windows, high *viga*-and-*latilla* ceilings, and indoor hot tubs built on spacious lots overlook the Rio Grande Valley. The slate-blue Jemez Mountains rise to the west and the majestic Sandias form a closer backdrop to the south.

Once past Placitas, NM 165 winds up the Sandia Mountains, following the tree-lined banks of Las Huertas Creek. The gravel road passes under tall pines, locust, and elder trees and alongside granite outcroppings covered with orange lichen. A turnout marks **Sandia Man Cave** where prehistoric spear points and scrapers were discovered in 1936 by Dr. Frank Hibben, then an anthropology student at the University of New Mexico. These tools were chipped by hunters who pursued bison and woolly mammoth throughout the middle Rio Grande Valley nearly 12,000 years ago. Known as Sandia Man, these early people were contemporaries of Clovis Man, another group of hunters who roamed southeastern New Mexico. It was through this cave's opening that small prehistoric hunters once came to seek protection and probably a place to eat their food in peace.

Today, an easy half mile trail leads to the cave, but once there a concrete staircase followed by a 12-foot spiral of metal steps scales the sheer rock face up to the opening. Inside, the narrow shaft has been sealed off to protect would-be explorers

Heavy winter snowfall is common in the mountains of northern New Mexico.

from getting stuck crawling on their bellies 300 feet to its end.

The narrow road continues weaving its way up through scrub oaks, ponderosa pines, and aspen groves until joining NM 536, a paved road that scales the mountain's eastern flank. Because of deep snow and a scant shoulder, NM 165 is closed during winter months.

■ ANCIENT PUEBLOS   *map page 59, A & B-2 & 3*

North of Bernalillo, NM 313 passes by the modern stuccoed homes of **Santa Ana Pueblo** before meeting up with I-25, which veers away from the Rio Grande as it heads north toward Santa Fe. Through this region, the river courses alongside three Keres-speaking pueblos: San Felipe, Santo Domingo, and Cochiti. While these pueblos share a language, each has its own dialect and is known for a special tradition: San Felipe for its Christmas Eve dances; Santo Domingo for its August Fourth Corn Dance, and Cochiti for its pottery. San Felipe and Santo Domingo are both very traditional pueblos; cameras and tape recorders are not allowed. Remember to ask permission at the governor's office before walking around the communities and striking up conversations with residents.

Clowns play an important role in the Corn Dance. These performed at San Juan Pueblo in 1935. (Museum of New Mexico)

Though many of **Santo Domingo's** ceremonies are closed to the public, on August Fourth visitors are welcome to view the elaborate Corn Dance. It begins mid-morning when the comic Koshare appear painted in black and gray stripes to warn the pueblo of attackers who are on their way to the village. Having done that, the dancers pantomime the ensuing battle, in which the Indians defeat the invaders. A steady drumbeat announces the arrival of the singers, about 50 Pueblo men who slowly walk into the enormous dirt plaza, chanting rhythmically. As they arrange themselves along one side, a line of dancers, both male and female, enters from the south after emerging from a *kiva* where they have huddled since early morning. This is the squash or pumpkin group, whose bodies are tinted in orange-tan colors. With measured steps, they move gracefully to the mesmerizing drum beat, shaking turtle and gourd rattles. This group moves out and is replaced by the turquoise group, dancers painted in blue who enter the plaza from the southeast. The men in both groups of dancers, which alternate their performances through-out the day, are dressed in kilts adorned with a foxtail at the waist and skunk skins and bells around each ankle. Women wear one-shouldered black dresses and color-fully painted stiff boards (*tablitas*) atop their heads. After a break for midday feast-ing on breads, pastries, chile, potato salad, and beans, the dancing continues until the sun sinks below the Jemez Mountains.

At **Cochiti Pueblo,** outsiders always are welcome to view the Church of San Buenaventura, its interior displaying tin candlesticks brought from Chihuahua and a larger-than-life painting of the patron saint that adorns the center wall above the altar. The pueblo also is recognized for its pottery, especially red-and-black "storyteller" dolls that depict little children crawling and clinging to an open-mouthed grandmother or grandfather figure.

Just north of Cochiti Pueblo's water tanks (painted to look like animal-skin drums), the Rio Grande backs up behind Cochiti Dam, creating a swimming hole and a haven for windsurfers. Don't bring a powerful motorboat in the hopes of waterskiing. Wakes behind boats are prohibited, leaving the waters to small sail-boats and fishermen trolling for bass, crappie, and pike.

Also near the water tanks, an other-worldly tableau of rock spires rises from the desert scrub. The area is known as **Tent Rocks,** a collection of cone shaped forma-tions eroded from volcanic debris spewed from the nearby Jemez Mountains *(see page 103)*. Trails, some only hip-wide, wind through this lunar landscape, offering one of the state's most unusual hiking outings. *505-761-8700.*

(following pages) The adobe church of Las Trampas. (Kerrick James)

■ TURQUOISE TRAIL *map page 59, A, B, & C-3*

More than a thousand years ago, Pueblo Indians in the Cerrillos Hills south of Santa Fe were using stone hammers to mine for turquoise—highly prized for its beauty, as well as its purported ability to ensure good fortune and a long, healthy life. This stunning blue mineral found its way to Canada and Mexico where, according to legend, Montezuma II, the powerful Aztec emperor, proudly displayed his pendants and necklaces of Cerrillos turquoise.

Later miners coaxed gold, coal, silver, lead, and zinc from the Ortiz and San Pedro mountains that extend south to Tijeras Canyon, a passage that bisects the Sandia and Manzano mountains east of Albuquerque. Today NM 14, now called the Turquoise Trail, connects these long dormant mining districts.

Tall yellow-green grasses mix with an occasional cholla cactus as the two-lane road leaves behind the bedroom communities of Cedar Crest and Sandia Park, once rural oases from Albuquerque, which sprawl on the opposite flanks of the Sandia Mountains. The air is scented with juniper berries, and hills are dotted with piñons and junipers, a refreshing change from Albuquerque's gas stations, burger stands, and auto parts stores. The snowcapped peaks of the Sangre de Cristo Mountains appear behind corners as the road wends its way to **Golden,** once a bustling gold-mining district on the northern edge of the San Pedro Mountains.

A general store and gift shop sit on the highway along with a few homes constructed of adobe, rock, and galvanized iron. Piñons sprout from the ruins of rock homes that proliferated in the mid-1800s when the town was booming with 22 stores and 100 houses. Still, nobody got rich because there wasn't enough water to wash the gold dust from the sand.

Golden's most impressive building is a little mission church atop a hill at the northern edge of town. Built in the late 1830s soon after the gold rush began, the adobe church honored St. Francis of Assisi. A hand-carved and carefully detailed figure of the church's patron saint was displayed inside for more than 130 years, until it was moved to the cathedral in Santa Fe. The well-worn saint was brought by *carreta* from Mexico to Golden in the early 1700s. A newer St. Francis has replaced the original, along with two statues, one a five-foot St. Peter. Services are conducted at the simple church twice a year—on June 29th for the Feast of St. Peter and October 4th for the Feast of St. Francis. Keep in mind that this is private property, so be sure to respect fences and closed gates.

Mission Church at Golden. (photo by Mark Middlebrook)

The slate-blue swell of the Sandia Mountains rises to the southwest, the ski runs of Sandia Peak Ski Area appearing from the distance like fairways divided by the deeper green pine trees. Pale-green lichen cover rock outcroppings as the road penetrates the Ortiz Mountains, then descends into the once-thriving coal mining district of **Madrid.** Charcoal-gray and pinkish-red tailings pile up underneath bare slopes, reminders of an era that began in 1889, when the mines produced 500 tons of coal a day, two-story wooden cabins lined the main street, and white picket fences protected groomed lawns and well-tended flower gardens. Company-owned Madrid boasted tennis courts, a seven-hole golf course, a shooting range, and a 30-piece brass band that marched in an annual Fourth of July parade.

In the 1930s, Madrid was so famous for its annual Christmas display that TWA pilots made detours to catch an aerial view of the town's 150,000 lights. Christmas decorations covered every inch of the main street, and the city ballpark was transformed into a giant toyland in which a miniature train carried children past the House that Jack Built and Peter the Pumpkin Eater. In recent years, Madrid residents have revived the Christmas light tradition.

During World War II, Madrid shipped 20,000 tons of coal to the secret mountain community of Los Alamos, where scientists were busy developing the world's first atomic bomb. By 1947, the demand for coal dwindled, and the mines closed.

In 1975, tired of waiting for another boom or a buyer for the entire town, owner Joe Huber sold Madrid piece by piece. It took 16 days. Artists, craftsmen, and back-to-the-earth characters purchased the 150 dilapidated buildings for between $1,500 and $7,500 each. Today, many of the miners' cabins and hillside adobe homes sport new roofs and windowpanes. Galleries and gift shops face NM 14. Mexican folk art, custom clothing and toys, jewelry made by Santo Domingo Pueblo craftsmen, and locally crafted pottery line the shelves of the quaint shops. You can still descend into an old mine shaft at the Old Coal Mine Museum. And in the summertime, strains of bluegrass and jazz waft from the ballpark during Sunday afternoon concerts.

A few more bends in the road and **Los Cerrillos** appears beneath leafy cottonwoods. Its boom days long over, this sleepy hamlet resembles a movie set, with its few faded storefronts, dirt streets, and rundown exteriors. (In fact, movies some-

North-central New Mexico continues to support a host of artisans. (Paul Chesley)

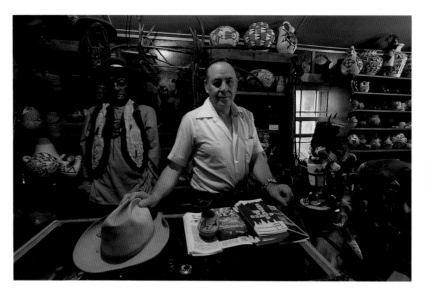

Trading posts such as this serve as an outlet for the artisans of New Mexico. (Paul Chesley)

times are filmed here.) In the late 1800s, when Los Cerrillos still offered lodging at hotels, and when the 21 saloons were filled with miners seeking their fortunes in gold, Thomas Edison paid a visit. He tried to extract gold from sand and gravel using static electricity, but he wasn't able to do it.

Today, the Casa Grande Trading Post sells souvenirs and gifts, and also features a turquoise mining museum and a homespun petting zoo in which goats, sheep, and burros await the caress of—and a hand-out from—soft hands. The Clear Light Opera House is now a recording studio.

If you're heading on in to Santa Fe, you might want to take a detour west on NM 586 to the Millennium Turquoise Mine where some of the world's highest-grade turquoise was first mined in A.D. 500. Once known as the Tiffany-Cerrillos Mines when the Tiffany Company of New York was part-owner, the site no longer is open to the public. But you can stand at the fence along this lightly traveled highway, gaze at the distant Jemez and Ortiz mountains on either side of you, and imagine those ancient Indian miners cracking the rocks with crude picks as they looked for turquoise.

■ EAST AND SOUTH OF ALBUQUERQUE

East of Albuquerque, I-40 bisects the Sandia and Manzano mountain ranges through Tijeras (Scissors) Canyon on its way to the eastern plains. One of the state's more interesting drives curves along the eastern foothills of the Manzano Mountains on NM 337 (old 14). Leaving Tijeras Canyon, the road climbs and dips, sometimes hugging lichen-covered granite outcroppings and other times passing through wide-open meadows of yellow wildflowers. Interspersed along this route is a collection of villages created as 19th-century land grants, with names such as Chilili, Tajique, Torreon, and Manzano. In 1829, at the mountain range's southern end, Spanish settlers built a small fort for protection from Apache attacks. They named their community **Manzano**, after a thriving apple orchard established there in 1800. Still bearing fruit today, this orchard is the oldest in the country. Manzano remains a sleepy community of tin-roofed adobe homes, some with horses in the yard, and a stuccoed adobe church. Two gravel roads wind away from the town, one leading to Capilla Peak and the other to a shady campground at the base of Manzano State Park, the starting place for hikers who wish to scale the mountains on foot. *505-847-2820.*

South of Manzano, the rolling slopes of junipers and piñons give way to the meadows of the Estancia Basin, traveled by prehistoric nomadic hunters who camped on the shores of a huge lake that filled the basin 12,000 years ago. Settlement came in the 10th century, when Mogollon Indians established villages alongside dependable streams and fresh springs. These early inhabitants grew corn, beans, and squash, hunted antelope and deer, and gathered piñon nuts and wild berries in nearby hills. They fashioned simple red or brown clay pottery and lived in pit houses, which later were replaced by *jacales.* Nearly 200 years later, the Anasazi arrived, bringing with them their stone and mortar architecture and multi-level homes.

At nearby salt lakes and beds, the Anasazi mined salt, which they bartered along with corn, beans, squash, piñon nuts, and cotton goods for buffalo meat, hides, flints, and shells from Plains tribes to the east and Rio Grande pueblos to the west. This area, at the southern edge of the Manzano Mountains, served as a major trade route, connecting tribes throughout the region. By 1300, outside influences had crept in: these Salinas Valley Indians raised turkeys and added bison and rabbit to their diet. Men wore breech cloths and bison robes. Both men and women wore antelope and deer hides and wrapped themselves in decorative blankets they wove of cotton and yucca fibers. They adorned themselves in turquoise and shell jewelry.

Juan de Oñate visited the area in 1598, but Spaniards didn't move in until Franciscan priests settled alongside Indians in the early 1600s. The missionaries wasted no time converting the pueblo residents to Christianity and forcing them to build churches. Indians hauled heavy slabs of limestone and sandstone from nearby outcroppings and laid them out to make smooth flagstone floors for the 40-foot-high stone churches with four-foot-thick walls. Initially the Franciscans tried to prohibit Indians from practicing their native religion, but their efforts failed, and the Indians eventually frequented both churches and their traditional *kivas*. The Spanish also taught the Indians how to tend orchards, vineyards, and wheat fields, and forced them to herd cattle, goats, and sheep.

◆ SALINAS PUEBLO MISSION NATIONAL MONUMENT *map page 59, D/E-3 & 4*

Three pueblos, separately situated in a 25-mile radius of the ranching center of Mountainair, have been preserved as **Salinas Pueblo Mission National Monument**. At Punta de Agua, a sleepy hamlet on NM 55, a gravel road veers off to the west, leading to the mission ruins at **Quarai**. Sandstone walls still loom 40 feet above a grassy plain, much as they did in 1630 when the church of La Purísima Concepción de Cuarac was completed. A well-marked trail passes by the unexcavated mounds of pueblo dwellings, covered with patches of grass. Entering the nave of the church, you are walking on some of the original flagstone set down by the pueblos. The dirt roof is gone, replaced by an azure sky. At the altar, you can picture the colorful altar screen that once decorated the wall, filled with *retablos* painted in red, blue, and yellow, and embellished with bits of reflective mica. Outside, a *kiva* is submerged into the earth. Additional rooms that stretch to the mission's far walls, which surrounded the pueblo, most likely served as stables, hay and storage sheds, and animal pens. Close by the settlement, a grove of towering cottonwoods indicates the springs that were so vital to Quarai's survival. Today, these trees provide shade to picnickers who sit at tables and gaze over at the imposing church, perhaps speculating about what the original residents might have had for lunch—beef jerky and corn tortillas with beans, washed down with goat milk?

Seventeen miles southwest via NM 55 and US 60, Indians at Abo erected their mission church in the late 1620s atop a rise in a wide valley surrounded by hillsides covered with piñon and juniper trees. Built of bright red sandstone, the **Abo church** is 30 feet high. Stone buttresses support two-foot-thick walls, an unusually sophisticated building technique for 17th-century New Mexico. The church also contained an organ, which was accompanied by a choir during services. The narrow Abo River gently flows nearby the Indians' three-storied rock-walled homes, now covered with red soil and patches of pale-green desert grass. Only partial walls show above the earth.

South of the town of **Mountainair**, NM 55 crosses vast fields of cholla cactus and brilliant orange-red Indian paintbrush. An occasional truck rattling along a lonely road disturbs the silence, and an occasional hawk floats in the sky. Then, looking up, you see the partial walls of the mission church at **Gran Quivira** rise majestically atop a distant mesa.

Early Spanish visitors who arrived with Juan de Oñate in 1598 named the community Pueblo de los Jumanos (Pueblo of the Striped Ones) for a stripe the Indians painted across their noses. Later explorers gave it its current name. Once, 1,500 people lived at Gran Quivira, growing beans and squash in fields that were well-served by rain. Though no water source is known within 30 miles, historians believe the Indians captured rainwater in natural limestone cisterns or tapped a spring that has since dried up. The Indians here also hunted bison, and fashioned pottery that they painted with black and white stripes.

In 1659, Indians erected the massive Mission of San Buenaventura, with 30-foot-high gray-blue limestone walls that were six feet thick. Nearby, they worshipped their traditional gods in underground *kivas*.

You can view generations of homes as you peer down into the multi-level ruins of the pueblo. At the lowest level, the rock walls are ill-fitting compared to well-crafted ones in the upper levels. Stone *metates* lie among grass that has grown up between low rock walls. After walking through the ruins and the immense church, you might want to sit on a stone bench, look out across the vast plains, and imagine children playing hide-and-seek among nearby stands of juniper trees or think of the woman who once ground the day's cornmeal on one of those worn *metates*. From atop this windswept mesa, the snow-capped peak of Sierra Blanca looms to the south and the deep-blue outline of the Manzanos to the north.

In the 1670s, besieged by Apache attacks and drought, the Indians of the Salinas Valley left their homes to take refuge at pueblos along the Rio Grande.

About 1,500 people once lived at Gran Quivira at Salinas Pueblo Mission.
(Kerrick James)

A visitor center for these three restored pueblos can be found on Main Street in Mountainair. *One block west of US 60 and NM 55; 505-847-2585.*

The small town of Mountainair was once known as the Pinto Bean Capital of the World. Like many of New Mexico's small towns, this ranching center has become popular among transplants from other states seeking an affordable and safer lifestyle. The town's showpiece is the **Shaffer Hotel,** a whitewashed building adorned with orange and black squares and black swastikas (the Indian symbol for happiness). This 1929 masterpiece of Pueblo Deco architecture was the brainchild of Clem "Pop" Shaffer, a local folk artist who lived nearby at the equally whimsical Rancho Bonito, where he created his colorful works. The hotel and dining room have frequently changed owners, and may be closed; do call ahead to see if it's open. It's worth it to see the antique metal light fixtures, the brightly painted geometric patterns on the walls, and the interesting fireplace; *505-847-2832.*

◆ ISLETA PUEBLO   *map page 59, C-2*

One of the oldest missions in the United States, **St. Augustine Church,** lies about 18 miles south of Albuquerque off I-25 in Isleta. Surrounded by adobe homes and rough shacks, the church has an other-worldly quality. Outside, the walls are high, white, and irregular; inside, a sense of mystery hovers among paintings of saints.

The pueblo itself dates from the 16th century and is one of the oldest and largest in New Mexico. Its history followed the generally tragic course of most Southwest Indian villages. Although its population acquiesced fairly amicably to the imposition of the Catholic faith and Spanish culture, this didn't protect the Indians from being decimated by disease, conflict, and forced relocation. A thriving town when the Spanish first arrived, by 1692 Isleta was home to only a handful of Indians—many of those refugees from other pueblos. Today, the pueblo has a population of 4,000.

TIME ENDING

*O*ne morning in the spring of 1942 I walked to the edge of the canyon and sat dreaming for awhile under the branches of a fir tree. The air was gossamer. A haze of subdued light lay over rock and tree. I watched thunderheads build up in the north over Tsacoma, the sacred mountain. A tiny spider spun a web from the twig of a barberry to my knee and back again.

But roughly upon the edge of peace that day an airplane droned, circling back and forth among the clouds, from the river to the mountain, south along the flowing hills on the horizon, out of sight, and then suddenly back again. It flew low, methodically. The sunlight glinted from its silvery structure. It was then I first knew without doubt that a time was ending. Not even here on these mesas was isolation possible. We too were vulnerable to change. The narrow trails cut in the ancient rock could not be defended against the invading future.

On the first of May we waked to the sound of an extraordinary wind. The sky that had been limpid at daybreak darkened. The sun was muffled, though there were no clouds. The bright air was choked with dust that stung our faces and burned our eyeballs. We women were too restless that day to stay alone in our houses. Each went to seek some neighbor for reassurance, and as we walked we leaned against the wind like ghosts. Tarpaper ripped from roofs whirled past our windows. Sheds were overturned. Paths and doorways were blocked by fallen trees. Before it died at evening the wind cut a wide swath of destruction across mountain and mesa.

When I next rode on the trail up the Guaje ridge northwest of Los Alamos I became for the first time in my life almost hopelessly lost. Trees lay scattered as though spilled from a giant matchbox. Great roots had been flung upward out of pits of earth. Picking my way through the ruined landscape I lost all sense of direction. My confused mare balked and trembled till at last I got off and led her. I knew that for the animal's sake, if not my own, I must not panic. I talked to her gently and turned from time to time to lay my hand on her sweating neck in reassurance. At the peak of despair I stumbled across a shattered root. Exposed in the gaping earth shone a black piece of carved obsidian. That unexpected pattern of symmetry could only have been formed by the hand of man. I picked it up and held it in my hand, an ancient spearhead, and suddenly felt that I was not alone. An age-old human instinct for finding order in the midst of chaos came to my rescue. In a few moments I found myself back on the homeward trail.

—Peggy Pond Church
The House at Otowi Bridge: The Story of Edith Warner and Los Alamos, 1960

NORTH CENTRAL
NEW MEXICO

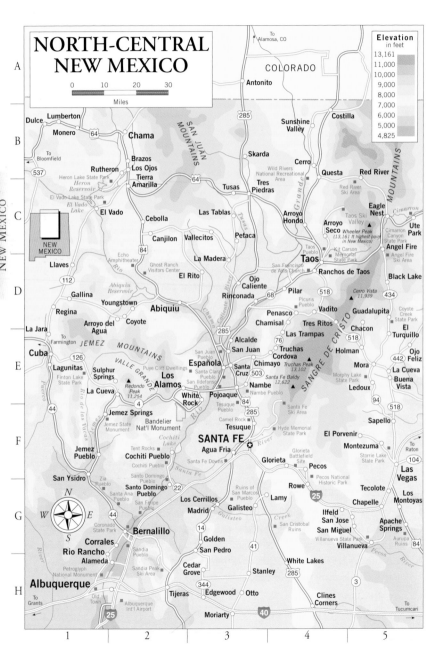

NORTH-CENTRAL NEW MEXICO

0   10   20   30
Miles

Elevation
in feet
13,161
11,000
10,000
9,000
8,000
7,000
6,000
5,000
4,825

COLORADO

To Alamosa, CO

Antonito

Dulce Lumberton
Monero 64 Chama
To Bloomfield
537
Brazos
Rutheron Los Ojos
Tierra
Amarilla
Heron Lake State Park
Heron Reservoir
El Vado Lake State Park
El Vado Lake El Vado
Cebolla
Canjilon Vallecitos
84
Echo Amphitheater
Ghost Ranch Visitors Center
Llaves
112
La Madera
El Rito
Gallina
Abiquiu Reservoir
Youngstown
Regina Abiquiu
Arroyo del Agua Coyote
La Jara
To Farmington JEMEZ MOUNTAINS
Cuba
126
Lagunitas Sulphur Springs
Finton Lake State Park
La Cueva Redondo Peak 11,254
44
Rio de los Vacas
Jemez Springs
Jemez State Monument
Jemez Pueblo
Cochiti Lake
San Ysidro Zia Pueblo
Tent Rocks
Cochiti Pueblo
Cochiti Pueblo
Santo Domingo Pueblo
Santa Ana Pueblo Santo Domingo Pueblo 22
San Felipe Pueblo
Coronado State Park
N Bernalillo
W E
S
Corrales
Rio Rancho
Alameda
Petroglyph National Monument
Albuquerque
To Grants Old Town
Albuquerque Int'l Airport
25

SAN JUAN MOUNTAINS

285
Skarda
Las Tablas
Petaca
Tres Piedras
Tusas
64
San Juan Pueblo
Española
Santa Clara Pueblo
San Ildefonso Pueblo
Los Alamos
White Rock
4 Pojoaque
Tesuque Pueblo
285
Camel Rock
Tesuque
SANTA FE
Agua Fria
Santa Fe Downs
Glorieta
Santa Fe
Ruins of San Marcos Pueblo
Los Cerrillos Lamy
Madrid Galisteo
14
Golden
San Pedro 41
Cedar Grove Stanley
344 Edgewood Otto
Tijeras
Moriarty 40

Sunshine Valley
Cerro
Wild Rivers National Recreational Area
Arroyo Hondo
Arroyo Seco
Taos Pueblo
San Francisco de Asis Church
Ojo Caliente
Rinconada
Picuris Pueblo
Pilar 68
518
Penasco
Chamisal
Tres Ritos
Las Trampas 518
Alcalde 76
San Juan
Santa Cruz 503
Chimayo Cordova
Nambe Santa Fe Baldy 12,622
Nambe Pueblo
Santa Fe Ski Area
Hyde Memorial State Park
Glorieta Battlefield Site
Pecos Pecos National Historic Park
Rowe
25
San Cristobal Ruins
Ilfeld San Jose
San Miguel
Villanueva State Park
White Lakes Villanueva
285 3
Clines Corners

Costilla

Questa Red River
Red River Ski Area
Eagle Nest
Taos Ski Valley
Wheeler Peak (13,161 ft highest point in New Mexico)
Kit Carson Memorial State Park
Taos
Ranchos de Taos
Black Lake
Cerro Vista 11,939
Vadito Guadalupita
Chacon El Turquillo
Holman
Ojo Feliz
Mora 442
Morphy Lake State Park La Cueva
Ledoux Buena Vista
94 518
Sapello
El Porvenir
Montezuma
Storrie Lake State Park 104
Las Vegas
Tecolote Los Montoyas
Chapelle
Apache Springs
Aurupa Ruins 84
To Raton
To Tucumcari

San Juan Mountains
Rio Grande
Rio Chama
Rio Grande
Rio Chama
SANGRE DE CRISTO
MOUNTAINS
Cimarron
Cimarron Canyon State Park
Ute Park
Angel Fire Angel Fire Ski Area
Truchas Peak 13,102
Coyote Creek State Park
Pecos River
Galisteo Creek

NEW MEXICO

N O R T H - C E N T R A L
N E W   M E X I C O

Food and Lodging begins on page 280.

NORTH-CENTRAL
NEW MEXICO

PINE FORESTS, ASPEN GROVES, AND THE CRAGGY PEAKS of the Sangre de Cristo and San Juan mountains combine with the gentler slopes of the Jemez Mountains to frame the north-central region of New Mexico. In between are the russet-tawny-lavender cliffs near Abiquiu, the placid Chama River and the more turbulent Rio Grande. Within this rugged, mountainous region, the state's spell is cast daily —in sunsets that transform deep green hillsides into golden, and then rose-red portraits. Coyotes howl and owls hoot as the slate blue of evening blanket the high country and lights switch on in the tiny villages.

Long ago, Indian agricultural communities flourished in the soft, crumbly tuff formed from volcanic ash and cinders left behind when a volcano exploded, creating the Jemez Mountains. Some of these communities are preserved at Bandelier National Monument and the Puye Cliff Dwellings. Today, a majority of the state's Indian pueblos are spread throughout this region, alongside and near waterways that flow from snowpacked mountains. These villages look like other rural New Mexican towns, with low-slung adobe buildings arranged around a central plaza. The northernmost pueblo is also the most spectacular: Taos Pueblo, a stunning multi-level structure that has been occupied since A.D. 1350.

Hispanic culture is pervasive here. Spanish is spoken as often, if not more, than English. Even the smallest hamlet displays a well-tended Catholic church, usually built of sturdy adobe, and some isolated ranches have their own chapels.

The Rio Grande makes a dramatic entrance into New Mexico from its head-waters in southern Colorado, cutting a 650-foot-deep gash through a sagebrush plain. The blue-green water kicks up through the Rio Grande Gorge, churning it-self into roiling rapids and deadly drops. One bridge passes over the deep volcanic chasm along US 64; another rugged gravel road with no designation follows the Rio Hondo, slicing through the gorge's middle. The only other access to the river here is by steep trails.

Once through the gorge, the Rio Grande mellows. Towns such as Velarde and Alcalde tap its water to irrigate apple orchards before the river piles up behind Cochiti Dam. The Rio Grande also flows past Española, which bills itself as the Low Rider capital of the world, and Bandelier National Monument.

Another of New Mexico's major waterways, the Chama River, enters the state at the western edge of this region. This gentle river, winding between alpine mead-ows and pine forests, backs up behind Heron, El Vado, and Abiquiu dams before joining the Rio Grande north of Española.

North-central's magical setting has drawn scores of artists who have been com-ing since the 1920s to paint, sketch, and write about its sandstone bluffs, silent, sagebrush plains, pine forests, and modest people rooted to the earth. Georgia O'Keeffe and D. H. Lawrence are the best known, but hundreds more have settled here. Galleries can be found in most small towns; in most of them exhibits feature paintings, pottery, weavings, and jewelry made by local artists.

■ INDIAN HISTORY

Beginning in A.D. 1100, the Anasazi Indians began leaving their multi-tiered homes in Chaco Canyon in northwestern New Mexico and southern Colorado. Most likely, they had despaired of unreliable seasonal storms needed to water their crops, so they began heading toward water they could count on. Most ended up along the Rio Grande or one of its tributaries. In some cases, these farmers joined tribes already growing corn and beans in the fertile lowlands. Others formed new communities, building multi-family dwellings and practicing irrigation methods developed at Chaco Canyon, such as diverting river water to crops through ditches. Some of these transplanted natives constructed their buildings with a new organizing

Deer Skull with Pedernal, *painted in 1936 by artist Georgia O'Keeffe, New Mexico's most famous artist. (Gift of the William H. Lane Foundation, courtesy Museum of Fine Arts, Boston)*

principle, breaking from earlier traditions of carving out homes in canyon walls or lining a valley floor with multi-storied structures. These new homes were built along streets and around open plazas.

During this transition, known as the Regressive Period, which lasted until 1450, ceremonial kivas varied from pueblo to pueblo, some remaining traditionally round, while others were rectangular. Also, pottery styles changed from black-on-white vessels to black- or white-on-red. Designs differed from pueblo to pueblo. By 1500, the Indians were concentrated in the Acoma-Zuni area and the Rio Grande Valley.

Sixteenth-century Spanish explorers found nearly 80 pueblos scattered throughout northern New Mexico, some with as many as 300 residents. They were impressed with the ingenious way each upper level was built behind the lower one so that access could be gained by climbing outside ladders. These flat-roofed buildings placed around plazas reminded explorers of the towns of their homeland, which is why they named their new settlements after pueblos.

Pueblo Indians used whatever materials were available to build a series of rectangular rooms with a central fireplace and a corner for grinding corn. Lower storage rooms were entered through the roof by a ladder, while additional ladders led to upper-story rooms, themselves entered through four-foot-high doorways. Along the river where building rocks were scarce, the Indians prepared adobe by mixing water with the clay and sandy soil, then spreading this paste over a framework of sticks and brush.

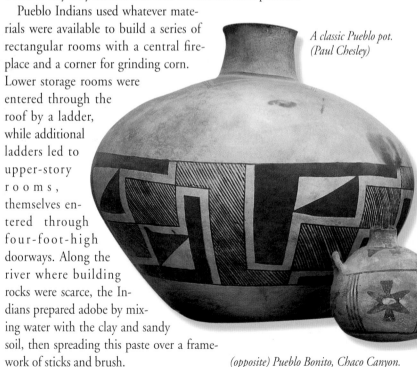

A classic Pueblo pot.
(Paul Chesley)

(opposite) Pueblo Bonito, Chaco Canyon.
(photo by Kerrick James)

Indian religion reflected a deep reverence for nature: the sun and moon were gods, while clouds, thunder, and wind were Pueblo spirits. Religious ceremonies dominated their lives. In the summer they centered on the growing of crops; in winter on hunting. Produce consisted of beans, squash, melons, and a large variety of corn: yellow, blue, white, pink, red, and deep purple. Fresh vegetables were a treat in the fall, but most were dried and stored for the cold winter. Likewise, the meat from buffalo was dried into jerky, and hides were used as blankets and coats.

■ SPANISH HISTORY

Juan de Oñate arrived in New Mexico in 1598 to settle the land for the Spanish crown. His slow-moving, cumbersome caravan followed, more or less, the Rio Grande until it reached San Juan Pueblo, situated in a small valley near the confluence of the Chama River and the Rio Grande. The Indians were friendly, and the settlers at first considered living alongside them, but eventually they opted for a site on the west bank of the Rio Grande that offered more room for expansion. On a low hill with the densely wooded Sangre de Cristo Mountains a distant backdrop, the settlement of San Gabriel was carved out. It would be nine more years before English colonists established their first permanent settlement at Jamestown, Virginia.

Eleven years later, in 1609, King Philip III of Spain designated New Mexico a royal colony, which placed it under direct control of the Spanish crown. Under this new designation, the Spanish government would pay the colony's expenses, along with those incurred by missionaries in their efforts to spread the Catholic faith. Pedro de Peralta was dispatched the following year from New Spain, with orders to establish a new capital. He chose a spot 30 miles south of San Gabriel in a grove of junipers and piñons, beside which ran a narrow stream that meandered down from the nearby Sangre de Cristo Mountains (named "Blood of Christ" for the rosy color they turn in the setting sun). At an altitude of 7,000 feet, the new capital, La Villa Real de la Santa Fe de San Francisco de Asís enjoyed crisp, clean mountain air and looked to the west at juniper-covered mesas and the soft curves of the Jemez Mountains.

De Peralta proceeded to establish a town council, assign house and garden lots to citizens, and order construction of the Palace of the Governors, a walled com-

(previous pages) Taos Pueblo, a magnificent structure dating from A.D. 1350.

pound that contained the governor's residence, government offices, and council chambers. From this fortress, 60 successive Spanish governors ruled New Mexico. All of this activity bore a sense of permanence, and Santa Fe to this day remains the capital of New Mexico, making it the oldest state capital in the country. The Palace of the Governors, now a museum, is the nation's oldest government building.

During the next 65 years, aptly called the Great Missionary Period, 250 friars of the Franciscan Order traveled among the pueblos, building churches and tirelessly working to turn the Indians into devout Catholics. Missions sprung up from Pecos to the western villages of the Hopi in eastern Arizona. Soon, the simple pueblo dwellings were dwarfed by colossal churches. Indians were ordered to erect these structures, assembling 30-foot-high walls with adobe bricks that weighed 60 pounds each, and topping them off with *latillas,* heavy *vigas,* dirt roofs, and a bell tower.

Church leaders didn't stop at converting the Indians. The Spaniards also taught them painting, Latin, blacksmithing, carpentry, weaving, and how to play small pipe organs that had been transported in wagons from Mexico. As the friars and priests focused on "civilizing" the natives, they also set out to destroy Indian civilization, raiding ceremonial *kivas,* desecrating altars, and burning masks, prayer plumes, and fetishes in the plazas. Soon they had outlawed all Pueblo religious rites, singing, and dancing.

The crackdown on Pueblo religions came to a head in 1675 when Gov. Juan Francisco Trevino ordered the arrest of 47 medicine men, whom Spanish priests regarded as little more than devil worshipers. Three were hung, another hung himself, and the rest were whipped and jailed. A group of Tewa warriors then descended upon the capital, demanding the release of the prisoners. Though Trevino obliged, the seed of revolt had been planted and Pueblo activists began plotting an uprising against the oppressive Spanish.

In 1680 that day came. Runners delivered knotted yucca cords to each pueblo. A knot was untied each day, until none were left, signifying the day for battle. Led by Popé, medicine man of San Juan Pueblo and one of those humiliated five years earlier by Trevino, Pueblo Indians across New Mexico attacked settlers, burning their homes and killing entire families. Years of tyranny-caused frustration welled up in the warriors as they directed their greatest wrath at the churches, where they killed priests at their altars and destroyed holy symbols, smearing them with human excrement. Eleven days later, Gov. Antonio de Otermin surrendered Santa Fe and led a string of battered, frightened settlers southward. The Indians let them go.

The shattered Spanish settlers retreated 300 miles to El Paso, but within a year, they had regrouped and were making attempts to retake the territory. Armed Indians turned them back three times during the next decade. With the Spanish safely deposed, Popé encouraged the Indians to shed all ties to the Europeans and to return to their traditional ways. He ordered everyone to wash in the river with soapweed to remove the taint of baptism. All Spanish influences were to be discarded, such as clothing, tools, livestock. Unfortunately for Popé and his followers, many Indians couldn't remember much about the days before the Spanish and their cattle, sheep, and horses. But at each pueblo, natives did revive the independence they had given over to the Spanish. Old feuds resurfaced, Popé lost his grip, and the nomadic Apaches, now on horseback, renewed raiding on pueblos to a degree not seen since the onset of Spanish rule.

In 1692, when Diego de Vargas, accompanied by 60 soldiers and 100 Indian helpers, marched northward from El Paso, he passed by one deserted pueblo after another before arriving in Santa Fe, which he found in a shambles. The Palace of the Governors had been converted into a pueblo.

The Indians initially countered his entrance into the city with a few bold refusals. But after a good long look into a couple of Spanish cannons, they surrendered, embracing de Vargas's promises of pardons and an unconditional return to the Catholic Church.

Despite this bloodless retaking, the next decade was rocked by more Indian uprisings—all unsuccessful. Thousands of Indians abandoned their Rio Grande homes rather than return to Spanish rule, and many of these rebels moved in with the Hopis in eastern Arizona. Some eventually returned to the river, but others stayed on in Arizona. The Hopis never did return to Spanish rule. As New Mexico's Indians readjusted to their Spanish conquerors and resumed their subservient roles, the church leaders likewise compromised: no longer did they raid sacred *kivas*, destroy religious symbols, or severely punish those Indians who embraced Christianity but retained their traditional religious practices.

Still, with their freedom gone forever, the Indians' spirits flagged. Diseases introduced by the Spanish continued to take their toll on the natives who had no resistance to measles, whooping cough, cholera, and smallpox. By the end of the 1700s, the pueblos had lost one-half the population of 100 years earlier. Only 19 pueblos remained of the nearly 80 that were flourishing when the Spanish arrived.

By contrast, the Spanish thrived. Land grants were issued to entice colonists to the untamed province. They settled in villas laid out in fertile river valleys, and on small ranches where they raised cattle and sheep, planted apple orchards, and cultivated squash, peas, and melons in fields irrigated by the Rio Grande, Chama River, and numerous streams that flowed from the mountains. As years passed, relations between the Indians and Spanish became more cordial. Indian women shared their traditional methods for cooking bread, corn, beans, and chile. Both cultures traded herbs and healing plants, and pottery-making and weaving methods. The Spanish adopted the pueblos' flat-roofed architecture. And the two groups intermarried.

Today, mud-brick buildings blend into the chamisa-covered earth, cornstalks reach for the sky, and sheep munch on grass in small villages with names such as Abiquiu, Canjilon, Vallecitos, Santa Cruz, and Tierra Amarilla. These towns, which never prospered, appear much as they did 100 years ago. Ansel Adams brought fame to Hernandez, with his world famous photo, "Moonrise Over Hernandez." A small cluster of adobe homes just north of Española, Hernandez's winter heating fires spread the sweet smell of piñon smoke across the valley. After a disappointing autumn day of photographing the northern New Mexico landscape in 1941, Adams was passing through Hernandez when he noticed a full moon hovering high above the snowcapped peaks of the Sangre de Cristos. Standing atop his station wagon, he snapped a shot in which the moon cast an eerie light on the town's church and houses, illuminating crosses in its cemetery. "Moonrise Over Hernandez" proved to be the photographer's best-known work.

■ PUEBLO CULTURE TODAY

Despite a similar culture, history, and physical appearance, Pueblo Indians are not a single tribe that speaks a common language. Today, 19 pueblos remain, sharing three language groups. Zuni is spoken at Zuni Pueblo. Keres is the language at Laguna, Acoma, Santo Domingo, Cochiti, Santa Ana, San Felipe, and Zia pueblos. The remaining 11 pueblos speak dialects of the Tanoan language family: Tiwa is spoken at Taos, Picuris, Sandia, and Isleta pueblos; Tewa is spoken at San Juan, Santa Clara, San Ildefonso, Pojoaque, Nambe, and Tesuque pueblos. Jemez Pueblo is the only one where Towa is spoken.

Pueblo Indians, stocky in build with piercing dark eyes, are reserved and very polite. They don't go for small talk, feeling that silence is part of the concentration that produces results. Therefore, many of their rituals are cloaked in silence. Because towns have sprung up near most of the northern pueblos, many tribal

Famed potter Maria Martinez applies slip on a bowl at San Ildefonso Pueblo in 1941. (Museum of New Mexico)

members work at city jobs, returning to the pueblo on weekends and for ceremonies. This balancing of traditional demands with modern-day pressures can creates inner turmoil as people struggle to exist in two distinctly different worlds.

Pueblo Indians carry on their centuries-old creative traditions, weaving willow wickerwork baskets, beargrass and yucca bowls, and colorful cotton belts and headbands. They fashion beadwork jewelry and leathercraft, and painstakingly shape pottery without the aid of a potter's wheel. Clays usually are dug from sandstone mesas, then strengthened with volcanic ash. The potter shapes a pancake-like base, then patiently lays on rolls of coiled clay, one atop the other, until the desired shape and size are reached. Using a smoothing stone, the artist smooths out the coils. Pots are polished and then fired outdoors over an open fire. If a red glaze is desired, the potter fires the pots with an oxidizing flame. To achieve the black-on-black pots made famous by San Ildefonso potter Maria Martinez, cow dung is piled around and over the upside-down pottery, permitting the carbon to permeate the porous clay. To decorate the wares, the artist uses spiked yucca or soapweed leaves that have been chewed until only the stiff fibers remain.

"Everything we do is sacred," says Craig, son of Blue Corn, a well-known San Ildefonso potter. He paints the designs on his mother's black- and earth-colored pots. "All designs have meanings. You learn by watching and memorizing the designs. Some designs take days to get the feelings. The design will come into your head and after that you try and work it onto the pot."

Most pueblos also host a few silversmiths who continue the tradition of jewelry-making. Although metals were not commonly used until the 19th century, Pueblo craftsmen have for centuries been carving turquoise, shell, and other gemstones for adornment. Turquoise, once plentiful in the knobby volcanic rock of the Cerrillos Hills south of Santa Fe, is said to contain benign powers: even a bead of the blue-green gemstone tied in an Indian's hair prevents disaster and ensures general well-being.

Another form of Indian artistic and religious expression can be found in *kachinas,* or *katsinas,* small doll-like figures carved from a single piece of pine. They are painted in bright colors, and dressed in deerskin, fur, feathers, and cloth. Each kachina is unique and a constant reminder of the "real" kachinas, supernatural beings who live in the mountains, lakes, and clouds. These messengers dispense blessings, such as rain and good crops. All kachinas wear masks. Doll-like figurines of buffalo, deer, eagle, and snake dancers are not kachinas, although they often are sold alongside them.

A dancer at a Taos Pueblo pow-wow. (Kerrick James)

Dances, held regularly, are the major measure by which Indians express their deep respect for nature. They dance to help the seasons follow one another in proper succession. They dance to promote fertility of plants and animals. They dance to encourage rain and ensure hunting success. Participation in these ceremonies is a duty and privilege of all Pueblo people, who are trained to take part from early childhood. Every item of clothing and adornment has a special significance, from hand-carried spruce or fir twigs that symbolize physical longevity and everlasting life, to feathers and tufts of down and cotton that are cloud and sky symbols.

At Jemez Pueblo, as at many of the state's pueblos, Christmas Day is spent dancing. Leading a throng of reindeer are three buffalo dancers—two men and a woman—who move steadily up and down the plaza to the beat of drums and a chanting chorus of pueblo men. The buffalo woman wears a black skirt, a one-shouldered top called a *manta,* and white moccasins. The men paint their skin dark brown and wear mustard-yellow shirts and dark pants. All don bushy head-dresses with horns and bells around their waists, and each carries eagle feathers and shakes a gourd rattle. Behind them are a few rows of reindeer dancers of all ages. They are decked out in white garments with red, black, and green woven trim and wear turquoise deer heads that seem to be made of papier maché. Each reindeer dancer leans on two sticks, meant to serve as front legs, and spruce boughs decorate their attire. Swooping around the animal dancers are a group of eagle dancers, comprised of teenage boys adorned with eagle feathers. Another animal group, young boys dressed as antelope, join in the dancing, then disappear into the pueblo's maze of earthen homes, only to reappear later. They wear tawny falcon or hawk feathers. Sometimes, Santa Claus even accompanies the drummers and chorus and hands out candy canes to spectators.

While some dances are open to the public, every pueblo has its own policy regarding guests. Some don't permit cameras or tape recorders, and those that do require approval from the governor's office. Ceremonies are highly sacred to the pueblos and customs must be respected. Guests should stay clear of Indian performers or spectators, enter homes only when invited, and speak in hushed tones. Approach these ceremonies as if visiting a church of which you aren't a member.

■ ABIQUIU   *map page 80 D-2/3*

Abiquiu began as a farming and cattle center on the banks of the Chama River and later served as a stop on the Old Spanish Trail, the tortuous trade route from

Santa Fe to Los Angeles. Shortly after Abiquiu's settlement in the 1740s, Spanish officials moved in a group of *genízaros* to help tame the barren land. These people were non-Pueblo Indians of mixed tribal blood but with Spanish surnames. Some had been captives of nomadic Apaches and Navajos who were sold to the Spanish as laborers and servants. At Abiquiu they struggled alongside Spanish settlers, regularly fending off attacks of Ute Indians who came down from Colorado to terrorize the colonists. Arable land was scarce and could only be cultivated as far back from waterways as irrigation ditches could be maintained. Timber was difficult to harvest because it had to be hauled long distances across open country. In between attacks, Ute Indians paid peaceful visits to Abiquiu, during which they traded deerskins for guns, horses, flour, and corn.

◆ RELIGIOUS IMPULSE

The serenity of this spectacular red-rock country seemed to tap the spirituality of its residents. Early manifestations took the form of witchcraft and what the Spanish referred to as "idolatrous worship." This wizardry was unacceptable to Fray

Juan José de Toledo, who was sent from Santa Fe to administer to the village's spiritual needs. He sent soldiers door-to-door to round up anyone engaged in sorcery. Eight perpetrators were flushed out, convicted of witchcraft, and sentenced to be servants of a prominent colonist.

By the turn of the century, another group of religious fanatics had formed. The Penitentes were a confraternity of the Catholic Church that believed in experiencing the suffering of Christ by flagellation. Formed by Spanish men isolated in rural towns without resident priests, this order (also known as the "Brotherhood of Light"), sought forgiveness for its members' sins, as well as for the sins of those who nailed

Saints and crucifixes at Martínez Hacienda.

Christ to a cross. Penitentes performed community service, assisting the sick and poor, comforting the bereaved, and counseling those who were troubled. By voting as a block, they wielded much political power. In Abiquiu, the Brotherhood built two *moradas,* or meeting houses—rectangular adobe structures that had few windows, one door, and a wooden cross in front. As curiosity spread among outsiders, Penitente gatherings and rituals became secret.

The high point of their year was Holy Week, and its climax was the re-enactment of the Crucifixion of Jesus. A procession of bare-backed men climbed a hillside, followed by a member chosen to be Christ. As they marched, the men whipped themselves until they bled. When they were no longer able to lash themselves, their companions took over the torture. The men screamed in pain, a flute player coaxed wails from his instrument, tin cans and chains rattled, all combining to create a mood of suffering and despair. "Christ" labored under a wooden cross

This rare photograph captures Penitentes flagellating themselves in 1896. (Museum of New Mexico)

that weighed as much as 100 pounds. Once atop the hill, the cross was erected and "Christ," bound tightly, hung there for about an hour. Supposedly, this re-enactment of the Crucifixion is no longer performed in New Mexico.

Dar Al-Islam Mosque at Abiquiu is a fine example of modern adobe architecture.

Another form of worship takes place atop a piñon-and juniper-covered mesa in the Chama River Valley at **Dar Al-Islam,** a Muslim community best known for its stark, ivory-colored, adobe mosque. The multi-domed structure with fluid walls was designed in 1980 by Egyptian architect Hassan Fathy. Next door, a series of barrel vaults covers a 10,000-square-foot Muslim school.

Farther south at Santa Cruz is a sizable Sikh community where white-clothed and turbaned families are a common sight. They work as lawyers and business owners in Española and Santa Fe. Each spring, the Sikhs sponsor a Peace Prayer Day during which they invite their neighbors to share songs and stories. A few miles upriver, at the end of an unpaved road sits **Christ of the Desert Monastery.** Here, Benedictine monks grow their own food, raise bees, weave, make pottery and furniture. They worship in a stunning adobe chapel with a floor-to-ceiling glass wall that seems to bring inside the nearby soft-hued red cliffs. The Presbyterians are also represented in this region of religious fervor at Ghost Ranch.

♦ GHOST RANCH   *map page 80, D-2*

Ghost Ranch, established in 1766, is a collection of adobe buildings nestled among maroon shales and dusty orange and purple sandstone hillsides. It was named for the *brujas* (witches), who are said to inhabit its numerous canyons. In 1934, Arthur Newton Pack, a wealthy Easterner, turned the working cattle operation into a fancy dude ranch where wild horses, burros, and mountain sheep roamed nearby, and where rattlesnakes hid in the cool shadows of rocks. One of his early customers, who turned out to be his most famous, was Georgia O'Keeffe—one of the most important painters of the 20th century. Once she set foot on Ghost Ranch, O'Keeffe never left it behind for long. Eventually, she bought a portion of the ranch and lived in a small U-shaped adobe house with whitewashed walls.

Today, Ghost Ranch is operated by the Presbyterian Church with a wide range of commitment to education and spiritual renewal. Several lodging options and a dining hall cater to those who want to take advantage of the programs. The conference center offers a multitude of workshops and seminars year-round on topics ranging from paleontology, astronomy, and theology, to pottery, wood carving, and conversational Spanish. There are also several land stewardship projects doing high desert, wetlands and ranch management research.

Three museums at Ghost Ranch highlight the area's natural history. **The Florence Hawley Ellis Museum of Anthropology** displays a re-created Spanish ranch house and interpretive exhibits of Indian pottery and crafts from people living in a 60-mile radius during the past 12,000 years. **The Ruth Hall Museum of Paleontology** was built around a fossil of *Coelophysis*, a six-foot-long dinosaur that was capable of remarkable speed when it came time to catch dinner. These dinosaurs roamed the Ghost Ranch region 250 million years ago, making them the oldest in the state. In 1981, *Coelophysis* was named the state fossil, and the dig at the museum continues.

From the ranch, a trail through fragrant juniper and piñon pines leads to the **Ghost Ranch Living Museum,** which, like the Living Desert Museum outside of Carlsbad, is home to a collection of animals native to the area. Black bears, bobcats, mountain lions, Mexican gray wolves, and elk roam about in separate enclosures. All have been injured, orphaned, or are ill and unable to survive in the wild. Take the self-guided tour past golden eagles, red-tail hawks, jet-black ravens, and a beaver pond, and learn about the region's ghostly rock formations and pastel striations in the "Up Through the Ages" exhibit. *Ghost Ranch information and brochures; 505- 685-4333.*

■ OJO CALIENTE   *map page 80, D-3*

The hot mineral waters that bubble to the surface at Ojo Caliente have been attracting travelers for thousands of years. The crumbling remains of three prehistoric Tewa pueblos sit atop a mesa overlooking a more recent chapel and an assortment of simple homes along the meandering Rio Ojo Caliente.

According to Tewa legend, Poseyemu, a mythical hero, sprang to life from piñon nuts gathered by a young virgin at one of Ojo Caliente's five springs. Every year, he returns to visit his grandmother who lives in the spring's curative waters.

In 1992, a fire at Ojo Caliente Mineral Springs destroyed the resort's early 20th-century bathhouses. Today, two bathhouses serve men and women, separately or together. Both indoor tubs and outdoor pools are open year-round, and they maintain temperatures from 98 to 113 degrees F. Owner Jerry Mauro claims that Ojo Caliente is the only place in the world where arsenic, iron, lithia, soda and sodium are found, each bubbling forth from a separate spring. All are good for drinking. The standard soak is followed by a sweat-inducing wrap in heavy wool blankets. Massages, herbal wraps, and facials are offered, as well as overnight accommodations at the resort and in town. *See pages 297 and 306.*

■ NORTH TO CHAMA   *map page 80, B & C-2*

North of Abiquiu, US 84 climbs along the side of a red-rock mesa as it heads toward Abiquiu Lake. From this incline, one of the most magnificent views in the state unfolds southward. Slate-blue mountain ranges line the horizon, and the sparkling blue Chama River wends its way among the square plots of tiny farms where horses graze in moss-green meadows and red-tail hawks circle overhead. Purple-yellow-pink cliffs fall away to the east.

Three miles north of Ghost Ranch stands a sandstone cliff face rounded by centuries of whipping wind and pounding rain. Called **Echo Amphitheater**, this is a lovely spot to enjoy a cold drink and sandwich at picnic tables maintained by the Forest Service. A 10-minute walk leads to the 200-foot-high beige wall. Be careful not to tell any secrets, because your conversation will be broadcast throughout the camping and picnic area.

Leaving Echo Amphitheater, the road climbs northward toward a stand of ponderosa pines before it drops into the Chama Basin, where the tin roofs of **Tierra Amarilla** homes glint in the sun. Here in the broad valley, churro sheep graze alongside cattle. Tierra Amarilla, named for the yellow-colored soil of the area, began as a land-grant settlement in the mid-1800s. But the village really took hold in 1865 when U.S. soldiers were dispatched to protect settlers from raids by Jicarilla Apaches and Utes. In 1872, both tribes were forced to relocate to reservations.

The town has gained a reputation as a seat of land-grant activism since 1967, when Reies Lopez Tijerina dramatized the plight of land-grant heirs who have lost

their claim to the land through sales to outsiders by what he views as trickery or fraudulent means. Tijerina, along with 20 followers, raided the Rio Arriba County Courthouse, wounding two policemen, attacking two others, and holding many more bystanders hostage for hours. When Tijerina's group escaped to the nearby mountains, it took 500 lawmen to flush them out. Although Tijerina faded into the background after serving eight months in prison, the land-grant movement continues to flare up now and then.

The tiny sheep ranching community of **Los Ojos** was struggling to survive in 1981 when residents put their heads together and created Ganados del Valle, a collectively run economic development corporation. Today, the village is home to Tierra Wools, where weavers work on looms in the back and shoppers can browse through clothing, tapestries, pillows, rugs, and piles of hand-spun yarn. Churro sheep produce the wool, and Los Ojos residents spin and weave it. Close by, the historic Parkview grocery store, reopened in 1990, operates as a general store that also sells locally made jams, tortillas, and handcrafts. Its coffee shop is the perfect place to sit and think about which rug to buy at the wool showroom.

Across the valley, the waters of the Rio Brazos tumble through the steep walls of the Brazos Box Canyon. A narrow road follows the river up to the mouth of the dead-end canyon where two lodges nestle among tall ponderosa pines, shimmering aspens, and spruce trees. From Corkins Lodge, the sheer granite face of the 11,000-foot Brazos Cliffs loom above. This land is private, so it's best to ask permission to prowl around.

■ CHAMA   *map page 80, B-2*

This small town at the base of 10,000-foot Cumbres Pass retains an outpost feel, a reminder of its formative days in the mid-19th century when a lace curtain in the front room and windowbox geraniums were signs of status. Residents don't have to store their home-grown vegetables in cool cellars anymore, but a hardy constitution helps to withstand sub-zero winter temperatures and the piles of snow that reach to the rooftops. Homes are still simple, folks still friendly, and the railroad (built in 1878) still runs into town.

Today the **Cumbres and Toltec Scenic Railroad** no longer hauls cattle. Instead, it carries summer tourists aboard one of the nation's few remaining coal-fueled, narrow-gauge trains. From mid-June through mid-October, a jet-black locomotive

A whisper can be heard from one side of Echo Canyon to the other due to its unusual acoustical configuration.

NORTH-CENTRAL
NEW MEXICO

The Cumbres and Toltec Scenic Railroad carries tourists to Antonito, Colorado. (Kerrick James)

pulls seven enclosed passenger cars away from the Chama station. Slicing through groves of golden aspens and struggling up the steep mountain pass, it belches charcoal-gray smoke. Golden eagles soar overhead, orange-lichen cover craggy volcanic outcroppings, and backpackers disappear along the banks of the meandering Los Pinos River. The train picks up speed as it emerges from the steep-sloped Toltec Gorge, sweeping past yellow-tipped chamisa and sweet-smelling sagebrush. The day-long journey ends in Antonito, Colorado, where passengers can either spend the night or return to Chama by van. *Call 505-756-2151 for reservations.*

River-runners, and those who'd like to be, should consider running the Chama River from just below El Vado Dam to Abiquiu Reservoir. This 33-mile stretch of the blue-green Chama winds its way between 1,500-foot hills past the dilapidated remains of an old homesteader's ranch and beneath dusty orange rock faces and sagebrush meadows. Rounded orange globemallow, red and purple penstemons, bright purple thistles, and brilliant red-orange desert paintbrush blossom from the riverbank. The current virtually disappears at Monastery Lake, a flat stretch that precedes Christ of the Desert Monastery, of the Benedictine order. (*see page 97*).

Once past the monastery, the river picks up speed and heads into a series of rapids with names like Skull Bridge, Gauge Station, Screaming Left, and Sidekick. Then, before you know it, you're back on shore.

■ JEMEZ MOUNTAINS   *map page 80, E-1 & 2*

One hundred and fifty million years ago the dinosaur *Seismosaurus*, which, at 120 to 140 feet long, was probably the longest creature to ever sprout from an egg and grow up, lumbered through the area of the Jemez Mountains. Ten million years ago, camels, elephants, and horses roamed the tall grasses of northern New Mexico. One million years ago, a mighty explosion—far greater than the blast that ripped the side off Mount St. Helens in 1980—changed the landscape forever. Ash and fiery lava oozed from a volcano that scientists estimate was between 14,000 and 27,000 feet high and that blew a hole in the ground 15 miles across and 3,500 feet deep. For thousands of years, eruptions poured forth, some ash hurtling up to a thousand miles away. This violent activity left behind an entire mountain range with its tallest point, Redondo Peak, a mere 11,254 feet.

Volcanic tuff from the massive explosion blanketed the landscape for miles, creating cone-shaped tent rocks and hoodoos (free-standing formations with a pancake-shaped rock on top). Black volcanic glass, called obsidian, covers some of the tuff. The long-extinct volcano also left behind an extensive network of geothermal pockets. Many remain locked in the earth, while others have burst forth in hot springs scattered throughout the Jemez Mountains. Ironically, the volcano's caldera, known as Valle Grande, has turned into a lush green meadow upon which cattle graze contentedly.

◆ BANDELIER NATIONAL MONUMENT   *map page 80, E/F-1/2*

In the late 1100s, ancestors of the Pueblo Indians found tuff-covered cliffs ideal for carving out homes. In **Frijoles Canyon**, these Indians began growing corn, beans, and squash alongside Frijoles Creek, which flowed through a narrow canyon. They wove cotton cloth and painted black geometric designs on their pottery. Eventually, they moved to the base of the cliffs, erecting a communal house called Tyuonyi, a three-story, free-standing masonry pueblo with 400 rooms. Only one entrance led into the community, which was built in a circle around a plaza. *Kivas* were dug into the open courtyard. A combination of famine, drought, soil-eroding flash

floods, and disease drove the Indians out, and by A.D. 1550 they had resettled along the Rio Grande.

Today, a 1.5-mile-long paved loop trail leads past the cliff dwellings and restored ruins. Rough-hewn ladders reach to the carved-out cliff faces where traces of ancient fires can be seen in faint black soot on ceilings. Ceremonial Cave sits 150 feet above the canyon floor and can be entered by climbing a series of spindly, but sturdy, ladders. Rather than the site of secret ceremonies, some anthropologists think the cool chamber once held tethered turkeys waiting to be dinner. The monument is named for Adolph Bandelier, a Swiss-born, self-taught historian who documented the history of the

Entrance to a ceremonial kiva at Bandelier National Monument. (Kerrick James)

Rio Grande Pueblo Indians. Between 1880 and 1886, Bandelier visited pueblos and talked to their residents, balancing their oral histories against written records. He also wrote "The Delight Makers," a fictionalized account of life in Frijoles Canyon when Tyuonyi was inhabited.

More cliff homes are preserved north of Bandelier on the Santa Clara Reservation. A steep staircase of stone steps leads to **Puye Cliff Dwellings,** which was once one of the most extensive cliffside villages. Some were mere caves, others had porches or open rooms attached. Wooden ladders and steps carved into the volcanic tuff were used to get from one dwelling to another and up to the pine-covered mesa above. Puye's residents, who lived there from A.D. 1450 until the latter part of the 16th century, constructed *kivas* on the cliff's edge, along its base, and on a ledge halfway to the top of the mesa. Their glazed red pottery was painted with serpents who were said to guard the springs that provided their lifeblood. The dwellings, which are closed in the winter, were the prehistoric home of the Santa Clara Indians, who now live nearby on more than 40,000 acres of rich farmland, rangeland, and forests. *Bandelier National Monument; 505-672-0343.*

To reach the Talus House at Bandelier, visitors must climb rickety ladders up dizzying heights to reach the cave entrances. (Kerrick James)

◆ JEMEZ SPRINGS   *map page 80, F-1/2*

NM 4 crosses the gently sloping Jemez Range, passing by the Valle Grande, mean-dering clear-blue streams full of brown and rainbow trout, and pine-covered hill-sides. On the mountains' western edge, a sulphur smell greets the nostrils, indicating that the supernatural-looking **Soda Dam** is right around the corner. Calcium carbonate and travertine deposits from a nearby hot spring have oozed into the river and hardened into a mushroom-shaped dam. Hot rocks near the surface cause the spring to bubble year-round, even when the rocks are covered with snow. In the winter, steam rises, adding to an already eerie atmosphere.

Two miles downstream is **Jemez Springs,** once the site of sheep wars, vigilante activities, and gambling enterprises, but recently a winner of a national All America-ca City award. In the early 1900s, this raucous village attracted swaggering Texas "gunslingers," who were tossed quickly from saloons by local ranchers and bar-tenders who found their bravado unimpressive. Today, the sleepy town, squeezed between steep, red, sandstone hills on the banks of the Jemez River, is known for its friendly atmosphere and its hot springs, among them the **Bodhi Manda Zen Center.** This center, which backs up to the clear waters of the shallow Jemez River and contains its own well-maintained hot spring, welcomes overnight non-Bud-dhist visitors, but please call ahead. *www.bmzc.org, 505-829-3854.*

Just north of town, the eight-foot-thick rock walls of the church of San Jose de los Jemez and the nearby prehistoric pueblo of Giusewa (a Tiwa word that means Place at the Boiling Waters) are preserved at **Jemez State Monument.** The massive church was founded in the early 1620s by Franciscan missionary Fray Alonso de Lugo. A self-guided tour takes you inside the fortress-like church, built with small windows for protection from anticipated invaders. Early twentieth-century excavations revealed one of the few fresco paintings in a New Mexico mis-sion church, but the fresco is gone and only stone now remains. A dirt path marked with small arrows leads past priest quarters and the low walls of the adja-cent Indian village. *505-829-3530.*

In the early 1630s, the missionary enterprise at Guisewa was abandoned, and Jemez Pueblo became the center for religious activities. Located 10 miles south of Jemez Springs, the pueblo's low adobe homes hug the brilliant brick-red earth. Coyote fences made with thin sticks form small corrals, and *hornos* the color of the rich earth appear beside nearly every home. Under shady *ramadas* that line NM 4 north of the pueblo, women sell bread they have baked inside these adobe ovens.

They also cook up frybread on the spot, and the pleasing smell of baking dough mingles with the sweet piñon scent from the fire. Young Jemez men are famous as cross-country runners and firefighters. Many spend their summers fighting forest fires throughout the United States.

■ LOS ALAMOS   *map page 80, E-2/3*

In 1918, Ashley Pond fulfilled a life-long dream by establishing a school where young boys were taught standard book-learning, but could also ride horses, cut wood, and learn the common-sense values that only ranch living can teach. The Los Alamos Ranch School was centered in a two-story log cabin designed by famed Santa Fe architect John Gaw Meem, hidden among tall pines atop the finger-like mesas of the Pajarito Plateau. A. J. Connell, an active Boy Scout leader from Santa Fe, became administrator and continued following scouting principles. Charted as Troop 22, the ranch school became the first mounted troop of scouts in the country.

During the summer of 1922, a young physics professor from Berkeley, J. Robert Oppenheimer, accompanied a pack trip from Frijoles Canyon into the Valle Grande. During subsequent trips into the Jemez wilderness, Oppenheimer often passed by the growing ranch school, occasionally stopping at Edith Warner's tearoom near Otowi Bridge that crossed the Rio Grande on present-day NM 502.

Twenty years later, when Oppenheimer was asked to help select an isolated site for a laboratory to develop the world's first atomic bomb, he thought of the ranch school. In 1941, it was forced to close to make room for the Manhattan Project. For the next three years, scientists secretly gathered in the ponderosa pine forests, sharing ideas. Prefabricated apartment houses and wooden barracks were erected to house hundreds of scientists and technicians who arrived by train, many not even apprised of their destination. They were issued driver's licenses with only numbers, no names, and all mail was sent to a Santa Fe post office box. People who applied to empty trash were only hired if they were illiterate. Even the scientists' families who accompanied them to the mountain outpost that came to be called "The Hill" didn't know exactly why they were there. But they made the best of it: wives taught in classrooms, shopped in Santa Fe, and attended ceremonies at nearby pueblos. Oppenheimer, Niels Bohr, and other scientists often stopped at Warner's tearoom, never letting on what they were doing up in the mountains. On July 16, 1945, the secret was out. The first atomic bomb was detonated in the pre-dawn desert at Trinity Site, 60 miles north of Alamogordo. (Edith Warner's 20 years as a neighbor of the San Ildefonso Indians and the secret community of Los Alamos is chronicled in *The House at Otowi Bridge,* by Peggy Pond Church.)

The Atomic Age had begun. After the war, Oppenheimer and his chief assistants moved out. But Los Alamos National Laboratory stayed behind, continuing in nuclear weapons research. The town that grew up to support the laboratory now is home to one of the highest concentrations of Ph.D.s in the country. Makeshift buildings have been replaced by permanent tan-colored concrete structures. The research has branched off into other areas besides nuclear energy. As the Cold War ended, scientists scurried to focus their research on ways to clean up hazardous-waste sites and develop alternative energy sources.

Although the laboratory maintains high security, the **Bradbury Science Museum** is open to the public. It documents the early days of Project Y, the code name given to the Manhattan Project. Replicas of the bombs dropped on Japan are on display, along with hands-on laser exhibits, and examples of current research into the nature of nuclei, atoms, and molecules. *15th and Central; 505-667-4444.*

The history of this once-secret community where nuclear energy was born is covered at the **Los Alamos Historical Museum.** Housed in Fuller Lodge (the original ranch school cabin), the museum has exhibits on physics and geothermal science; in addition, the museum has Anasazi artifacts and a bookstore well stocked with titles on Los Alamos and the Southwest. *1921 Juniper; 505-662-4493.*

Fortunately, none of these buildings were damaged when a wildfire swept through the city in May 2000, destroying more than 200 homes and charring nearly 50,000 acres of nearby forest.

■ ENCHANTED CIRCLE   *map page 80, C-3 & 5*

An 86-mile loop strikes out from Taos, heading north between the craggy rim of the Rio Grande Gorge and the western edge of the Sangre de Cristo Mountains. It then cuts through the tall ponderosa pines and douglas firs of the rugged range, and drops into the serene, spacious, ridge-rimmed Moreno Valley before returning to Taos along the meandering Rio Fernando de Taos. The Enchanted Circle winds around the state's tallest peaks: at 13,000 feet, Wheeler Peak is the highest.

Arroyo Hondo, the remains of an 1815 land grant, straddles the rushing Rio Hondo, a runoff stream from the nearby mountains. The first Hispanic settlers put in vegetable gardens along the fertile river plain and grazed cattle and sheep in tall grass meadows. A number of Penitente *moradas,* marked by wooden crosses in front, are an indication of the strength this religious confraternity maintained here during the mid-1800s.

It didn't take long for an enterprising Anglo to disrupt the tranquil lives of the settlers. In 1830, Simeon Turley established a prosperous cattle and sheep ranch in Arroyo Hondo. He also planted acres of corn and wheat. Turley dammed the Rio Hondo, built a grist mill, and hired Hispanic settlers and Taos Pueblo Indians to work for him. He was probably best known for the "Taos Lightning" that he distilled. This moonshine often was the cause of disruption at fiestas in northern New Mexico.

During the uprising of 1847 *(see page 122),* Turley escaped after a two-day battle at his ranch, during which his mill was burned. He sought refuge at a neighboring ranch, only to be killed there by his pursuers.

In the 1960s, canvas tepees appeared in the village at the New Buffalo commune, which sprung up near the earthen adobe homes. Part of the back-to-the-land movement, commune members dreamed of leaving behind modern urban life and returning to a more cohesive existence unencumbered by social mores with which they disagreed. Today, only a few members remain. A dirt road leads to the Rio Grande, passing by small gardens, barking dogs, and disinterested sheep. During the spring, trucks hauling hypalon rafts share the bumpy road with residents. At the John Dunn Bridge, which crosses the river where the Rio Hondo flows into it, boaters put in to run the Lower Taos Box, a 17-mile stretch of the Rio Grande that passes underneath the 600-foot-tall Rio Grande Gorge Bridge and through exhilarating boulder-choked rapids. Once beyond the gorge bridge, no roads enter the steep volcanic canyon until the end of the trip. The remoteness and challenging whitewater combine to make this the premier one-day river trip in the state.

North of Arroyo Hondo, atop a gravel ridge, **Questa** has changed from a farming and trade center to a community focused on mining. Molybdenum (an element used in the manufacture of lightbulbs, television tubes, and missile systems) is removed from an ancient volcanic caldera on the steep banks of the blue-green Red River. The only trading Questa shares in anymore is at its few gas stations, restaurants, and motels. The tiny village also markets honey, which can be purchased from the beekeepers themselves at their homes north of town.

NM 38 passes alongside slopes scarred by the mining operation as it follows the Red River to a town named for the blue-green waterway that runs red after rainstorms. Surrounded by hillsides blanketed in tall pines, **Red River** was platted in the late 1800s by the Mallette brothers, who sought to take advantage of a mining boom in the area. By 1905, the town supported 15 saloons, four hotels, two newspapers, a barbershop, hospital, and thriving red-light district. The failure of any big strikes spelled the end of Red River's mining era. But prosperity arrived in the 1920s when flatland vacationers came looking for relief from their homes among the dusty plains of Oklahoma and Texas. They found it in cool, clear streams, radiant aspen groves, and stately pine forests—not to mention dust-free air. Fishing, hiking, bicycling, and pack trips have since lured vacationers to the cool slopes in the summer. Construction of the Red River Ski Area in 1958 turned the town into a year-round resort. Shops, restaurants, and motels line the main street, making Red River a pleasant place to walk around and browse.

A few stone walls and cemetery grave markers are all that remain of **Elizabethtown,** the scene of an 1866–1875 gold rush during which thousands of prospectors feverishly scoured the flanks of 12,500-foot Baldy Mountain. The rowdy mining town was named after the daughter of Capt. William Moore. A Union soldier stationed at Fort Union, Moore opened up the town's first store in 1867. Two hotels, four more mercantiles, and seven saloons quickly followed. Gold worth millions of dollars was removed from claims staked in the pine-studded hills before the ore played out. In 1903, a fire destroyed much of the dying town's business district. Baldy Mountain endures, of course: a rounded bare knob that still stands like a beacon overlooking the tall grasses of the Moreno Valley.

In 1919, Charles Springer, a prominent cattleman, banker, and engineer, decided it was time to provide a stable water source for the vast fields of the Moreno Valley. He designed and built Eagle Nest Dam at the head of Cimarron Canyon. Today, a five-mile-long lake, named after the dam, is tapped for irrigation. The lake holds some of the state's biggest rainbow trout and kokanee salmon, which anglers go after even in winter through holes in the ice. A year after the dam went up, a village followed. The abundance of soaring golden eagles in the mountains that surround the lush Moreno Valley inspired residents of Thermal to rename their town **Eagle Nest.** For years, Eagle Nest was the largest town in the valley, but today has been relegated to the status of a stock-up and overnight stop because of newer developments nearby.

JEWISH TRADITION IN NEW MEXICO

In 1492, when Columbus set sail for Asia (and came upon America instead), Ferdinand and Isabella of Spain issued the infamous Edict of 1492, which forced Spanish Jews to choose between exile or conversion. Some Jews became "new Christians," many only pretending to convert, and in the early years of the Conquest, emigrated to Mexico. When the Inquisition reached the New World, the "new Christians" found themselves once again under suspicion, and many began moving to the farthest reaches of the empire, into what is now New Mexico.

Ostensibly practicing Catholics, these Jewish families clung in private to their traditions: lighting candles on Fridays, baking unleavened bread, and keeping the Sabbath. Recently, Jewish families searching for their roots have found hundreds of gravestones with Hebrew inscriptions in isolated cemeteries across the state.

Although the oldest synagogue in the United States was founded in New York in 1645, it may be that its first *minyan* was held in New Mexico.

The **Vietnam Veterans National Memorial** sweeps upward from a hillside at the south end of Eagle Nest Lake. The solemn white structure, with 50-foot-high front walls was raised piece-by-piece by the family of Dr. Victor Westphall, whose son was killed in a 1968 enemy ambush in Vietnam. The chapel—the first memorial to Vietnam vets built in the United States—was completed in 1971. It is open 24 hours a day, and is now recognized as a major national Vietnam veterans memorial. Special programs take place on Memorial Day and Veteran's Day

After a shaky start in the mid-1970s as a ski area, **Angel Fire** has blossomed into a year-round resort that offers golf, fishing, tennis, hiking, and horseback riding. From the ski area's 34 miles of trails, the vast Moreno Valley unfolds below with snowcapped Wheeler Peak visible in the distance. *See page 304.*

■ PECOS NATIONAL HISTORICAL PARK   *map page 80, F-4*

By A.D. 1450, Indians in the Pecos River Valley were living in a tiered village on a rocky ridge overlooking the river and pine-studded mesas beyond. Dwellings rose five stories high and were divided into 600 rooms and 22 *kivas*. These Towa-speaking Indians cultivated corn, squash, beans, and cotton in the fertile valley and foraged for wild berries and nuts in the foothills of the Sangre de Cristo Mountains. By today's standards they were a small people; most women stood under five feet. Men draped themselves in animal skins, and women wore one-shouldered dresses and turkey feather robes.

When Franciscan friars arrived at the pueblo in the 1620s, they ordered the Indians to build the 170-foot-long, 90-foot-wide Mission de Nuestra Señora de los Angeles de Porciuncula. In addition to introducing Catholicism to the Indians, the friars taught them the Spanish way of life. They organized weaving rooms, tanneries, classrooms, and a carpentry shop, planted gardens of flowers and vegetables and fruit orchards, and brought in small bands of goats, sheep, cattle, and horses. In exchange, the Indians submitted to baptism and provided labor to maintain the community. That the Indians didn't much appreciate the new lifestyle became evident when they enthusiastically participated in the 1680 Pueblo Revolt, burning the church and joining in the attack on Santa Fe. When they were reconquered 12 years later, the Indians built a smaller church. By this time, repeated attacks by Comanches on the pueblo village, coupled with smallpox outbreaks, had severely reduced the population. Eventually, Pecos residents moved into nearby villages or joined their brethren at Jemez Pueblo, the only remaining Towa-speaking community. In the mid-1800s, when travelers passed by on the Santa Fe Trail, all that remained were the crumbling ruins of the once-proud pueblo.

The partial walls of the massive church still stand, testament to long hours of Indian labor. To the north are the ruins of the extensive pueblo. At a restored *kiva,* a ladder leads into a musty chamber that holds memories of many secret ceremonies. Push a button on one of the vertical support beams, and drumbeats and chanting voices fill the dank room, much as they might have hundreds of years ago. The Fogelson Visitor Center, named after the area's large landowner (actress Greer Garson's husband) provides both an excellent introduction and in-depth look at the Indian and Spanish eras. *Pecos National Historical Park is situated four miles north of I-25 on NM 63; 505-757-6414.*

Two miles past the park, the tiny village of Pecos supplies campers and fishermen heading into the Pecos Wilderness. NM 63 follows the narrow, slow-moving Pecos River, penetrating the tall pines of the forest until ending at the hunting and fishing resort of Cowles. A few dude ranches and camps are spread out along the river, which is stocked with rainbow and brown trout.

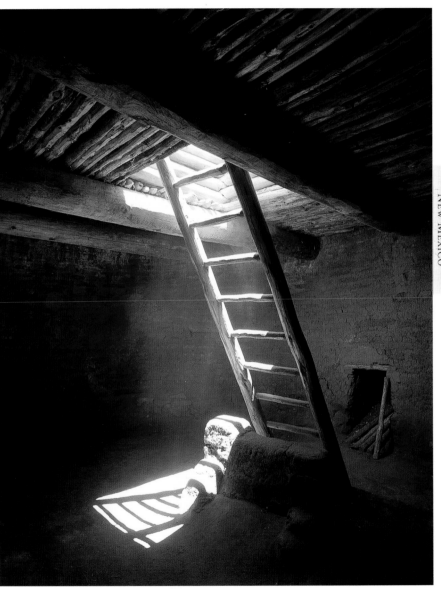

Interior of kiva at Pecos National Historical Park. (Kerrick James)

NORTH-CENTRAL
NEW MEXICO

GEORGIA O'KEEFFE

That first summer I spent in New Mexico I was a little surprised that there were so few flowers. There was no rain so the flowers didn't come. Bones were easy to find so I began collecting bones. When I was returning East I was bothered about my work—the country had been so wonderful that by comparison what I had done with it looked very poor to me—although I knew it had been one of my best painting years. I had to go home—what could I take with me of the country to keep me working on it? I had collected many bones and finally decided that the best thing I could do was to take with me a barrel of bones—so I took a barrel of bones. —Georgia O'Keeffe

On a warm May day in 1929, Georgia O'Keeffe stepped off a train at the small station in Lamy, New Mexico, and beheld a pale-green landscape covered in bushy piñon and juniper trees, gray-green in the brilliant New Mexico sunshine. She was 41 years old and had ventured west without her husband, Alfred Stieglitz, to spend the summer painting whatever the dry, dusty desert offered as a subject. By then an established painter, O'Keeffe instantly was enamored with the radiant light and the sharp edges of mountains, trees, and flowers caused by the thin, dry air. "No one told me it was like this!" she told her host, Mabel Dodge Luhan, a wealthy art patron who owned a sprawling compound in Taos.

After one of her paintings sold in New York for $6,000, O'Keeffe bought a black Model A Ford, which she used to explore the countryside. One day, motoring with Charles Collier, the son of the director of the Bureau of Indian Affairs, O'Keeffe reached the lavender, dusty orange cliffs of Abiquiu, about 60 miles west of Taos. Collier was searching for Ghost Ranch, a place he thought the painter would enjoy, but they never found an entrance. "This is my world, but how to get into it?" O'Keeffe remembered thinking at the time.

A few years later, she found the ranch, a cluster of low adobe buildings set in the shadows of a sandstone mesa speckled with piñons and junipers. Owner Arthur Newton Pack had just purchased the working cattle ranch and was turning it into a fancy dude ranch. O'Keeffe moved into a cottage and returned there every summer until 1940, when she purchased Rancho de los Burros, a U-shaped adobe house Pack had built for himself three miles from the main house. Whitewashed rooms surrounded a patio, and a huge bedroom window overlooked a flat-top mesa called the Pedernal, which lay 10 miles to the south. Behind the house to the north, rosy red, pale yellow, and coral cliffs rose to meet an azure sky. The colors of these corrugated cliffs shifted as the sun moved across the sky. The artist replaced adobe walls with huge panes of glass, and while the interior remained sparsely furnished, it overflowed with bones, rocks, shells, pine cones, driftwood, and feathers she collected on daily walks through sandstone canyons and piñon-juniper forests.

> The unexplainable thing in nature that makes me feel the world is big far beyond my understanding—to understand maybe by trying to put it into form. To find the feeling of infinity on the horizon line or just over the next hill.

In 1945, O'Keeffe purchased a dilapidated house that overlooked the Chama River in the nearby village of Abiquiu. She had the place rebuilt to her specifications—once again, glass walls replaced older adobe ones, fireplaces were installed in every room, and village women plastered mud on the rounded fireplace walls.

The following year, Stieglitz died in New York, and shortly thereafter, O'Keeffe moved to New Mexico for good. She continued to paint the soft curves of Abiquiu's hills and flowers, casting many in ethereal poses. "Two walls of my room in the Abiquiu house are glass and from one window I see the road toward Española, Santa Fe, and the world. The road fascinates me with its ups and downs and finally its wide sweep as it speeds toward the wall of my hilltop to go past me," she said to describe two 1964 paintings of US 84.

In 1972, a young impoverished potter came asking for work. After a few rebuffs, the aging artist hired him to do odd jobs at her Abiquiu home. Juan Hamilton subsequently became her constant companion, and as her eyesight failed, he managed her affairs. Their friendship lasted until O'Keeffe's death in 1986. She was 98. The house is open to visitors, but tour reservations must be made well in advance; *call 505-685-4539.*

Georgia O'Keeffe near the "Pink House," Taos, 1929. (Museum of New Mexico)

GREATER SANTA FE

SANTA FE & TAOS

■ HIGHLIGHTS

Central Santa Fe map on page 130.
Downtown Taos map on page 144.
Food and Lodging begins on page 280.

BROWN ADOBE HOUSES, SOME NEARLY 200 YEARS OLD, line narrow dirt streets as reminders of a past that doesn't feel too far away in the town of **Santa Fe**. Laid out in the protective foothills of the Sangre de Cristo Mountains, Santa Fe's crooked streets follow the contours of the uneven earth. Most buildings are one story high, and painted in all shades of brown—from tawny to ginger to coffee. Even though many are of frame construction, nearly all reflect the flat-roofed, box-shaped, adobe building style that dominated the city's early architecture. Yards are often small, and shabby exteriors frequently belie elaborate interiors with pine *vigas*, corner *kiva* fireplaces, polished brick and tile floors, and fluid, curving walls and doorways. Due to this indigenous architectural style, taken from Indian pueblos, the town blends in with the rolling landscape of piñon and juniper. At odd moments in the spare desert light it seems to have sprouted from the earth.

The town of **Taos**, 70 miles north of Santa Fe, was built on a high plateau between a deep chasm carved by the Rio Grande and the majestic peaks of the Sangre de Cristos. This smaller version of Santa Fe maintains the tradition of low-slung homes along winding dirt streets, which are rarely identified by signs. With its small population (5,300) and its isolated location, the village tends to be less fashionable and "hip" than Santa Fe. People choose lifestyles that meet basic needs and activities revolve around the Rio Grande and nearby mountains. Recycling takes on new meaning in homes built of old tires and empty aluminum cans. It's easy to be yourself in Taos, no matter how unusual you might be.

Both Santa Fe and Taos attract artists, writers, natural healers, psychics, and other creative minds from around the world whose spirits respond to the soft golden light of early morning and the dusty red of evening. The hustle-bustle of modern life is tempered, as people linger over cappuccinos or spend a day chopping and hauling piñon wood from the nearby mountains. Blue jeans and cowboy boots are de rigueur.

Both towns boast an inordinate number of lodgings, galleries, museums, gift shops, bookstores, and restaurants. Taos attracts individualists with a keen appreciation of its outpost character, while Santa Fe is more for the idiosyncratic cosmopolitan and gourmet.

Both towns, however, are in danger of losing what makes them so appealing: their tri-cultural mixture of Indians, Hispanics, and Anglos. As urban outsiders descend upon the two communities, seeking clean air, simpler lifestyles, and aesthetic sophistication, many long-time residents have been forced to leave, taking traditions with them. But those traditions—of roasting and freezing chile, slapping out fresh tortillas, and sharing in the springtime ritual of clearing out irrigation ditches—continue to thrive in the small communities that dot the roads between Santa Fe and Taos.

■ HISTORY

Ancestors of today's Taos Pueblo residents lived nearly 1,000 years ago in small villages throughout northern New Mexico. By 1350, they had settled along the shallow waters of the Rio Pueblo where they erected, tier by tier, the stepped walls of Taos Pueblo. Nearby they grew squash and beans, and corn that women ground between two rocks and then cooked into flat corncakes. Men hunted deer, rabbits, and squirrels in the nearby mountains. Due to the isolation of this northernmost pueblo, Taos was a major target of raiding Comanche and Ute Indians who scoured the northern plains. But this same seclusion also kept away Spanish missionaries. Even though a mission church was built there in 1617 and the Pueblo Revolt of 1680 was plotted at Taos, few Spanish moved into the area until the eighteenth century.

Rather, missionaries concentrated on pueblos closer to Santa Fe, established in 1610 as the capital of the new Spanish colony. During its formative years, Santa Fe was maintained primarily for the purpose of bringing the Catholic faith to New Mexico's Pueblo Indians. In 1680, however, the Indians rebelled against the Spanish and their religion. Colonists who escaped from their homes fled to the

Palace of the Governors, an enclosed one-story compound that housed the governor, the town's chief political officers and their offices, a military chapel, shops, and work rooms. As the surviving colonists huddled together inside the governor's palace, the Indians outside set fire to a church and other prominent buildings around the plaza, dancing and shouting victory chants. Once the Spanish were cornered and sufficiently frightened, the Indians allowed them to depart, and they marched in good order for 300 miles until they reached El Paso, where they remained for the next 12 years.

La Conquistadora, who accompanied Spanish colonists in their reconquest of New Mexico from the Indians. (Museum of New Mexico)

Diego de Vargas, a member of one of Spain's leading families, was assigned the task of restoring Spanish rule to New Mexico. In 1692, he led a squad of soldiers and Indians up El Camino Real to Santa Fe. There he surprised a group of Indians who had turned the governor's palace into a pueblo. After minor resistance, the Indians surrendered peacefully, returning the battered capital to the Spanish. Every September since 1712, this reconquest has been celebrated as Las Fiestas de Santa Fe.

After securing the capital, De Vargas returned to El Paso, where he gathered colonists to resettle the territory. In October 1693, he ushered northward a ponderous entourage that included 70 families, 18 friars, 100 soldiers, 2,000 horses, 1,000 mules, and 900 head of cattle. Eighteen carts hauled heavy supplies, including three cannons. A small wooden statuette of the Virgin, known as La Conquistadora, accompanied this excursion. La Conquistadora originally had been brought to the capital in 1625, but was carried down to El Paso by the retreating Spaniards in 1680.

Upon arrival, De Vargas discovered the Indians had, in his absence, changed their minds and decided to keep Santa Fe and resist the Spanish. Well-armed and organized, De Vargas's men succeeded in taking back the capital by force. Tradition has it that De Vargas attributed his success to the Virgin Mary through La Conquistadora, and today she stands on a gilded altar in the north chapel of St. Francis Cathedral. Every June, La Conquistadora is paraded through town to Rosario Chapel, the site of De Vargas's camp during the reconquest. A novena of masses is said before a procession returns her to the cathedral.

After a few more Indian uprisings were quickly quashed, the conquering Spanish moved in by droves, settling the protective hills near the new capital and the high Taos Plateau where they grew vegetables, wheat, and barley alongside streams that flowed from the nearby mountains. In 1617, Fray Pedro de Miranda built a mission near Taos Pueblo. An important landowner in the region was Fernando de Chávez, whose family was slain during the Pueblo Revolt. Chávez didn't return after the reconquest, but his name was attached to the land; and in 1710, when Cristóbal de la Serna petitioned for a land grant, he identified Chávez as the previous owner. Thus, the Spanish settlement became known as Fernando de Taos. In 1716, a second community was established a few miles south and is known today as Ranchos de Taos.

Typically, homes were joined together by a solid rear wall that provided protection from raiding Comanches, who continually threatened settlers. During 1759, for example, 50 Spanish women and children were abducted by Indians. The following year, Spanish soldiers bent on revenge fought and killed 400 Comanches among the tall grasses of the high plains.

A tradition that persisted during these unsettled times was the annual Taos Trade Fair, at which Ute, Apache, and Comanche Indians, laden with buffalo hides, jerky, and buckskins, pitched tepees outside of town, and traded for Spanish guns, knives, and ammunition, as well as vegetables and grains cultivated at the pueblos. Ill feelings were set aside during this boisterous occasion, and large amounts of local moonshine, called Taos Lightning, were consumed. By evening, everyone had joined together at an all-night fandango.

Sign language was used to secure deals. Goods were bartered—no money changed hands. Spanish or Indian captives often accompanied the Indian traders who sought to trade goods for their release. Sometimes the Spanish governor led a retinue from Santa Fe to oversee the noisy gathering. As soon as the fair ended and

St. Francis of Assisi Mission, Ranchos de Taos. (Kerrick James)

parties departed, however, tribes began plotting upcoming raids. During the nineteenth century, the trade fair brought mountain men of French descent with beaver pelts, and Missouri merchants freshly arrived on the Santa Fe Trail with calico, jewelry, handkerchiefs, furniture, glassware, paper and ink, spices, and medicine. Today, the fair is reenacted in late September at the Martínez Hacienda, followed a week later by the feast of San Geronimo at Taos Pueblo, which commemorates a pueblo trade fair that dates to prehistoric times.

By 1821, Mexico had declared its independence from Spain, and Santa Fe became a far-flung outpost (nearly 1,400 miles north of Mexico City) of the struggling new nation. In the mid-1800s, the United States' doctrine of Manifest Destiny brought Gen. Stephen Kearny and his troops to the Southwest to claim the territory for the United States. While most of New Mexico rolled over and let him fly the Stars and Stripes, a group of headstrong Taoseños loyal to Mexico mounted a resistance effort. On a wintry January night in 1847, Hispanic settlers and Taos Indians converged on the Taos residence of Charles Bent, governor of the new U.S. territory of New Mexico, killed him, and paraded his scalp on a board through the streets. A week later, soldiers arrived from Santa Fe and defeated the insurgents who had barricaded themselves inside the Taos Pueblo mission church.

Independence from Spain also opened doors to trade with the United States. Under Spanish rule, the northern province could trade only with Mexico, but Mexican leaders relaxed that edict and encouraged a business relationship with the United States. The Santa Fe Trail was quickly established as a major trade route between Santa Fe and Independence, Missouri. Caravans rolled across the prairie, bringing cloth, tools, furniture, and dishes, along with adventurous American settlers.

The 1848 Treaty of Guadalupe Hidalgo ceded New Mexico to the United States, which immediately began wielding its influence. Lawyers, newspapermen, and shopkeepers flocked to the newly opened frontier. In Santa Fe, Archbishop Jean Baptiste Lamy arrived in 1851 and promptly began molding New Mexico's laid-back clergy into disciplined church leaders. He also designed a cathedral in the Romanesque style of his native Auvergne, France. Begun in 1869, it took 17 years to complete St. Francis Cathedral, which today dominates the end of San Francisco Street in downtown Santa Fe. Built of light-tan volcanic stone quarried in hills south of town, the cathedral stands as a monument to Lamy, who went on to build 45 more churches and bring a handful of parochial schools to the wild New Mexico Territory.

SANTA FE & TAOS 123

SANTA FE TRAIL

William Becknell knew a good deal when he saw one. Part of a carefree fivesome trapping and hunting horses in the Southwest in 1821, the veteran Indian fighter paid close attention to the dizzying profits his group reaped when they were invited to Santa Fe that September to celebrate Mexico's newly won independence from Spain.

Under Spanish rule, New Mexicans were forbidden to trade with anyone other than Mexico. Traders loaded carretas and pack mules with bearskins, piñon nuts, tallow candles, and wool and slowly made their way along the Chihuahua Trail, traveling 550 miles to Chihuahua City or another 900 miles on El Camino Real to Mexico City. There they exchanged their frontier goods for spices, chocolate, shoes, writing paper, and ink. Large caravans usually made the rough trip twice a year.

Because of this isolation, Santa Fe's residents rarely saw new wares. But once word reached the frontier capital of Mexico's independence, New Mexico's borders were flung open to traders. In no time, Becknell and his party sold their supply of brightly colored blankets, knives, kettles, and looking glasses brought along to trade with Indians. And their profits were three-fold!

Soon thereafter, Becknell hightailed it back home to Franklin, Missouri, where he restocked and headed west again. This time, instead of following the Arkansas River into southeastern Colorado and then into New Mexico along the steep slopes of Raton Pass, Becknell veered south across the Arkansas River about 20 miles west of Fort Dodge, Kansas, crossing the Oklahoma panhandle and the Cimarron River in a straight shot that led to Santa Fe.

For the next 59 years, Becknell's Cimarron Cutoff was the principal trade route to the Southwest. The main arm of the Santa Fe Trail continued into Colorado, where Bent's Fort became the largest trading post of the West. This mountain branch was longer, but wood and water were plentiful, compared to the Cimarron Cutoff, which cut 10 days off the trip but entailed crossing the 60 miles of bone-dry desert and hostile Indian country between the two rivers.

The Santa Fe Trail was the first major Western trade route and preceded by two decades the more northern Oregon and California trails. By 1831, oxen were replacing mules as the preferred beasts of burden on the trail. Eight of the slow but steady animals could pull 2-plus tons of cooking pots, calico cloth, knives, and tools in a wagon with iron-rimmed wheels as tall as a man's head. Each spring, 100 of these wagons gathered in Missouri for the 900-mile trek across the plains of Kansas and

SANTA FE & TAOS

the tall-grass prairies of northeastern New Mexico. The lumbering caravans averaged 15 to 20 miles a day and in New Mexico passed by Rabbit Ears Mountain, Starvation Peak, the abandoned Pecos Mission (now Pecos National Monument), and Pigeon's Ranch. At the end of the trail in Santa Fe, tired oxen were traded or sold for fresh ones and the Conestoga wagons were loaded with gold, silver, wood, and furs.

This opening up of the West was not without its hazards. Pawnee, Apache, Comanche, and Ute Indians, unhappy with these intrusive caravans, often killed traders they encountered. In mid-July 1828, just inside what was to become the state of New Mexico, two scouts riding ahead of a caravan curled up for a nap on a bank of the North Canadian River as they waited for the wagons. A raiding party of Pawnees spotted the sleeping men, and creeping silently, seized their rifles and shot Capt. Daniel Munroe and Samuel McNees, just as the wagon train rolled down the opposite bank. As the men were being buried, six Comanche Indians rode up. No questions were asked and all but one was killed. The spot became known as McNees's Crossing. Today the crossing is only a dry river bed in the middle of a cow pasture.

In 1849, when Dr. J.M. White, his family, a servant, and four men left a wagon train near Point of Rocks, a rugged 150-foot-tall promontory near Farley, New Mexico, to push on by themselves, a group of Apaches approached the group asking for gifts. Dr. White refused. The Indians shot all of the men and took the women captive. Led by legendary Indian fighter Col. Kit Carson, a group of men chased the band. (Carson himself had made the western trip 23 years earlier as a 16-year-old.) Just as they were closing in on the Apaches, the Indians shot Mrs. White to death with arrows. The servant was never found.

Yet another battle ensued near the Point of Rocks when some 200 Comanches set upon a wagon train on January 1, 1833. After slaughtering all of the party's mules and horses and wounding most of the 12 traders in the caravan during a 32-hour period, the Indians let them go.

After the New Mexico territory had won its independence from Mexico in 1848, forts were erected to protect traders from the bitter Indians. The Civil War delayed the coming of the Santa Fe Railroad, but in 1880 the iron horse began inching its way across the Mountain Branch of the Santa Fe Trail, tunneling through mountains in Raton Pass and chugging across northern grasslands before it reached Lamy, outside of Santa Fe.

Today, tall grass covers deep indentations carved into the soft earth from years of wagon wheels creaking across the now-silent prairie. These ruts that stretch to the eastern horizon and ghosts in the wind are all that remain of the first major trade route that connected New Mexico to the eastern United States.

Recently, Congress honored the Santa Fe by designating it a National Trail and providing funds to preserve and mark the vestiges of this once-vital lifeline.

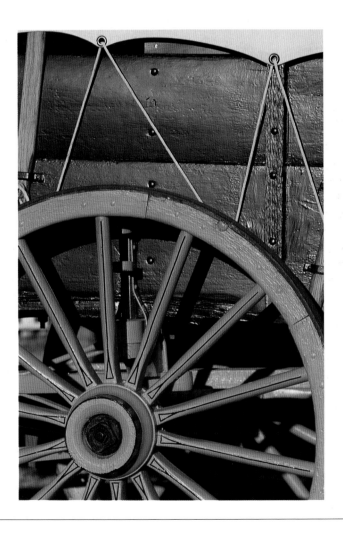

Outside of Santa Fe, however, New Mexico continued to be ruled by the smoking gun. In 1878, President Rutherford B. Hayes appointed Lew Wallace as governor to enforce law and order. In between trying to negotiate the capture of Billy the Kid and administer the state, Wallace penned *Ben Hur* in 1880 while living at the Palace of the Governors.

In 1879, the Santa Fe Railroad reached Lamy, 18 miles south of Santa Fe (the closest passenger trains ever came to Santa Fe itself). With this comfortable and efficient mode of travel, ever more immigrants from the U.S. arrived, bringing with them their own ideas and traditions. Red-brick Victorian houses with double-hung windows were soon being built alongside brown adobes with rough-hewn panes.

Seventy years later, in 1949, Ernie Blake arrived in Santa Fe to help build the Santa Fe Ski Basin on the western slopes of 12,409-foot Lake Peak. The Swiss-born mountaineer managed the small ski area for five years, until he discovered the perfect location for his dream ski resort at the abandoned copper mining camp of Twining, north of Taos. Against the advice of friends who warned him the slope was too steep and would scare off skiers, Blake installed the first lift in January 1956 and went on to mold Taos Ski Valley into one of the world's most popular resorts. Today, the mountain offers skiers some of the most challenging terrain in the West.

■ ARTISTS ARRIVE

In 1848, two Philadelphians, Edward and Richard Kern, arrived at **Taos,** and if their stay was brief, the brothers earned the distinction of being the first artists to visit the town. Fifty years later, a broken wagon wheel detoured painters Bert Phillips and Ernest Blumenschein, who were on their way to Mexico, into the dusty town. Once there, they found themselves enthralled with the handsome, chiseled faces of the Taos Indians, the deep-dark eyes of Hispanic farmers, and the layers of pine-covered mountain ridges. They stayed to establish what came to be known as the Taos School—a group of painters who displayed throughout the world spiritual canvases of Indians and mountains, awash with the ethereal New Mexico light.

Taos became firmly established as an art colony in 1915 when the Taos Society of Artists was formed. In addition to Phillips and Blumenschein, members were J. H. Sharp, Oscar Berninghaus, E. Irving Couse, Victor Higgins, Walter Ufer, and Kenneth Adams. The following year, a bored wealthy Easterner by the name of

Mabel Dodge Sterne moved to Taos. In 1923, she married a Taos Indian, Tony Luhan. To her wide circle of friends back East she wrote of sunsets transforming the high plateau and pine-clad mountains into a rose-red tableau, and of Indian people living a simple life of survival in multi-level adobe structures with no electricity or plumbing.

Artists who came at her invitation included Ansel Adams, Andrew Dasburg, Georgia O'Keeffe, Marsden Hartley, and John Marin. Perhaps her greatest visitor arrived in 1922. D.H Lawrence and his wife Frieda spent that fall and winter and the spring of 1924 at Kiowa Ranch north of Taos, a gift of the generous Mabel Dodge Luhan. Even though his time in New Mexico was short, Lawrence wrote that the state changed him forever.

> All those mornings when I went with a hoe along the ditch to the Cañon, at the ranch, and stood, in the fierce, proud silence of the Rockies, on their foothills, to look far over the desert to the blue mountains away in Arizona, blue as chalcedony, with the sage-brush desert sweeping grey-blue in between, dotted with tiny cube-crystals of houses, the vast amphitheatre of lofty, indomitable desert, sweeping round to the ponderous Sangre de Cristo mountains on the east, and coming up flush at the pine-dotted foot-hills of the Rockies! What splendor! Only the tawny eagle could really sail out into the splendor of it all.

Lawrence left behind half a dozen paintings—stylized figures displaying an amateurish quality unlike the sophisticated prose of his novels and essays. The paintings now hang on the walls of the manager's office at La Fonda, a hotel on the plaza in the town of Taos. For $1, you can view the bare breasts of plump women with piercing eyes. Just as interesting are photographs, many signed, of Taos' famous residents, including film actor and director Dennis Hopper, Frieda Lawrence, and Cubist painter Andrew Dasburg.

In 1930, Lawrence died in France from tuberculosis. A few years later, his wife Frieda returned to Taos with his ashes and her new lover, Angelo Ravagli. Today, the ashes are housed in a small chapel at the ranch that Frieda bequeathed to the University of New Mexico. Her own grave is nearby.

Most artists and writers who came to the state arrived by train, and many of them preferred the juniper foothills of **Santa Fe** to the plateau outpost of Taos. They included Willa Cather, Mary Austin, and Oliver La Farge, who won a 1929 Pulitzer Prize for a Navajo love story called "Laughing Boy."

One group of Santa Fe artists—who met while painting the high desert country-side and the people of Santa Fe—formed Los Cinco Pintores (The Five Painters). Their goal was to "bring art to the people," and members were Jozef Bakos, Walter Mruk, Will Shuster, Willard Nash, and Fremont Ellis. The group's first exhibition was in 1921 at the Museum of Fine Arts. All built homes on Camino del Monte Sol and worked in studios along and near Canyon Road, today the most concen-trated art district in the city. They were dubbed "the five nuts in five mud huts." Ellis's works are for sale at his Canyon Road studio, which is open by appointment.

Will Shuster briefly broke away from painting in 1926 to help create Zozobra, a menacing 40-foot-tall wooden puppet that has come to symbolize Las Fiestas de Santa Fe. The weekend celebration, which commemorates the 1692 re-occupation of Santa Fe by Diego de Vargas, begins at dusk on the Friday following Labor Day. Zozobra, also known as Old Man Gloom, eyes gleaming with anger, waves his arms and groans in anguish at Fort Marcy Park, trying to dissuade the Fire God from igniting his papier-maché body with a flaming torch. The effigy always loses and goes up in a burst of flame to the cheers of 40,000 spectators, gleeful to see gloom disappear for another year.

Many others followed these early artists to northern New Mexico, including woodcutter Gustave Baumann, Russians Leon Gaspard and Nicolai Fechin, and painter Robert Henri.

The growth of the Santa Fe and Taos art colonies fostered a new respect for Indian artists, such as Allan Houser, Dan Namingha, Michael Naranjo, and Pablita Velarde, whose works hang in museums and galleries.

Blumenschein House in Taos is a fine example of "Santa Fe style."

D. H. LAWRENCE IN TAOS

D. H. Lawrence and his wife Frieda spent the fall/winter of 1922–23 and the summer of 1924 at a ranch outside Taos.

We leave the ranch quite wild—only there's abundant feed for the five horses. And if we wanted to take the trouble, we could bring the water here as McClure did, and have a little farm.—There's quite a lot of land, really—I'd say 180 acres, but it takes a terrible long time to go around the fence, through the wild forest.—We got lots of wild strawberries—and we still get gallons of wild raspberries, up our own little canyon, where no soul ever goes. If we ride two miles, we can get no farther. Beyond, all savage, unbroken mountain.

We get our things from Taos—17 miles—either by wagon or when someone is coming in a car. Our road is no road—a breaking through the forest—but people come to see us. Every evening, just after tea, we saddle up and ride down to Del Monte Ranch for the milk, butter, eggs, and letters. The old trail passes their gate, and the mailman, on horseback, leaves all the mail in a box nailed on a tree. Usually we get back just at dusk. Yesterday we rode down to San Cristobal, where there is a cross-roads, a blacksmith, and a tiny village with no shop, no anything, save the blacksmith —only a handful of Mexicans who speak Spanish—we went to get Frieda's grey horse—the Azul—shod. They call him in Spanish *el Azul*—the Blue. During the day there's always plenty to do—chopping wood, carrying water —and our own work: sometimes we all paint pictures. Next week the Indian Geronimo is coming up to help me mend the corral, and build a porch over my door, and fix the spring for winter, with a big trough where horse can drink. I want a Mexican to come and live here while we are away, to keep the place from going wild, squirrels and bushy-tailed pack-rats from coming in, and to see the water doesn't freeze for the horses. It gets very cold, and snow often knee deep. Sometimes, for a day or two, no getting away from the ranch.

There, I hope that's all you want to know.

—D.H. Lawrence in a letter to his niece, 1924

■ SANTA FE SIGHTS AND ATTRACTIONS

In the early days, their isolation caused Santa Feans to remain a part of three worlds: that of the spiritual Indians, the sensuous Spanish, and Anglo adventurers. For example, they adopted the earthen building styles of their neighbors, the Pueblo Indians in order to deal with an intense summer sun, spring winds that whipped up the sandy soil, and a white winter carpet that turned streets into mud bogs when it melted away. But they steadfastly retained the colorful dress of their forefathers to the south in Mexico or across the Atlantic Ocean in Spain.

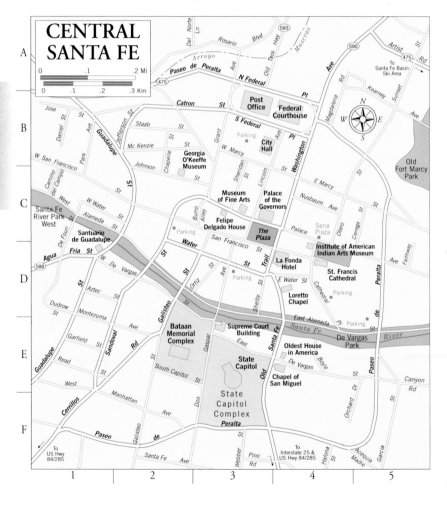

Unwittingly, these hardy and ingenious people derived a unique and indigenous fashion statement known as "Santa Fe Style" that today can be found in all corners of the United States. While dirt-and-straw adobe bricks survive only in dry climates, *vigas* and *latilla* ceilings and red-brown clay tiled floors go anywhere, most notably, perhaps, in the restaurants of Los Angeles and New York.

But it's in New Mexico where they seem to belong. Cozy corner *kiva* fireplaces warm cold nights, flat roofs become gardens during summer months, and doorways curve into adobe benches underneath cobalt-blue wood-trimmed windows. Navajo and Chimayo textiles adorn walls and floors. Chairs, tables, and cupboards are intricately carved in the old Spanish Colonial style. Tin light fixtures and frames hang on white plaster walls.

In the early 1900s, a group of Santa Fe painters, writers, architects, businessmen, and politicians began a movement to preserve this Spanish-Pueblo architectural style, with its flat-roofed adobe buildings. The movement resulted in important new buildings that celebrated their vision: the Museum of Fine Arts, La Fonda, the New Mexico School for the Deaf—all sporting *vigas,* deliberately uneven walls, and *kiva* fireplaces.

But as Santa Fe Style has gained in popularity, so have its travesties multiplied. One newcomer to Santa Fe, an apartment manager, wanted to erect a 15-foot-high, turquoise-colored coyote outside the apartment complex because she thought it was the town's symbol. After all, coyotes howling at the moon are everywhere in the "City Different," one of Santa Fe's labels. These wooden sculptures come in a multitude of colors, from fire-engine red to seafoam green, and often wear a contrasting bandana around their necks. Another cliché is brightly painted wooden snakes, writhing as if to escape their cuteness. Add to these new arrivals a 20-pound squash blossom necklace with enough turquoise to fill a small safe, finely worked silver concha belts, and cow and ram skulls with horns, and you've got what many people refer to as "Santa Fe Tacky."

Tacky or stylish, Santa Fe is different and unlike "the deadly monotony of 10,000 American towns," as Santa Fe painter Carlos Vierra described the rest of the United States in 1917.

◆ GALLERIES AND SHOPS

More than 200 galleries line the plazas and winding streets of Santa Fe. They are stocked with items ranging from the sublime to the ridiculous, including Western landscape paintings, cowboy portraits, acrylic abstracts, old and new pottery, bandana-bedecked howling coyotes, bronze buffaloes, and the works of a few European masters. Roy Rogers floor lamps stand next to glass cases stuffed with exquisite Hopi silver bracelets and earrings. Ancient Mimbres pottery and yucca water baskets are for sale next door to a shop that displays saddles and silver spurs . In many galleries and shops, a friendly hound or cat extends the initial greetings.

A stroll up the winding **Canyon Road,** an old Indian trail that leads into the piñon foothills, is an immersion into the town's eclectic art world. Nearly 100 galleries, shops, and restaurants line the narrow road.

In 1998, the **Gerald Peters Gallery,** a longtime Santa Fe fixture, moved into a sprawling new building on the edge of the city's historic district. This elegant space, filled with many works by distinguished artists, feels more like a museum than a gallery. In addition to sculpture, the 8,500 square feet of exhibit space is dedicated to western, wildlife and contemporary art, and paintings by artists of the early Taos and Santa Fe arts colonies.

The sweet smell of piñon smoke wafts from *kiva* fireplaces, which provide welcome warmth on a chilly winter day. The uncluttered, wood-floored interior

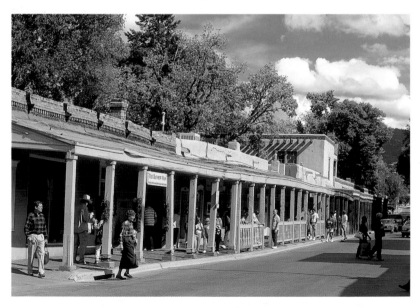

Santa Fe Plaza offers boutiques, fine hotels, excellent cafes, and sidewalk crafts. (Kerrick James)

of the **Turner Carroll Gallery** and its international modern art collection contrasts with the homey feeling at **Kania-Ferrin Gallery,** where you walk through the kitchen to view a Fiji war club. **Bellas Artes** offers a wide range, from pre-Columbian art to abstract expressionist works by Robert Rauschenberg and Ellsworth Kelly. Two horse chestnut trees and a turquoise picket fence mark **El Zaguán,** a 19th-century hacienda that has been turned into private apartments. The west garden of this rambling adobe with its three-foot-thick walls was designed by Adolph Bandelier in the late 1800s, and its peony bushes were imported more than 100 years ago from China. The garden's wrought-iron benches are a pleasant place to rest and listen to the springtime songs of birds and the hum of traffic along the narrow road. On Christmas Eve, votive candles called *farolitos* are set in dirt inside paper bags and line walls, rooftops, and the narrow streets. Those strolling among the flickering lights may stop to warm their hands at small bonfires of stacked piñon wood, called *luminarias.* Neighbors play guitars and share hot apple cider and *bizcochitos*—small anise-flavored sugar cookies.

In spring, the white and pink blooms of cosmos mix with other wildflowers along Canyon Road, leaving barely a sidewalk for folks on foot. Coyote fences (wooden posts strung together with wire) and stone walls ensure privacy for the few residents along this scenic thoroughfare. Where Canyon Road joins Camino Cabra, **Cristo Rey Catholic Church** stands as a memorial to Francisco Vásquez de Coronado. Dedicated in 1940 to commemorate the 400th anniversary of the Spanish explorer's travels in the Southwest, the massive adobe structure was built primarily to house a magnificent stone *reredos* (altar screen)— the most famous piece of ecclesiastical art created in New Mexico during Spanish colonial times. Clearly the focal point of the otherwise austere sanctuary, the faded colors and weathered white stone elicit a feeling of reverence. This screen, commissioned in 1760, served as the prototype for the numerous wooden altar screens found in churches throughout the state. A total of 180,000 adobe bricks were used in construction, all molded from the soil on which the building stands.

Farther into the foothills, on Upper Canyon Road, artist Randall Davey's home has been turned into regional headquarters for the **Audubon Society,** and nature trails wind through its grounds at the mouth of **Santa Fe Canyon.** *1800 Upper Canyon Rd.; 505-983-4609.*

■ Museums

Palace of the Governors

More than 450 years of New Mexico history is represented in this nearly 400-year-old structure, which remains the oldest public building in the nation. The block-long adobe palace was built around a courtyard, and its rooms attach to each other, beckoning exploration from one to the next. Exhibits follow a chronological order and feature ancient Indian pottery, a rebuilt two-wheeled *carreta,* maps of 18th-century Spanish America and a 19th-century chuck wagon. *105 W. Palace; 505-476-5100.*

Outside the restored government building, Indian artists sit patiently on the brick sidewalk beside blankets spread with their crafts and art work. Rain or shine, warm or cold, these artisans display their handmade jewelry every day of the year. Prices are reasonable and the artists enjoy talking about their work.

Museum of Fine Arts

Across the street from the palace is a building as wonderful as the art contained within. This museum houses a permanent collection of more than 8,000 works, including seven paintings by Georgia O'Keeffe and other regional pieces by Gustave Baumann, Will Schuster, John Marin, Marsden Hartley, and painters from the Taos School. Completed in 1917, this massive structure was the first example of the Pueblo Revival style to be built in Santa Fe and acted as a stimulus to the development of the city's emerging art colony. Changing shows display works from the permanent collection, along with contemporary local and regional painting, sculpture, and photography. *Lincoln and Palace; 505-827-4455.*

Museum of International Folk Art

Located southeast of downtown among juniper and yellow-tipped chamisa this museum is a whimsical, fascinating world of toys, textiles, and crafts collected from 100 countries. A walk through the wonderful Girard Wing takes you past a mesmerizing fantasy world of African puppets, antique dolls from around the world, Russian icons, and table settings complete with plastic vegetables and rubber hamburgers. Tiny figurines depicting people of all ages shop and work in a detailed miniature Mexican village that includes green shrubbery. Doll houses line the streets of a typical American town, and an array of intricately carved boats, mostly Oriental, line up in a busy harbor ready to unload their wares. The 106,000 items of folk art make up the one-of-a-kind Girard Collection, gathered by architect Alexander Girard and his wife, Susan, during a lifetime of travels.

The Hispanic Heritage Wing houses the largest collection of Spanish colonial folk art in the United States. Changing exhibits display tinwork, Spanish colonial furniture making, folk costumes, and textiles. *Bultos* and *santos* reveal an evolution of style through nearly three centuries. *706 Camino Lejo; 505-827-6350.*

New Mexico Museum of Indian Arts and Culture

Across the parking lot from the Museum of Folk Art, this museum details the history and contemporary lives of Pueblo, Apache, and Navajo Indians. Their story is told through displays of Clovis points, ancient cookware, clothing, and diagrams. Exhibits draw from collections of the 60-year-old Laboratory of Anthropology, located next door, including the first black-on-black pot fired by famed potter Maria Martinez of San Ildefonso Pueblo, a bridle that belonged to Apache leader Cochise, a 151-foot-long hunting net made of human hair and fiber dating to 1100, and more than 50,000 baskets, items of pottery, jewelry, weaving, and carving. In addition, modern Indian artists demonstrate their craftsmanship, weaving on looms and molding pottery. *710 Camino Lejo; 505-827-6344.*

Wheelwright Museum

This museum, located next door to the Museum of Folk Art, is dedicated to preserving and nurturing the spirit of Navajo ceremonialism. Walking into it gives the impression of walking into a giant Navajo hogan, a circular one-story structure used for ceremonies and residences. As in all Navajo dwellings, the entrance faces east, to best achieve a sense of harmony with the sun streaming in every morning. This private museum is dedicated to preserving and furthering the traditions of Native Americans and contains textiles, baskets, pottery, jewelry, folk arts, fine arts, and clothing, mostly of Navajo origin. In addition, the Wheelwright's collection of 600 Navajo sandpainting reproductions is the largest in the world. Pueblo, Plains, and Apache Indians also are represented in the exhibits, which include the Case Trading Post, a replica of an early 20th-century reservation store. *704 Camino Lejo; 505-982-4636*

Georgia O'Keeffe Museum

This downtown museum is dedicated to the work of Georgia O'Keeffe, one of the 20th century's most influential women painters. The private museum houses the largest single concentration of the pioneering modernist painter's work. *217 Johnson St.; 505-995-0785.*

◆ SANTA FE WALK

The winding streets of Santa Fe, which often seem too narrow for cars, are perfect for a leisurely stroll. Following is a suggested walk that starts at the St. Francis Cathedral. This taste of old Santa Fe represents only a partial look into the romantic city's past. Nearly every street surrounding the Plaza contains its own treasures and is worth exploring.

Built of sandstone and a lightweight volcanic rock, the towering Romanesque **St. Francis Cathedral** looms at the end of East San Francisco Street, in stark contrast to nearby low earthen-colored adobe buildings. Originally, plans included building a 160-foot steeple on each of the two towers, but today the only visual evidence of such intentions are supports that jut from the left tower.

As you enter the grounds, you'll see the statue of Archbishop Jean Baptiste Lamy, the driving force behind this mammoth undertaking. Inside, 55-foot-tall taupe walls are decorated with intricate geometric designs painted on the many sweeping arches that reach up to support the vaulted ceiling. The brightly colored stained-glass windows are finely crafted and exquisitely detailed. The serene La Conquistadora, who accompanied Spanish colonists to Santa Fe in the early 1600s, stands proudly on her own altar in her own chapel. She wears a delicate lace veil and a billowing gown that is changed with the season or holiday: at Christmas it is kelly green.

Another of Archbishop Lamy's projects, the **Loretto Chapel** was designed to meet the spiritual needs of Loretto Academy, founded in 1853 by New Mexico's first six nuns. The small Gothic chapel, fashioned after Sainte Chappelle in Paris, offers a lot for its size: European-made stained-glass windows, Italian statues depicting the stations of the cross, and a faux-marble wooden altar. But most impressive is a 33-step wooden staircase that twists in a double helix—and was built without a nail, screw, or any support. Known today as the "miraculous staircase," this wondrous feat of carpentry contains no imprint of its master builder, a mysterious man equipped with a hammer, saw, and a T-square. His only request was for two tubs of water. He accepted no payment and disappeared after completing the project. Some say he was St. Joseph, the carpenter saint. Others say he was Yohon Hadwiger, a carpenter visiting from Vienna, Austria. *219 Old Santa Fe Trail.*

Heading south, Old Santa Fe Trail crosses the Santa Fe River, which rushes with water in the spring, but becomes a dry ditch by fall due to dams and reservoirs high up in the mountains.

Across the river is **Barrio de Analco**, Santa Fe's oldest neighborhood, originally settled in the 1600s by Tlaxcalan Indian servants from Mexico who accompanied early Franciscan missionaries and Spanish officials to the new territory. Narrow brick sidewalks buckle and porch roofs slant, showing their age. The **Chapel of San Miguel** stands in the center of this historic district. A finely crafted stone wall protects the simple adobe chapel from the busy street. Inside, an animated gilded statue of St. Michael, the church's patron saint, stands centered on an ornate wooden altar.

Cottonwoods provide shade, and a cloyingly sweet fragrance emanates from purple wisteria blossoms as the ancient narrow De Vargas Street leads west to the **Santuario de Guadalupe** at the corner of Agua Fria and Guadalupe streets. Built sometime between 1776 and 1795, this adobe shrine to Our Lady of Guadalupe, patron saint of Mexico, displays one of the finest *reredos* in the Southwest. Painted in 1783 in Mexico, this oil-on-canvas altar screen was made expressly for the Santa Fe chapel and was hauled up the Chihuahua Trail in an oxcart. Carved *vigas* and corbels adorn the high ceiling, and the windows are stained glass. Today, the small chapel is still in use and is often the site of theatrical and musical performances. Crossing back over the Santa Fe River, Guadalupe Street intersects with San Francisco Street, which leads back to the Plaza.

San Miguel Chapel, Santa Fe.

◆ EATING IN SANTA FE

Finding a great place to eat in Santa Fe is never a problem, but during the summer, getting a seat in a restaurant can be a different story. More than 175 restaurants (not including chains and franchises)—with menus offering everything from dim sum to pasta, from bean burritos to rabbit confit enchiladas with orange-jicama salsa—can be found along major thoroughfares or tucked into back-alley adobes. The cuisine represents the city's varied cultures, especially the newly transplanted ones. *Restaurant listings begin on page 300.*

The tony **Coyote Cafe**, while beyond the pocketbooks of most Santa Feans, is likely the city's most famous eatery. When chef Mark Miller opened his cafe in 1987, his unique combination of ingredients and techniques from Mexico, New Mexico, France, and Berkeley (birthplace of California cuisine) won near-instant success, and helped foster the Southwestern cooking craze. Tapas (Spanish hors d'oeuvres) are served in the cozy confines of **El Farol,** and the mocha cake at either **The Shed** or **La Choza** (owned by the same folks), is worth saving room for. Despite the town's 20th-century influences, breakfast burritos, chile rellenos, tamales, and enchiladas remain the food of choice. At **Old Mexico Grill,** a comfortable eatery with tiled floors and a copper-covered grill, Mexican paella and shrimp marinated in tequila bring to mind balmy ocean breezes and the stone streets of Puerto Vallarta.

To entice its trendy visitors, the **Zia Diner** replaces mundane pinto beans with sleeker black ones, and blue corn tortillas have nearly run the traditional yellow variety out of town. British visitors and anyone else just needing a rest from shopping may enjoy high tea, which is served daily in the lobby of the St. Francis Hotel. In Santa Fe, you can expect to pay a few dollars more than anywhere else in the state, but after all, location is everything.

■ THE HIGH ROAD   *map page 80, D & E-3 & 4*

Most of the small Hispanic farming villages that line what has become known as the "high road," linking Santa Fe and Taos, were settled in the eighteenth century. Remarkably, these picturesque hamlets—with their weathered log barns, thick, adobe-walled homes, and tin roofs that reflect the shimmering sunlight—appear much as they did 200 years ago. Most people speak Spanish as easily as English. Every spring, members of community *acequia* associations gather: armed with shovels, rakes, and pitchforks, they clear debris from irrigation ditches and ensure an uninterrupted flow of mountain runoff throughout the summer. Fall brings a harvest of beans and apples, followed by day-long wood-cutting expeditions to the nearby mountains.

Heading north out of Santa Fe, this scenic route starts out by passing **Tesuque, Pojoaque,** and **Nambé** pueblos. At Nambé, hikers can walk to a series of three waterfalls five miles up Nambé Creek and listen to a ranger tell of a time long ago when a pueblo maiden was courted by two rivals—a warrior and a hunter. When the jealous warrior killed the hunter, both were swallowed up by the earth. The falls were formed by the girl's tears as she wandered and wept in mourning.

In between the pueblos, the town of Espanola boasts the state's most concentrated population of low riders, automobile aficionados devoted to customizing their vehicles with chainlink steering wheels, hydraulic suspension systems and one-of-a-kind paint jobs. As you make your way through town, you'll likely be slowed by one or more of these custom cars showing off its individuality.

◆ CHIMAYÓ TO PEÑASCO   *map page 80, D & E-3 & 4*

Winding among rolling hills dotted with piñon pines and junipers, the high road drops into the village of Chimayó, which is tucked into a cottonwood-shaded valley. Here, Hispanic weavers craft brightly colored clothing and blankets, characterized by bold stripes. Originally, Spanish colonial artisans wove these beautiful textiles for their own use. Interest in the craft flagged and in the early 1800s, Santa Fe residents sent to Spain for expert weavers to revive the art and teach their children. Two of these artisans, Juan and Ignacio Balzan, rejected the capital city for the sheltered hamlet of Chimayo. There, they taught the craft to Chimayo residents who continue the tradition today. Ortega's Weaving Shop is now headed by David Ortega, a member of the sixth generation to live and work in this spot. His two sons are also weavers.

This peaceful town is also known for **El Santuario de Chimayó,** which attracts thousands of pilgrims every year during Holy Week. Some worshipers walk along the shoulders of freeways and two-lane highways from as far away as Albuquerque, 80 miles south. They come to express their faith at the adobe chapel whose bell towers rise above ancient cottonwoods. Inside a small, candlelit anteroom built onto the structure, they collect from a tiny hole in the ground a sample of the *tierra bendita* (sacred earth) that many believe has healing powers. According to ancient legend, fire and smoke erupted near where the sanctuary stands today, leaving a pool of mud. Pueblo Indians used the soil for medicinal purposes, eating it or smearing it on their bodies.

The family chapel was built between 1813 and 1816 by Bernardo Abeyta who, legend has it, was deathly ill when a vision led him to a spot where immediately he was cured. He erected the small church atop the spot to give thanks. Testaments of healing, such as discarded crutches, hang from the adobe walls of a small room that attaches to the main chapel.

Before leaving town, a perfect rest stop is **Rancho de Chimayó**, the restored 1880 home of the Jaramillo family, now a restaurant. A strain of chile grown only in the fields of this area is featured in the New Mexico cuisine here. Diners can bask in the warmth of a *kiva* fireplace in a wooden-floored dining room, or sip a margarita in cool shade on the outside patio. Another Jaramillo family home has been turned into a quaint bed and breakfast. The operations are run by descendants of the Jaramillo family, who were early Chimayó settlers. *See page 288.*

(above) El Santuario de Chimayó is visited by thousands of religious pilgrims every Holy Week.

(opposite) The family chapel, built by Bernardo Abeyta between 1813 and 1816, has become a local pilgrimage site. (both photos by Kerrick James)

Córdova, a tiny enclave tucked into a narrow valley, has long been home to traditional woodcarvers. Look for signs that mark their workshops.

With the stunning 13,000-foot Truchas Peaks as a backdrop and the Rio Grande Valley in the distance, the tin roofs of **Truchas** (Trouts) rise from fertile vegetable and bean fields. Wild herbs, scrub oak, and cattails prosper in back yards. It's easy to see why, in the mid-1980s, Robert Redford filmed *The Milagro Beanfield War* in this bucolic setting. Many trails branch out of town into the piñon and ponderosa pine hills of the Carson National Forest.

One of the finest eighteenth-century Spanish Pueblo-style churches survives at **Las Trampas,** on high ground next to the road. In contrast to the more refined restoration at the Chimayó sanctuary, San José de Gracia at Las Trampas retains a rustic simplicity. The Las Trampas church initially was known as the Church of the Twelve Apostles, and it has been said that only 12 men at a time were permitted to erect its four-foot-thick adobe walls. The church, which stands 34 feet tall, was built with an outside choir loft so the chorus could move outside to sing during religious processions. Inside, plain wooden benches rest on uneven wood-planked floors. Painted *vigas* and corbels, along with elaborate paintings, add decoration to the stark interior. If the church should be locked, visitors need only ask a neighbor to open the heavy wooden doors that lead to its cool interior. *(See photo on pages 68 and 69.)*

Picuris Pueblo is a small, yet growing, pueblo situated in an open valley along the Rio Pueblo. A tribal museum tells the story of the isolated pueblo, which today has 150 residents. Guides take visitors past the remains of its prehistoric village that stands near modern-day residences.

Abandoned movie theaters and car dealerships attest to the long-lost commercial prosperity once enjoyed by the village of **Peñasco.** Originally established in 1796 as three settlements along the Rio Santa Barbara, Peñasco still stretches along the waterway. But as its younger residents move away in search of better jobs, the small farms and ranches that gave the village its identity are disappearing. Many historic adobe homes, dance halls, and restaurants remain, but some are no longer occupied.

A dirt road follows the shallow, tree-shaded Rio Santa Barbara into the **Pecos Wilderness** to campgrounds surrounded by fields of wildflowers and trails that lead to mountain lakes and the high peaks that protect the valley settlements.

◆ NM 518 to Taos   *map page 80, D-4*

The paved road that leads to Taos, NM 518, climbs steeply, leaving behind the fertile valleys and entering into tall pine forests and mountain meadows of the Taos Plateau. **Fort Burgwin Research Center** straddles the road. Restored and run by Southern Methodist University, the fort was built in 1852 to protect Taos from raiding Comanche and Ute Indians. Research focuses on the ruins of Anasazi dwellings on the site that date to A.D. 1100. During summer months, music and theater presentations, along with seminars, are offered. *505-758-8322.*

The road ends at **Ranchos de Taos,** a few miles south of the village of Taos. This small village was established in 1716 by Spanish homesteaders. Comanche raids made life unpredictable for settlers until the end of the nineteenth century. Many fine adobe buildings have been restored in this hamlet, and it is home to one of the most photographed and painted 18th-century missions, the Church of St. Francis of Assisi, built in 1730 to convert Taos Indians. Burros hauled huge adobe bricks up earthen ramps. A fortress-like church, its walls are 13 feet thick at the base and are supported on the outside by heavy adobe buttresses. Like most churches of its day, the Ranchos Church supports two bell towers. Unlike many, however, the left tower is slightly taller than the right, a testament to New Mexico's disregard for symmetry. One artist attracted to the irregular lines of the church's walls was Georgia O'Keeffe. "Most artists who spend any time in Taos have to paint it, I suppose, just as they have to paint a self-portrait. I had to paint it—the back of it several times, the front once."

Inside, enormous *vigas* and corbels support a high ceiling. Most notable among a collection of European and New Mexican artwork is a painting that is said to glow in the dark.

■ Taos Sites and Attractions   *map page 144*

Easy to inspect on foot, most Taos galleries hug the narrow streets and historic sites surrounding the central plaza. Occasionally a crow calls from the treetops above the **Charles Bent home** where New Mexico's first American governor was killed and scalped during the Taos Rebellion. Pink plaster is peeled away where his wife and two other women dug into the thick adobe wall in their attempt to escape Bent's killers. The women were spared. A black-cloth Penitente mask and leather whip are protected in a glass case as a reminder of the days when that self-torturing Catholic confraternity flourished in northern New Mexico. A broad-backed Bent family wooden chair with leather seat sits in a room next to a marble-topped dresser. *117-A Bent St.; 505-758-2376*

At the **Old Taos County Courthouse,** which faces the plaza, 10 allegorical murals depicting classical animated scenes with moralistic messages such as Reconciliation and Transgression grace the walls of the second-story courtroom. The impressive 1934 frescoes were the work of Emil Bisttram, Bert Phillips, Victor Hughes, and Ward Lockwood, and were commissioned by the Works Projects Administration. An eleventh mural by Frederico Vigil was added in 1995.

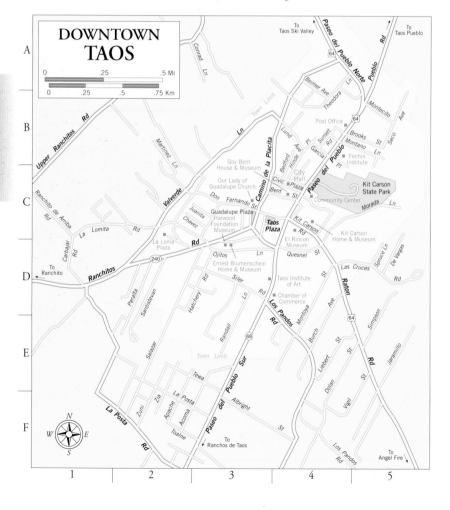

DOWNTOWN
TAOS

SANTA FE & TAOS

Kit Carson and his wife Josefa fed their eight children out of this kitchen.

Friendly shopkeepers encourage browsers interested in custom women's clothing, deep purple cellophane-looking duffel bags, or seventeenth-century maps. More than 50 galleries are scattered throughout the town's dusty streets. Mixed media pieces by Larry Bell hang at **New Directions** on the plaza, and R.C. Gorman's pastel portraits of Indian women line the walls at his **Navajo Gallery** on Ledoux Street. Gorman, a Navajo artist, has lived outside of Taos since 1968.

At the **Taos Book Shop**, you can pick out a book and curl up with it in a comfortable overstuffed chair in front of a warm fire.

Kit Carson, who at age 16 signed on with a wagon train heading across the Santa Fe Trail, made his home in Taos. Even though the famous trapper and Indian fighter spent most of his time on the road, in 1843 he presented to his new bride, Josefa Jaramillo, a 12-room adobe home near the central plaza. Seven of the Carson's eight children were born inside the 30-inch-thick adobe walls of the U-shaped building, occupied by the family for 25 years. Today, the **Kit Carson Home,** built in 1825, is one of three historic museums operated by the Kit Carson Foundation. A walk through the meandering dirt- and wood-floored rooms provides a glimpse of life in the Carson household where the couple's children played and helped their mother prepare meals, and where Carson met with traders, dignitaries, and military men who passed through New Mexico. You'll see shotguns that probably accompanied the Kentucky-born scout on his many missions into the wilderness. You'll also see one of Josefa's narrow-waisted tan and brown silk dresses and a fringed beige shawl on display inside a glass case. The living room, with Carson's black wooden desk in a corner and wooden organ along a wall, seems to be awaiting the return of its inhabitants. *113 Kit Carson Rd.; 505-758-4741.*

The fortress-like adobe walls of the **Martínez Hacienda,** two miles outside of Taos, alongside the Rio Pueblo, were built for protection from Indian attacks. Construction of the home, begun in 1804, was often interrupted by Comanche and Apache raids. Even after completion, tending sheep outside its protective walls was hazardous. Antonio Severino Martínez, one of the area's chief traders, hauled over the Chihuahua Trail to Mexico tallow candles, piñon nuts, jerky, beaver pelts, wool, and woven belts in two-wheeled carretas and atop pack mules, bringing back cloth, nails, tools, sugar, and chocolate. Martínez, who also served as mayor of Taos, turned his home into a showpiece, with 21 rooms surrounding two courtyards. Each room reveals a different latilla construction of split pine, juniper, or aspen pole, all hauled from the nearby mountains. A shepherd's fireplace, set deep enough into the adobe wall so that large pots could fit inside, takes up one corner of the kitchen. A carreta, with wooden wheels worn smooth from its travels, is sheltered under a covered *zaguán* (entryway). Today, local weavers and quilters spin wool, work on wooden looms, and sew in rooms off the rear courtyard, much as they might have done 150 years ago. *On Ranchitos Rd.; 505-758-1000.*

From 1919 until his death in 1960, artist Ernest Blumenschein, along with his wife Mary, lived and worked in a 12-room, 18th-century adobe home in downtown Taos. Today, the **Ernest Blumenschein Home** appears much as it did when the painter lived there. Wooden armoires shipped from France stand against adobe walls, and a cedar table and matching sideboard, made by a Taos craftsman, fill the dining room. Paintings by Blumenschein, his wife, their daughter Helen, and other Taos artists line the walls. *222 LeDoux; 505-758-0505.*

Millicent Rogers, a Standard Oil heiress, came to New Mexico in 1948 for a short visit and, caught by its spell, built a home in Taos. For the next five years, until her death in 1953, Rogers amassed an extensive collection of ancient Indian pottery, 19th-century Navajo blankets, kachinas, jewelry, and Spanish Colonial *bultos,* pressed tin light fixtures, and frames. In 1956, her son, Paul Peralta Ramos, established the **Millicent Rogers Museum,** which includes one of the largest collections of black-on-black pottery created by San Ildefonso potter Maria Martinez. One large deer-motif pot dates to 1919, the year Maria and her husband, Julian, devised the technique. One room is dedicated to Maria and her family, some of whom are also potters. Photographs depict the precise, time-consuming process of coiling the clay and achieving the shiny black glaze by firing the piece over an outdoor fire covered with metal and cow manure. *1504 Millicent Rogers Museum Road, 4 miles north of the plaza on NM 64; 505-758-2462.*

◆ EATING IN TAOS

Taos restaurants are less interesting than those in Santa Fe. Apart from innovative pastas and seafood at the **Apple Tree,** smoked lamb sirloin on goat cheese souffle at **Doc Martin's,** and the lightness of fresh fish topped with vegetable relishes at **Lambert's,** the choices are mostly traditional New Mexican. In keeping with its Pueblo-Spanish decor, even the fast-food outlets boast stuccoed mud-colored exteriors. No golden arches reach for the sky. For something in between, try a Greek pizza at the **Outback,** bangers and mash at **Eske's Brew Pub,** or a club sandwich at the **Bent Street Deli.**

Breakfast cooks seem to think everyone is on their way to the ski slopes. At **Michael's Kitchen,** a popular local hangout, no matter what you order, you'll get more than you can eat. You can catch up on the local gossip over chile and eggs at **El Pueblo Cafe** north of town in the village of El Prado. *Restaurant listings on pages 302-303.*

NORTHWESTERN
NEW MEXICO

Food and Lodging begins on page 280.

SANDSTONE BLUFFS AND MESAS RIMMED IN MUTED SHADES of red and gray rise above the box canyons and grama grass meadows of northwestern New Mexico. Parched riverbeds that swell with muddy water after a summer cloudburst and then dry up again meander throughout rangeland dotted with chamisa and saltbush. This gentle landscape is interrupted by the rugged El Malpais lava flow, with its chilly ice caves and hardened tubes of lava. In the Bisti Wilderness, the fossils of horned dinosaurs lay strewn among eerie mushroom-shaped spires, and Shiprock, a basaltic core that once filled the center of a volcano, now stands like a beacon in the desert. Nearby flows the blue-green water of the San Juan River as it wends its way toward Utah.

Among these strung-out mesas, abrupt rock cliffs, and buttes is a treasure trove of Native American dwellings, old and new. Ragged remains of ancient Indian villages lay scattered throughout broken mesas and cliffsides. Some have been excavated and preserved, others are covered with mounds of windswept soil. Indian influence, past and present, is greater here than anywhere else in the state, and much of the land belongs to New Mexico's three major Indian groups: the Navajo, Apache, and Pueblo.

The Anasazi, ancestors of the Pueblo Indians, lived alongside riverbeds that once flowed year-round, where they cultivated beans and corn and erected rock buildings held together with mortar. The excavation of 11 of these sites has

NORTHWESTERN NEW MEXICO

UTAH — COLORADO — ARIZONA

NORTHWESTERN NEW MEXICO

0 | 10 | 20 | 30 | 40 | 50

Miles

Elevation in feet

13,161
12,000
11,000
10,000
9,000
8,000
7,000
6,000
5,000
4,000

revealed the most extensive ancient Indian ruins in the country. Little evidence, on the other hand, remains of the ancestors of the Apache and Navajo, nomadic hunters and gatherers, who moved about in search of food.

Northwestern New Mexico is still largely rural, with many modern-day Indians living in small communities or on isolated ranchos spread across their reservations. Of the few sizable towns, Gallup, at the southern end of the Navajo Reservation, is the major trading center for Indian wares, and Farmington at its northern border serves as a business hub.

■ CHACO CANYON   *map page 149, D-3 & 4*

Today, most of the state's 19 pueblos hug the Rio Grande, clustered in north-central New Mexico. But it wasn't always that way. Between A.D. 900 and 1200, the ancestors of these Indians made their homes alongside the flowing Chaco River and atop high desert mesas. More than 2,000 sites have been documented throughout the northwestern region, and it is likely there are more to be found. We know these early people as the Anasazi, a Navajo term that means "Enemy Ancestors." We also know that during the Chaco years, this primitive culture made a giant evolutionary leap in its approach to life, which never was surpassed by following Native generations.

As many as 5,000 small, brown-skinned Indians grew corn, beans, and squash in irrigated fields beneath sandstone walls in Chaco Canyon during what has become known as the Anasazi Golden Age. They built multi-story stone and mortar homes with rooms several times larger than those in the previous stages of their culture. River water was diverted through complex irrigation systems into ditch-fed fields. An elaborate road network connected more than 75 pueblos scattered throughout the region. These 30-foot-wide roads were laid out in straight lines unimpeded by rough terrain, and where they passed over bare rock the roads were bordered by masonry walls or a line of boulders. This 400-mile transportation and trade route probably was used by communities spread throughout northwestern New Mexico to exchange crops, pottery, and clothing made from deer, elk, and antelope hunted in nearby mountains. Seashells, copper bells, and the remains of parrots and macaws found in the crumbling ruins prove the Indians also had contact with tribes as far south as Mexico.

The large number of kivas found in Chaco's pueblos indicates that religion was central to the culture and suggests that Chaco served as a religious center for the numerous outlying villages. Astronomy also played a major role as shown by the placement of small corner windows built into the thick walls at Pueblo Bonito, the largest excavated ruin. A sun priest in charge of planting and harvesting rituals could schedule those events based on the play of light along an interior wall at the pueblo.

By A.D. 1000, Chaco had established itself firmly as the political, economic, and possibly the religious center of the northwestern plateau. As improved farming methods provided abundant food, these productive people had the leisure to develop their artistic abilities. They etched petroglyphs of snakes and spirals into the soft sandstone, wove baskets and sandals from desert grasses, and fashioned clay bowls, pitchers, water jars, and mugs with detailed black-on-white geometric designs.

The Anasazi mysteriously disappeared from the canyon by the 14th century. Theories abound as to why they abandoned their pueblos at the height of their culture. Archaeologists attribute the exodus to drought, to disease, to roving bands of Indians who continually threatened these people, or to outbreaks of fighting among the Anasazi themselves. One thing is certain. A drought struck the region

Consisting of more than 600 rooms, Pueblo Bonito is considered one of the most sophisticated examples of Anasazi architecture. (Kerrick James)

in 1276 and lasted 25 years. They may have traveled south to build new homes near more reliable sources of water, such as the Rio Grande.

When the Navajo entered the area in the 1770s, they found the broad basin unoccupied. The once-flowing river was dry and ran only after summer rainstorms. The fields of corn and beans had been overtaken by desert grasses and sagebrush, and the voices of a vibrant culture were silent.

Today, the wind whistles through the canyon and carries new voices, those of visitors at **Chaco Culture National Historical Park.** Extensive rock ruins blend with towering sandstone cliff faces that provided the ancient masons with their building materials. Along the banks of the bone-dry riverbed, partial walls appear rust red against an azure sky, steel gray under a blanket of clouds, or dull umber when covered with snow.

At Pueblo Bonito, Anasazi masons shaped thousands of rocks of all sizes with crude stone hammers and axes in the construction of more than 600 rooms and 40 kivas. The varying construction techniques reflect the order in which these carefully crafted walls were built. For example, the oldest walls were one-stone thick with generous applications of mud mortar. Later walls had thick inner cores of rubble topped off by a veneer of stonework so precisely fitted that little mortar was needed. Stone bases remain that once steadied masonry pillars supporting heavily beamed four-story roofs.

Across the dry wash from Pueblo Bonito is the giant *kiva* of Casa Rinconada, which was built apart from other communities, indicating that it was possibly used as some sort of community center. An occasional gust of wind disturbs the silence and the musty smell of sandstone mingles with imagined memories of the many ceremonies that must have taken place here at one of the largest "great *kivas*" in the Southwest.

Behind Pueblo Bonito, Pueblo Alto sits atop a mesa. Its location at the junction of several prehistoric roads suggests it served as a trade and distribution center.

Tours are offered daily, and pamphlets for the self-initiated also are available at each of eight restored ruins connected by well-marked hiking trails. There are two gravel roads leading to the park. The road from I-40 to the south is not recommended although it is usually passable by four-wheel-drive. The preferred route is to come in from NM 44 to the northwest, but check with the visitors center for accessibility, as storms can create impassable conditions. The only accommodation at the park is a campground and there is no food available, only a pop machine. *505-786-7014.*

♦ CHACO OUTLIERS   *map page 149, A & B-3*

While most of the prehistoric villages served by the Chaco road network have remained unexcavated, two outlying sites are preserved and partially reconstructed.

The communal dwellings at **Aztec Ruins National Monument** were built on a rise overlooking the blue-green Animas River in, what is now, the town of Aztec. The ruins reveal construction methods similar to those used at Chaco Canyon. (The crumbling walls and rectangular rooms were named by nineteenth-century settlers who mistakenly assumed the pueblo was built by the Aztec Indians of Mexico.) A walk through the largest pueblo, a U-shaped village that covered two acres and contained 500 rooms in three stories, allows you to look across the decaying walls into a maze of square and rectangular adjoining rooms and to crawl through tiny doorways. You can peer into subterranean kivas, built with thousands of soft taupe sandstone slabs. Anchoring the pueblo is the Great Kiva, constructed in the twelfth century and reconstructed in 1934. The grand underground space was broken only by massive columns that supported a roof estimated at 90 tons.

NORTHWESTERN
NEW MEXICO

Morning light in the Great Kiva at Aztec Ruins National Monument. (Kerrick James)

This is the only reconstructed great kiva in the Southwest. As you descend into the flat-top, underground sanctuary, push a button to hear recorded Native American music, take a seat on the mud-brown rock bench, and try to recapture the solemnity that must have pervaded Anasazi religious ceremonies.

Much of this site remains unexcavated under sandy mounds scattered in the shade of cottonwood trees. No one knows if the mounds cover dwellings or trash heaps. *505-334-6174.*

Salmon Ruins sits atop a bluff overlooking the farmland of the San Juan River valley two miles west of Bloomfield. A well-traveled Chacoan road leads directly north from Chaco Canyon for 50 miles through dusty arroyos and across desert mesas to the C-shaped, 250-room pueblo. Most building materials here were imported: sandstone was quarried at sites 30 miles distant, and timbers used for the vigas (roof beams) were hauled from southern Colorado. Nearby petroglyphs depict ears of corn on a stalk, and some archaeologists speculate that the small community was developed as an agricultural center to serve the main Chaco Canyon villages. Salmon Ruin was named for George Salmon, an 1880s homesteader who protected the site from vandals and thieves in search of ancient pottery. His home still stands nearby.

The pueblos of Aztec and Salmon were abandoned by the mid-12th century, only to be reoccupied in the early 13th century by Indians from the nearby Mesa Verde culture of southwestern Colorado. But they, too, left later that century, never to return.

◆ AZTEC   *map page 149, B-3*

Aztec is a town of tree-shaded streets filled with Victorian brick buildings. Shops and businesses along Main Street have retained an early twentieth-century Midwestern appearance, and the only modern touches are a few pastel-painted storefronts.

Aztec boasts two claims to fame: first, it's home to "6,000 friendly people and six old soreheads." No doubt there are 6,000 friendly people, so where did the soreheads come from? The sorehead tradition began in 1969 when a good-natured Chamber of Commerce erected the first welcoming sign that listed 4,000 residents and six old soreheads. Townsfolk loved the idea, and many clamored to become designated a sorehead. Secret ballots were sent to the town's clubs and organizations seeking nominations. The winners posed for the local newspaper with bags over their heads and their backs to the camera. Their identities never were revealed, although many residents claim to be one of the originals. Since 1987, the honor has been spread around as ballots are sent out every year to add six new soreheads to the roster. Only now they remove the bags.

Aztec's second claim to fame is as an All America City, an award it received in 1963 after the town's citizens built NM 173, a two-lane road that connects Aztec with the San Juan River just below Navajo Dam. No government funds were used in construction: businesses donated supplies, men and women volunteered labor, and children held fundraisers to help cover expenses.

■ JICARILLA APACHES   *map page 80, B-1*

Jicarilla is a Spanish name meaning "Little Basket." The colonials were impressed by the beautiful baskets, especially two-handled vessels coiled and stitched with sumac twigs and small woven drinking cups (*jícara* means "small cup"), fashioned by this band of Apache, which roamed the forests and canyons of northwestern New Mexico.

A century ago, when the federal government placed the Jicarillas on 722,000 acres of land that included deserts and forests along the Continental Divide, it was clear to everyone that the Indians had received a bad deal. First of all, they were accustomed to a nomadic existence—hunting deer and gathering nuts and berries (later pillaging wagon trains) for their survival. Accustomed to roaming freely, the Apaches had a difficult time settling down to an assigned spot and, having little experience in farming, their attempts at cultivating the sandy soil they'd been given were not always successful. But at least their new home had variety, with its pine-covered mountains, tall grass meadows, canyons, mesas, and sagebrush prairies. As it turned out, the land also was rich in fossil fuels, namely oil and natural gas. The sale of leases has made the Jicarilla the richest tribe in the state.

The Jicarilla have also capitalized on their dynamic landscape. At Stone Lake Lodge they cater to fishermen and especially to hunters who flock like geese to the reservation for its prize deer, elk, turkey, cougar, and waterfowl. North of the lodge at the capital of Dulce, most of the tribe's 2,000 members make their homes. At the tribal gift shop, few of the Jicarilla's namesake baskets are for sale, but oil paintings, leather craft, and intricate bead work are plentiful. *On US 64; 505-759-3242.*

■ THE FARMINGTON AREA   *map page 149 B-2*

To the Navajos, the area of present-day Farmington was known as "To-tah," which means "Among the Waters." Three of the region's major waterways meet three miles apart: the gently flowing Animas River skirts Farmington's eastern edge, then empties into the wide San Juan River south of town. The smaller La Plata enters the San Juan west of town after irrigating fields of hay and corn.

When local residents think of the Farmington area, they think of an outdoorsman's paradise: great skiing, fishing, and hiking. When business folks do so, they may be considering the large deposits of oil, natural gas, and coal that lie in the San Juan Basin, beneath some of the most unusual land formations found in the state. The main thoroughfares of Farmington are crowded with small businesses, restaurants, shops, and some fine places to stock up on coolers and tackle boxes.

World-class downhill skiing, backpacking, and hiking are accessible an hour's drive north in the southern Rocky Mountains at Durango, Colorado. Three marinas with boat docks service boaters at Navajo Lake State Park 34 miles east of

Known to the Navajo as Tse Bida'hi *(Winged Rock), Shiprock rises 1,500 feet from the desert floor. (Kerrick James)*

town. Just downstream from Navajo Dam is the finest trophy stream fishing in New Mexico in the clear, cold, blue-green waters of the San Juan River. A nearly four-mile stretch called the Quality Waters harbors big, fat trout that will give you a fight to the finish. Strict restrictions apply. Fishermen must use barbless hooks and may not take home more than one 20-inch lunker. The locals say once you've fished these waters, no other New Mexico stream will ever satisfy you.

◆ SHIPROCK   *map page 149 B-2*

Along the wide, placid San Juan River heading back to Farmington and beyond toward Shiprock, fertile fields fed by the river suggest the origins of Farmington's name. Today, small farms and orchards of apple, pear, and peach trees flourish, but it's the vast deposits of coal, oil, and natural gas that have come to dominate the area's economy. Farmington sits at the edge of the Navajo Reservation with the dusty town of Shiprock set squarely within it. Both are more interested in serving their residents than attracting tourists.

To the southwest of the town of Shiprock, a 7,178-foot jagged rock monolith dominates the semi-desert landscape. **Shiprock** begins as an apparition, fuzzily coming into view. But once you've spotted it, this volcanic core of an extinct volcano commands your attention. You can't take your eyes off the massive form that rises from a dusty plain. Navajos call the mystical rock Tse Bida'hi (the Rock with Wings) and many tribal legends surround it. Numerous rock climbers have scaled it, and two have died trying. Shiprock has been closed to climbers since 1970.

◆ BISTI BADLANDS   *map page 149 C-3*

Nearby is yet another natural marvel, the **Bisti Badlands,** a 3,968-acre wilderness of giant mushroom-shaped spires surrounded by red, green, and bone-white cliffs located 32 miles south of Farmington in the San Juan Basin. The eerie desolation of this wild moonscape is all that remains of what once was a shallow sea bordered by swamps and forests and inhabited by dinosaurs. Eons of wind and water have carved the sandstone and shale formations. The Bisti, along with the nearby 19,922-acre **De-na-zin area,** are rich in fossils, left behind from the days 75 million years ago when duckbill and horned dinosaurs sloshed along the seashore. Huge conifers towered above a jungle of ferns and palms. Salamanders, snails, worms, sharks, and crocodiles choked the waterways.

(following pages) Today the Bisti Badlands, south of Farmington, are an eerie, desolate moonscape accented with giant mushroom-shaped rock formations. Long ago, this was the bottom of a shallow sea. (Eduardo Fuss)

NORTHWESTERN NEW MEXICO

Today, snakes and lizards scurry across the hard rocks, which are absent of any vegetation, a reminder of the days when their ancestors dominated this barren sandstone wilderness. Unfortunately, billions of tons of coal lie near the surface underneath the Bisti, posing the constant threat that this magical, unspoiled land could be destroyed by open-pit mining.

■ GALLUP   *map page 149, F-2*

Gallup, as one of the nation's foremost trading centers for Native American arts and crafts, calls itself the Heart of Indian Country. And for good reason: the town is 25 miles southeast of Window Rock, Arizona, capital of the Navajo Nation; 98 miles southwest of Chaco Canyon, home of the ancient Anasazi; and 38 miles north of Zuni Pueblo. Most of the Indians you see along the streets of Gallup have come in from the nearby Navajo Reservation to shop, sell their wares, and sometimes to have a few drinks. Liquor sales are prohibited on the reservation.

At one time, this gritty little town was the epitome of the Wild West. Its first building was the Blue Goose Saloon, constructed in the 1860s near a stagecoach stop. After coal was discovered north of Gallup in the late 1870s, miners from across Europe, including Slavs, Czechs, Austrians, and Italians, converged on the town. The immigrants worked hard in the sooty mines, digging out jet-black lumps of carbon. After railroad tracks reached the community in 1881, mining camps sprang up outside of town, appearing much like today's suburbs. Some homes were built of stone, and some camps had schools and saloons for miners who didn't want to make the few-mile trip to Gallup. The coal mines were closed in 1950.

Within two years after the Santa Fe Railroad arrived in Gallup, 22 saloons (including the Bucket of Blood) and two dance halls were competing with the Blue Goose for business. David Gallup was paymaster of the railroad, which ended at the western outpost. Come payday, workers would say they were going to Gallup's to collect their wages. The name stuck.

During those early years, prostitution and gambling were in an exuberant (if illegal) state of availability. Soldiers, lumberjacks, cowboys, railroad workers, and miners were regular customers. In 1895, a bevy of respectable East Coast women arrived at Gallup to work for a Harvey House restaurant and according to some, improved the town's reputation. Many of these women married and settled in Gallup, turning the wild outpost into a quiet family town.

Navajo weaver Nellie Mae Davis cradles her grandson. (Paul Chesley)

Beginning in the 1930s, Hollywood directors descended upon Gallup to use its unspoiled red-rock canyons and majestic piñon-covered mesas as backdrops for Westerns. These included *The Big Carnival,* starring Kirk Douglas; *Four Faces West,* with Joel McCrea; and *The Bad Man,* starring Wallace Beery, Lionel Barrymore, and Ronald Reagan. To house the stars in style, R. E. Griffith, brother of director D. W. Griffith, built the El Rancho Hotel in 1937. The two-story oversized ranch house still boasts its original motto: "Charm of Yesterday, Convenience of Tomorrow." The entrance opens onto a brick-floored lobby where guests can share a bench with a wooden Indian, and marvel at the deer heads, Navajo rugs, and loads of Indian and Western art tacked to the walls. A gallery of autographed photographs of the stars lines a second-floor balcony. Rooms are named after the Hollywood stars who slept in them—Betty Grable, Burt Lancaster, Lee Marvin, to name a few.

Route 66 bisected Gallup in 1926, and many of the shops and tourist courts that sprang up to entice a new world of motorists are still in business.

A showpiece from that era, the El Morro Theatre, has been refurbished to its original grandeur of 1928, when it opened on Coal Avenue. Named for nearby Inscription Rock, El Morro reflects a Spanish Colonial Revival style, with Spanish Baroque plaster carving and bright polychromatic painting. Locals come here for second-run Hollywood movies, as well as dance performances.

Gallup's most popular event is the **Inter-Tribal Indian Ceremonial** held anually in August. Begun in 1922 when a contingent of Gallup businessmen invited a group of local Indians to dance and display their crafts at the McKinley County Fair, the show now attracts Native American dancers, craftsmen, and cowboys from throughout North America. For a Saturday parade that weaves through downtown, different tribes bring out their finery. Members wear ornate turquoise necklaces, feathered headdresses, and buffalo masks, and they pause often to dance a few steps to the rhythmic beat of drums. In the All-Indian Rodeo saddle bronc competition, professional rodeo cowboys from across the country try to stay atop bucking horses , or bind together the legs of squeamish calves in the calf roping contest. Nearby, there's Indian frybread topped with plenty of sugar and honey, or Navajo tacos—frybread covered with mutton, cheese, lettuce, and tomatoes. Indian crafts range from traditional Navajo blankets, silver jewelry, and beadwork to modern sculpture and painting. During the fair, the town's population of 20,000 doubles, and lodging is virtually unobtainable without reservations months in advance. *East of town at* **Red Rock State Park;** *505-863-3896.*

A marvelous way to travel through New Mexico is on the **Southwest Chief,** the Amtrak train that travels daily between Los Angeles and Chicago. A Navajo tour guide boards the train in Gallup and spends the two and a half hoursride to Albequerque imparting some of the tribe's lore and legends to interested passengers. As the silver train rumbles past vermilion mesas, the guide may point to a traditional Navajo hogan and explain why it is built facing east. "The philosophical reason is because we believe that all good things in life come from the east when the sun rises in the morning. But it also has practical purposes. Obviously, if you've got the sun shining at your door in the morning, it's going to warm your house up a little faster." *Amtrak; 800-USA-RAIL.*

If you're curious about Navajo weaving, you might want to attend the monthly

Navajo weavers outside a hogan on Navajo tribal lands. (Museum of New Mexico)

Crownpoint rug auction, where bidding is lively and the artisans are on hand to discuss their work. Typically the auction takes place at the Crownpoint Elementary School on the third Friday of the month. *505-786-5302.*

■ ZUNI PUEBLO   *map page 149, G-1*

The radiant desert sunsets that have been attracting people to New Mexico for years proved to be the undoing of 16th-century Zuni Indians living at Hawikuh, a settlement 12 miles south of the present-day pueblo. It was here that in 1539 Fray Marcos de Niza, searching for the fabled Seven Cities of Cibola, caught a glimpse at sunset of the walls of the pueblo's dwellings, turning gold in the waning light. Gifted with an excitable imagination, the man of God thought he saw gold-plated walls and envisioned treasure-laden streets. Returning to Mexico, he passed on his account to Antonio de Mendoza, viceroy of New Spain. Mendoza enlisted the financial assistance and energetic support of Francisco Vasquez de Coronado, the young governor of a New Spain province. The next year, Coronado arrived at Hawikuh to find flat-roofed mud huts and angry Indians who tried to resist his troops. The "cities" turned out to be Zuni villages.

The Zunis had things much more valuable than gold: they had an integrated and sophisticated civilization, a sacred land, their religion, and ancient traditions. They grew corn, beans, and squash alongside the Zuni River in the slate-blue shadows of surrounding mesas; they raised turkeys and kept eagles in captivity for their feathers. They traded turquoise and salt with Plains Indians for buffalo hides and with Mexican tribes for parrot plumes; they thought nothing of running 20 miles round-trip to carry messages.

Although the Zunis grudgingly accepted the Spanish presence, allowing them to build churches and erect crosses, they never fully embraced the Christianity that was forced upon them. Occasionally they burned mission churches and killed priests who wouldn't stop harassing them. Even today, Christianity takes a back seat to their own ancient religion, and the Zunis maintain an elaborate ceremonial organization. Because they believe the sun is the source of life, the most revered man in the tribe is the Sun Priest, who oversees solstice ceremonies. Other esoteric cults include the rainmaker, ancestor, kachina, beast, and war gods. Sacred Zuni fetishes, which include quartz crystals, turtle-shell rattles, and seashells were used by the priest in charge of each cult to carry out his duty.

The Zunis took part in the Pueblo Revolt of 1680, killing a friar and burning

SHALAKO DANCE AT ZUNI PUEBLO

As the short winter day gives way to evening, residents at Zuni Pueblo excitedly anticipate the final celebration of their ceremonial year. Huddled in doorways, wrapped snugly in wool blankets against the chill of the fading light, the Zunis occasionally glance to the south, listening for a loud clacking sound that comes from a wooden beak. They are awaiting the arrival of the Shalakos, six 10-foot-tall gods who will spend the night blessing six houses built in their honor during the previous year and offering prayers so that the tribe may enjoy fertility, long life, prosperity, and happiness.

The Shalako ceremony is a reenactment of the creation and migration of the Zuni people to Heptina, or the "Middle Place," which was destined to be their home. This is the most elaborate and unique of any pueblo ritual, beginning at dusk and lasting throughout the night. The date, in late November or early December, is determined in the fall. Outsiders are sometimes invited to witness the symbolic night-long dances only if they agree not to take photographs, or make sketches or tape recordings of the event. It's best to check with the pueblo before venturing out.

Serious organization for the ceremonies begins shortly after the Zuni New Year in the first part of January, almost a full year earlier. Tribal ceremonial leaders select impersonators of the dance characters, and families accept responsibility for building or remodeling houses that will be used to entertain the gods. In addition to the six Shalako houses, two more are built each year: one for the Council of the Gods—the Longhorn House—and one for the Mudheads, or Koyemshi, a group of 10 dancers who wear knobby, adobe-colored masks and paint their bodies with pinkish clay, creating the effect of distorted creatures. During the year, religious and house-building activities of the Mudheads take up so much of their time that they do not take other jobs.

Shalako Day begins with women baking bread in beehive-shaped *hornos* and stirring great pots of chile and beans that will serve the visiting gods and guests. These women also grind corn into sacred meal that the gods will use to bless shrines and the Shalako houses. In addition, six shrine sites throughout the pueblo must be readied for the various performers who will visit them later in the day.

In mid-afternoon the Fire God makes his appearance, accompanied by his ceremonial Godfather. A 10- to 14-year-old boy is chosen as Fire God and is identified by a black mask painted with yellow, blue, red, and white dots and by numerous turquoise necklaces. Fire God and his Godfather visit sacred shrines in the pueblo and then retire to the Longhorn House where they wait for the four-member Council of Gods. These gods follow the Fire God to the shrines, performing prayers and rituals at each one. Each of the gods wears a distinct mask and costume that identifies him as either the Rain Priest, the Hututu, or one of the two Yamuhaktos, each representing one of the four directions of the compass.

At dusk the Shalakos slowly walk over the top of a hill on the south side of the Zuni River. Two horns and wooden eyes jut from the spectacular turquoise mask that is adorned with a profusion of feathers: eagle feathers for the headpiece and downy feathers that run from the ends of the horns down the back. These imposing bird-like creatures are robed in white embroidered ceremonial clothing, and a massive ruff fashioned from glossy raven feathers.

They proceed to their sacred shrine, located southwest of the laundromat. Occasional clacks can be heard from their wooden beaks snapping together. As the skies darken, red firefly-like lights flicker from cigarettes smoked by the gods and their assistants. Well after dark and after cold temperatures have numbed onlookers' feet, the Shalako follow a special footpath to the river and then pick their way across. They never use a nearby bridge. Members of the crowd fall in behind one of the Shalako, following the dancer to the house that has been prepared for him.

Solemnly, the Shalako plants prayer plumes and seeds inside the threshold and deposits seeds in baskets in front of an altar at the west end of the room. An excavation below this altar signifies the fourth womb in the world, through which the Zuni people emerged in their creation. Then the Shalako mask is placed in front of the altar where it remains until the dancing begins shortly after midnight. Numerous rituals follow, including a feast for invited Indians, during which the Shalako impersonator takes a little food from each bowl passed to him and wraps it in *piki* —a paper-thin bread made from blue corn. He also walks to the river where he makes sacrificial offerings to tribal ancestors.

Shortly after midnight, a group of men gathered about a large drum in a corner of the room begin a rhythmic pounding that continues until sunrise. Others shake rattles and begin chanting. The Shalako dancer dons the awkward mask and begins moving in time to the drumbeat. He gracefully dips and sways, and swoops from one end of the room to the other, often clacking his protruding beak. The dance is interrupted only when the Shalako's understudy assumes the beat, giving the main dancer a break.

During the night-long ceremony, the Mudheads travel in pairs to each Shalako house, singing and providing comic relief, often taunting the towering Shalako dancers. In the morning, the Shalakos leave their houses and proceed back across the river, returning to their ancestral homes, leaving behind enough blessings and good will to sustain the Zunis for another year.

the mission church, but feared the certain retaliation of the Spanish. After the rebellion, they took refuge on Towayalane, or Corn Mountain, a majestic mile-long multi-colored sandstone mesa that stands three miles southeast of the present-day pueblo. They built three-story rock houses alongside a shallow wash where the mesa makes a slight dip. The Indians remained here, continuing to farm the lowlands, for 12 years, until Diego de Vargas reclaimed the territory for Spain. Then the Zunis came off the mountain and settled at the site of the present-day pueblo.

As time went on, Zuni craftsmen became famous for making extraordinarily beautiful jewelry, in particular silver pieces inlaid with turquoise, shell, and jet. They have also made a craft of animal fetishes fashioned out of carved minerals, glass, and stones, embellished with gemstones. In addition, Zuni "needlepoint" is the placement of tiny gemstones (most often turquoise) close together in intricate patterns set in silver.

Zuni Pueblo has 8,000 members, making it the largest in New Mexico. It appears much like any other small New Mexican town, with a maze of low, flat-roofed houses, small vegetable patches, and dusty unpaved streets. A few craft

Shalako dancers at Zuni Pueblo in 1897. (Museum of New Mexico)

shops are mixed in among stores and businesses. If in the morning you notice the delicious smell of baking bread, follow your nose and you'll find yourself standing beside a *horno,* a beehive-shaped clay oven of ancient design built at the side of nearly every home.

Tribal permission is required if you wish to visit two nearby places of interest—the crumbling ruins at Hawikuh and the unexcavated Village of the Great Kivas, three ancient pueblos located 18 miles north of Zuni.

■ THE WAY TO GRANTS   *map page 149, G-3 & 4*

Indians from Zuni and Acoma pueblos knew their way through pine and juniper forests and across a massive lava flow, the remains of five major eruptions from nearby volcanoes, that sprawls between the two pueblos south of the present-day town of Grants. (As recently as 700 years ago, rivers of molten rock and flying cinders oozed across the sandstone and limestone valley. Indian legends tell of rivers of "fire rock.") Carrying precious loads of salt and turquoise, the natives walked the jagged landscape—warm black rocks under an intensely blue sky. They filled wide gaps in the hardened lava with boulders to create bridges and erected cairns from the sharp rock so they wouldn't lose their way across the unrelenting terrain.

Early Spanish and American travelers rarely ventured across the hardened lava. Leading their horses around it, they called the 114,000-acre lava-rock valley El Malpais (The Badlands). In 1988, the federal government recognized the unique geological features of the area and established **El Malpais National Monument and Conservation Area.** *The visitor center is located 10 miles south of Grants on NM 117. 505-285-4641.*

The valley's violent past can be seen along a portion of the trade route marked by the Indians. Aptly called the Zuni-Acoma Trail, the 7.5-mile path crosses all five of the major lava flows that blanket the broad valley, giving hikers a chance to walk on chunky lava called *'a'a* and ropey lava known as *pa'hoe'hoe* (both Hawaiian terms). A network of four-by-four wooden posts connects the ancient rock cairns, providing easily spotted trail markers—the undulating lava flow looks the same in every direction, so it's easy to lose the trail. Before striking out from one marker, be sure to have the next one in sight.

The volcanoes that once spewed blistering hot lava still brood above the scene.

The crater of one of them, Bandera Crater, can be seen at the end of a one-half-mile-long trail carpeted in soft cinder. Peering down 800 feet into the extinct volcano, it's reassuring to know that the last time it erupted was about a million years ago. All that remains are rust-colored scree walls with an occasional ponderosa pine stretching for the sun. A ghostly silence is disturbed only by a dislodged basalt pebble tumbling toward the crater's center. Nearby, a sturdy wooden staircase leads 75 feet below the jagged surface of broken basalt to the opening of an ice cave. The cave was formed when molten lava, within a crust of cooling and hardening lava, flowed through. Afterward, moisture seeped through the cracked and porous basalt and froze in the cold cave. A blast of chilly air emanates from the opening, which is coated with thick layers of mossy green ice. Icicles dangle from the ceiling, and steady droplets of water drip from them into a blue-green pool. This brisk, 31-degree F air prevents lengthy visits. Heading upward toward the warm 80-degree F sunshine, the staircase passes by brilliant orange, yellow, and brown lichen draped across volcanic boulders.

At the eastern edge of the flow and visible from NM 117 is a magnificent natural arch aptly called La Ventana (The Window). Years of wind pounding against the soft sandstone and water seeping into cracks have left a 125-foot-high opening in the rock. Black and red striations of color called desert varnish play on the underside of the 165-foot span. A short walk to the giant window is well worth the effort.

The ancient Indian trade route, which NM 53 roughly follows, also passes by a massive 200-foot-high sandstone mesa visible for miles, atop which sit two Zuni pueblos, one unexcavated and one with partial walls showing. It's been preserved as **El Morro (The Bluff) National Monument.**

At the base of the pale cliff is a natural basin filled with water, replenished by summer rains and winter snows. A natural rest stop for nearly a thousand years, travelers couldn't resist leaving their marks on the nearby smooth sandstone surface. Indian petroglyphs were first, followed by signatures and messages written by Spanish explorers and later Anglo settlers. Two years before Jamestown, Virginia, was founded in 1607, Juan de Oñate left an inscription: "Passed by here the Governor Don Juan de Oñate, from the discovery of the Sea of the South on the 16th of April 1605." The "Sea of the South" was the Gulf of California. When Diego de Vargas was on his way to reclaim Zuni after the Pueblo Revolt, he too left his mark: "Here was the General Don Diego de Vargas who conquered for our Holy Faith, and for the Royal Crown, all of New Mexico at his own expense, year of 1692." Through the centuries, explorers, traders, soldiers, surveyors, and settlers carved messages as they passed by. Thus the name Inscription Rock seems most appropriate.

El Morro National Monument's fine visitor center, with a museum featuring ancient tools and pottery, is open year-round. *Located between Grants and Zuni on NM 53; 505-783-4226.*

■ GRANTS   *map page 149, G-4*

Set on a flat plain in the protective shadows of the towering Mount Taylor, an 11,300-foot ancient volcano, Grants is once again a busted mining town trying to revive itself. One main street pretty much takes care of the sights in this dusty community, named after the three Grant brothers, Angus, Lewis, and John—who won a contract to build the section of the Atlantic and Pacific Railroad between Isleta Pueblo and Needles, California. Grants's entire economic history, in fact, has been one of boom and bust. First it boomed in 1881 as a camp for railroad workers, when 4,000 men and 2,000 mules hauled ties for the tracks. With the completion of the railroad, the town's population dwindled; by the late 1920s it was 350. Revitalized by the construction of Bluewater Dam on the nearby Rio San Jose, Grants bloomed as an agricultural community. The town went crazy for carrots—lush-topped ones, the kind Easterners craved. By 1941, the water from the dam had helped to produce about 2,000 train carloads of carrots a year, valued at $2.5 million. When their competitors began encasing carrots in colorful cellophane wrapping, the Grants farmers didn't follow suit and demand dropped.

The town's next wave of prosperity began in 1950 when Paddy Martinez, a Navajo sheep rancher, found an unusual-looking yellow rock at the base of Haystack Mountain, adjacent to one of his pastures. Convinced it was uranium and worth at least $10,000, he rode his horse into Grants where he showed it to a merchant friend, who scoffed at the idea it was the valuable ore. Martinez staked a mining claim anyway, thus setting the stage for another Grants comeback. In 1960, Grants was incorporated and for the next 30 years, it was sustained by the uranium industry.

Ancient Indians and Spanish explorers left drawings and messages at El Morro.
(Paul Chesley)

Paddy Martinez, by the way, never mined the uranium. He only rented the land around Haystack Mountain to the Santa Fe Railroad, which paid him a monthly sum for his discovery. With his monthly check, Martinez moved to the shores of Bluewater Lake and continued to graze sheep.

By the early 1980s, the demand for uranium had dropped. The last Grants-area mine closed in January 1990, but not before boosters had opened the **New Mexico Mining Museum** at Grants so people wouldn't forget the golden days of uranium. There, visitors can visit a simulated uranium mine, complete with an elevator that imitates a 900-foot descent into the earth. The town's latest endeavor is the Mt. Taylor Winter Quadrathlon, a grueling 75-kilometer race held in February in which nearly 600 competitors bike, run, ski, and snowshoe up 11,301-foot Mt. Taylor and back to town.

The Grants Chamber of Commerce is located at the New Mexico Mining Museum and can provide information about the museum, the quadrathlon and the region; *505-287-4802 or 800-748-2142.*

◆ LAGUNA PUEBLO   *map page 149, G-5*

About 27 miles east of Grants, **Laguna Pueblo** is visible along I-40. Laguna, named for a nearby lake that has since become a meadow, actually serves as the center for six farming villages. Although the area has been occupied since 3,000 B.C.E., the pueblo has proven its adeptness at adapting to the modern world. In the 1870s, pueblo residents—influenced by nearby Anglo settlers who married into the tribe—adopted a tribal constitution modeled after the U.S. Constitution. And in recent years, the pueblo has been successful in business. In its modern form, the pueblo was established in 1699 by the Spanish governor Pedro Rodriguez Cubero. Later that year, the San José de Laguna Church was completed, making it the last of the early mission churches to be established in New Mexico.

Today, the imposing stone church stands on a hill overlooking simple pueblo dwellings. The ornate and colorfully painted pine altar carved by Indian craftsmen is flanked by paintings of St. Barbara and St. John Nepomucene, and an animal hide attached to the ceiling is colored with Indian symbols of the rainbow, sun, moon, and stars.

■ ACOMA PUEBLO   *map page 149, H-4*

At the same time the Anasazi were at the peak of their civilization, residents at Acoma were building adobe and rock homes high atop the 357-foot Rock of Acuco. This multi-colored sandstone mesa rises from a sandy plain dotted with chamisa and juniper trees southeast of present-day Grants. Some historians estimate Acoma Pueblo has been occupied since A.D. 1075, making it the oldest continuously inhabited city in the country.

The Acomas say their ancestors arrived in A.D. 600 from Mesa Verde in what today is southern Colorado. According to legend, the Indians were told by Iatiku, mother of all Indians, to seek a mesa resembling the tip of an ear of corn. They found Enchanted Mesa and built a rock-walled village atop the majestic mountain. Only one route led up the precipitous 430-foot cliffs of the desert monolith, and another legend has it that one day, when most of the tribe was tending fields on the plains, a violent storm moved in, wiping out the path to the top. A young girl and her grandmother were stranded on top. Rather than starve, they leapt to their deaths. The tribe moved to the nearby Acuco Mesa.

Some historians believe the early dwellers chose to build atop Acuco for its protection from marauding tribes. The solitary citadel served the tribe well in 1540 when Spaniards came searching for the Seven Cities of Cibola and mistakenly thought they saw those riches reflected in the pueblo's mica window panes. Though their attempt to scale the mountain was unsuccessful, the soldiers killed 100 Acoma men.

At one time, several thousand Indians lived in multi-story rock-walled dwellings crowded onto the 70-acre mesa. They must have wakened to a dawn in which a brilliant sun illuminated a distant snowcapped peak (now called Mt. Taylor) and fields below of corn, beans, and squash—much the same view as today. Descending a steep staircase carved from the soft rock, they would have set about their various occupations—gathering wood from nearby woodlands and tending to their fields. Every night they would have climbed the steep mountain to the village.

Acoma residents successfully held off intruders until 1598, when the pueblo voluntarily submitted to the Spanish. This peaceful acquiescence was short-lived, however; the Indians killed Juan de Zaldivar and 12 soldiers who were seeking cornmeal. Unfortunately for the Indians, Zaldivar was a nephew of Juan de Oñate, Spanish governor of New Mexico. Seventy men quickly avenged Zaldivar's death, killing at least 100 Acoma men and kidnapping 60 young Indian girls to sell in Mexico as slaves. They also severed a foot from each of the remaining Indian men.

With the Indians securely subdued, the Spanish soon were overseeing construction of the San Esteban del Rey Mission, completed in 1640. Forty-foot-long roof beams were cut in the Cebolleta Mountains, 30 miles south, and carried on men's backs up the rugged slopes of the mesa.

Today, you can walk inside the mission where stark, white-washed walls contrast with a wooden altar painted in bright reds, blues, yellows, and greens. Each year, prior to San Esteban's feast day, which honors the patron saint, the walls are freshly painted with traditional yucca and sheepskin brushes. The paint is ground from pink and white sandstones quarried at nearby mesas.

About 13 Acoma families reside at the pueblo, which has never had running water or electricity. All of life's essentials, even dirt for the pueblo's cemetery, must be hauled up from below. An occasional antenna attached to a generator-driven television rises above the ancient dwellings and keeps the inhabitants up to date on world events. Most of the tribal members have opted to live in the nearby villages of Acomita, McCartys, Laguna, or Paraje, where they can bathe in hot water from a spigot and are closer to schools and work.

The only way outsiders can see the mesa-top village is on a guided walking tour, which departs regularly from a visitor center at the base of the mountain. A tribal member acts as a guide, leading guests into the mission church and its cemetery, then through the narrow streets that wind among the multi-storied rock and adobe buildings. Ladders reach to upper stories and ceremonial *kivas.* Around every corner, artisans display for sale the tribe's precise thin-shelled pottery painted with orange and black pigments taken from sandstone and rich alpine soil. An occasional truck rattles by, ascending the mountain on a narrow road financed in 1941 by a movie company so that parts of the film *Sundown* could be shot at the pueblo. Fake trees and real ostriches were imported as set designers turned the dusty pueblo into a jungle city in the film that starred Gene Tierney.

Each guide embellishes the tribe's legends as her mood dictates. As you stand at the edge of the mesa, wondering which tale to believe, a breath-taking panoramic view spreads out before you. Below, a carpet of yellow-tipped chamisa periodically gives way to red-tinted sandstone buttes and boulders. An occasional raven soars nearby, uttering a hoarse, lonely call. Peering over the sheer cliff face that surrounds the mesa, it's easy to see how Acoma Pueblo kept outsiders away for so long.

After the hour-long tour, you can take the path of the original inhabitants back to the visitor center. An ancient rock stairway used for thousands of years by the Indians leads you along narrow, often steep, passages through the soft sandstone. Natural steps have been worn smooth, along with handholds carved over years of use into the weathered sandstone walls. *Call 505-470-4966 or 800-747-0181 for information.*

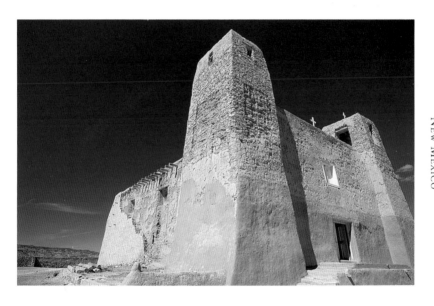

Mission Church, Acoma.

NAVAJO GIRL

Some of the men of Jemez rode out to meet the Navajos. John Cajero was one of them. He was then a man in his prime, a Tanoan man, agile and strong in his mind and body, and he was a first-rate horseman. He was mounted on a good-looking gray quarter horse, which he handled closely and well, and he cut a fine figure upon it in his blue shirt and red headband, his manner easy and confident. He singled out old friends among the Navajos, and soon there was a cluster of riders holding up on the side of the road, convened in a high mood of fellowship and good humor—and a certain rivalry. Then John Cajero was holding the coils of rope in his hands, shaking out a loop. Suddenly he leaned forward and his horse bolted into the road between two of the wagons, nearly trampling over a dog; the dog lunged away with a yelp and ran at full speed, but the horse was right upon it, bunched in motion, and the rope flashed down and caught the dog up around its hips and set it rolling and twisting in the sand, jerking it up then into the air and slamming it down hard, as the horse squatted, jamming its hooves in the earth, its whole weight cracking against the bit. And John Cajero played out a little of the rope from his saddle, and the dog slithered out of the noose and ran ahead, its tail between its legs, and went crouching and wary under its wagon. John Cajero laughed, and the others, too, though their laughter was brittle, I thought, and the Navajos watched evenly the performance, the enactment of a hard joke, and considered precisely what it was worth. There was a kind of trade in this, a bartering of nerve and arrogance and skill, of elemental pride. Then, getting down from his horse, John Cajero drew a dollar bill from his pocket, folded it once lengthwise, and stuck it down in the sand. He gestured to the others; it was a beckoning, an invitation, but I did not understand at first what he meant them to do. He swung himself up into the saddle and gestured again, pointing down to the money on the ground. No one moved; only they were watchful, and he urged his horse away, prancing, a little distance. Then he turned the horse around and set it running—or loping, rather, not fast, but easily, evenly—and reached down from the saddle for the dollar bill. It seemed that his fingers brushed it, but he could not take hold of it, for the stride of the horse was broken slightly at the crucial moment. It was the barest miss— and a beautiful, thrilling thing to see—and he was upright in the saddle again, his motion and the motion of the horse all of a piece. I was watching him so intently that I did not at first see the girl. She came from nowhere, a lithe, lovely Navajo girl on a black horse. She was coming up fast in John Cajero's dust, faster than he had come, and her horse was holding steady in a long, loping stride, level and low. When I saw her she was already hanging down nearly the whole length of her arm from the saddle horn, her knee cocked and her long back curved like a bow, her shoulders close against the deep chest of the horse; she swung her left arm down like a scythe, and up, holding the dollar bill with the tips of her fingers until it was high over her head, and she was standing straight in the stirrups, and her horse did not break stride. And in that way she rode on, past John Cajero, along the wagon train and into the village, having stolen the show and the money, too, going in beauty, trailing laughter. Later I looked for her among the camps, but I did not find her. I imagined that her name was Desbah Yazzie and that she looked out for me from the shadows.

—N. Scott Momaday
The Names, a Memoir, 1976

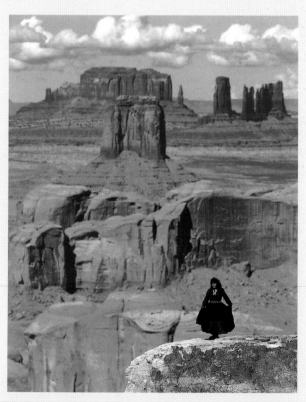

S O U T H W E S T E R N
N   E   W   M   E   X   I   C   O

■ HIGHLIGHTS

Food and Lodging begins on page 280.

FROM THE AQUAMARINE WATERS OF ELEPHANT BUTTE LAKE and the cactus prairie near Lordsburg to the pine-clad mountains of Silver City, southwestern New Mexico offers a vibrant diversity of landscape. The bone-dry desert is relieved by the Rio Grande, which wends its way through the region, creating wetlands for migratory birds and providing sustenance to fields of onion, cotton, and chile. Pale-green hillsides dotted with piñon and juniper rise to the dense woods of the Gila National Forest, once home to the Mimbres Indians and still home to mountain lions and black bears. You can drive for miles without seeing another car and if you do, it'll probably be a pickup truck with a gun rack in the cab.

Like a hazy mirage, rugged mountain ranges soar upward from the flat, desolate landscape where wide expanses of desert grasses mix with the crooked branches of mesquite trees. Vast stretches of cracked earth covered with clumps of grass are marked by isolated ranches and barbed-wire fences that extend in long lines against the hills.

Along NM 9, which dips close to the Mexico border, immigrants illegally slip across the open range in the dark of night. Water flows steadily in irrigation ditches along US 85, which passes cotton fields displaying their unmistakable white bolls. Just across the road, a dark-green carpet of chile fields provides a stunning contrast. In the fall, the chile's pungent odor assaults your olfactory nerves and is a reminder that winter is just around the corner.

SOUTHWESTERN NEW MEXICO

Elevation
in feet

13,161
12,000
11,000
10,000
9,000
8,000
7,000
6,000
5,000
4,000

0   25   50 Miles

0   25   50   75 Kilometers

The past, too, is never far away. Here you'll find the remains of ancient Indian cliff dwellings, the crumbling ruins of 19th-century forts, and the tattered shacks of once-thriving mining camps.

In recent years, the quiet, slower-paced lifestyles of ranching and farming, along with a mild climate have been attracting retirees. Nowhere else in the state are motorists more apt to lift a hand across a steering wheel as a greeting in passing, or a sales clerk to inquire where you are heading. Many towns are so small, every stranger who stops is noticed.

■ HISTORY

As early as 3000 B.C.E., the ancestors of the Mogollon Indians learned how to cultivate corn and squash from their southern neighbors in Mexico. By 300 B.C.E., they had added red kidney beans and were shaping pottery and living in pit houses dug four feet underground and covered with timber and dirt. In the first centuries of A.D., the Indians moved into large caves along the Gila River where they continued to grow corn, beans, and squash. Others built free-standing masonry dwellings deep in the mountains. One branch of Mogollons, the Mimbres, developed exquisite black-on-white pottery and created designs that ranged from geometric patterns to stylized reptiles. These fragile pots are usually found with a hole punctured in the bottom at grave sites. Through this hole, the pot's spirit, thought to be part of its maker, is released. An extensive permanent exhibit of this prehistoric pottery can be seen at Western New Mexico University Museum in Silver City.

By A.D. 500, the Mogollon culture had peaked. But the Indians continued to hunt and farm in the mountains and valleys of southwestern New Mexico until the early 1300s, when they left the Gila to resettle along the Rio Grande and other drainages of the region. One of their cave settlements has been preserved at the Gila Cliff Dwellings National Monument, 44 miles north of Silver City.

◆ APACHES AND GERONIMO

By the early 1300s, bands of Apaches had entered the region to hunt deer and bison. Women supplemented their diet by gathering berries, roots, and seeds as they moved about. Historians tend to lump the southern Apaches into two main groups: the Mescaleros, who lived in animal-skin tepees, and the Chiricahuas, who erected grass and brush huts called *wickiups*. Young girls wound their hair around two willow hoops, worn over their ears, while some older women adopted the style of Plains Indians and braided their hair in long plaits. The women sewed deer-skin robes and animal-skin moccasins, which could be pulled up to the knee for warmth, or folded down to protect against thorns and rocks.

Of the Mescaleros, the late C. L. Sonnichsen wrote:

> They owned nothing and everything. They did as they pleased and bowed to no man. Their women were chaste. Their leaders kept their promises. They were mighty warriors who depended on success in raiding for wealth and honor. To their families they were kind and gentle, but they could be unbelievably cruel to their enemies—fierce and revengeful when they felt that they had been betrayed.

In the 16th century, Spanish explorers investigating New Mexico passed through the southwest on their way north. At that time, several groups of Pueblo Indians were living in earthen homes along the southern Rio Grande. They were probably both alarmed and amused by the cumbersome entourages led by armored conquistadors that traipsed by looking for gold. After giving up on this fruitless venture, the Spanish concentrated on colonizing what today is northern New Mexico. As a result, southwestern New Mexico was well-traveled but rarely settled. Towns such as Socorro and Mesilla served as stations on El Camino Real, "the King's Highway," a 1,500-mile trade route that connected Mexico City with the provincial capital of Santa Fe. The northern part of this trail, from Chihuahua to Santa Fe, became known as the Chihuahua Trail.

Entire families made this arduous journey, carrying household goods and chickens in carretas and herding cattle and churro sheep. Accompanied by soldiers and priests, these caravans inched along a dirt path that hardly could be called a road. Clouds of dust and the loud creaking of the two-wheeled carretas marked their progress. As more people made the grueling journey to Santa Fe, they began to notice the fertile fields of the Mesilla Valley.

The noisy caravans drew the attention of the roaming Apaches, who resisted the Spaniards from the outset. The Indians attacked the travelers, stealing water, food, and animals, and sometimes taking captives.

One Apache warrior in particular carried with him his entire life a hatred for the intrusive Spanish. Born a member of the Bedonkohe Apache band sometime in the late 1820s, his given name was Goyahkla, but later he became known as Geronimo. As a child, before he even saw a Spaniard, Geronimo heard stories of campaigns in which they acquired the Apaches as slaves or killed them outright. When the Apaches retaliated, the Spanish turned other tribes against them.

When he was 17, Geronimo was designated a warrior, which gave him the right to accompany his tribe into battle. He spent 60 years traversing the wooded canyons outside Silver City and the desolate cactus plains that spilled into Arizona and Mexico, alternately living peacefully and fighting for his people. By the mid-1850s, he had lost two wives and four children to the Spanish.

As early as 1855, the United States government was coercing Indians to sign treaties giving away their land, but Geronimo didn't trust the white man's word, nor did he like the idea of living on a reservation. As U.S. soldiers gradually reduced his domain, capturing Indians and sending them to reservations, however, Geronimo realized his days of freedom were numbered, and he began negotiating with the American officers. During this time he tried unsuccessfully to live on the San Carlos Reservation in Arizona. Finally, on September 5, 1886, the aging warrior, his conditions met, surrendered for the last time to Brig. Gen. Nelson Miles at Skeleton Canyon, on a rugged raiding route between Mexico and the Arizona mountains. "We placed a large stone on the blanket before us. Our treaty was made by this stone and it was to last until the stone should crumble to dust; so we made the treaty and bound each other with an oath," Geronimo said.

General Miles promised the great warrior cattle, horses, mules, and farming tools, along with a house and a large tract of land covered with timber, water, and grass. Geronimo was also guaranteed a reunion with members of his tribe already in the government's custody.

Instead, Geronimo and a few other warriors were sent by train to Florida. They spent the next eight years either incarcerated or working for the federal government in Florida and Alabama. Many died of tuberculosis. Finally, in 1894, they were reunited with their families and relocated to Fort Sill, Oklahoma, where they were given

The great Apache warrior Geronimo, in 1885. (Museum of New Mexico)

houses, land, and animals. During the following years, Geronimo became a celebrity, making appearances at regional conventions and fairs. At the Louisiana Purchase Exposition at St. Louis in 1904, he was a main attraction, selling his photograph for 25 cents and signing autographs. "I often made as much as two dollars a day, and when I returned I had plenty of money, more than I had ever owned before," he said. The defeated warrior died in 1909 after falling off a horse.

◆ SETTLEMENT AND THE RAILROAD

Settlement came to the region in the 19th century after the Treaty of Guadalupe-Hidalgo was signed in 1848, ending the Mexican-American War and designating the Rio Grande as the boundary between the two countries. As the town of Mesilla sat on the west side of the river, it was relegated overnight to the status of a Mexican border town. The burgeoning community swelled further as Mexicans flocked north to the area's lush cropland. In 1854, the United States signed the Gadsden Purchase and for $10 million bought from Mexico all land west of the Rio Grande. Mesilla now flew the U.S. flag and the town boomed: mule trains, stagecoaches, and miners en route to the silver and copper mines of the Gila Mountains stopped for supplies and horses at what now was a safe haven. Mesilla was also an important way station on the Butterfield Trail, a stagecoach route established in 1850 to transport passengers and the mail twice a week 2,800 miles from Tipton, Missouri, to San Francisco. In 1863, the river changed its course after a flood, and Mesilla found itself on the eastern side of the Rio Grande where it sits today.

After the Mexican-American War, the U.S. government concentrated its energies on the Apaches, who continued to attack stagecoaches and wagon trains. Uncertainty as to what the Indians might do added a sharp edge of fear to all journeys through this wild territory. Sometimes the warriors killed their victims, but most often they took firearms, food, supplies, livestock, and horses. One stagecoach driver, Bigfoot Wallace, was once forced to walk 80 miles to town after the Apaches purloined his mules. On another occasion, he came limping into El Paso with his stage stuck full of arrows.

In an effort to calm travelers' nerves, the federal government erected numerous forts in the region during the 1860s and '70s. The remains of one of these, Fort Selden, built 12 miles north of Las Cruces in 1865, has been preserved as a state monument. During its 25 years of service, the fort's soldiers saw little action with the Apaches. Its claim to fame is that Gen. Douglas MacArthur learned to ride and shoot there before he learned how to read and write. His father, Capt. Arthur MacArthur, served as commander at the military post.

In the 1880s, the Southern Pacific Railroad began wending its way east across the Southwest into New Mexico, and the towns of Lordsburg and Deming sprang up as railroad camps. In 1881, the Atchison, Topeka & Santa Fe Railroad, which made its way southward through New Mexico, joined its competitor the Southern Pacific at Deming to form the second transcontinental railroad route in the country.

Mesilla, which had been the largest city of the region, began to decline when the railroad bypassed it, choosing instead to locate a depot at the county seat of Las Cruces. There, Victorian homes with screened-in porches were built alongside traditional single-story adobes for tuberculosis patients who came for the clear dry air of the Southwest. They came in far greater numbers once they could ride in the comfort and safety of railroad cars. Many of these "lungers" enjoyed the mild climate and rural valley so much that they stayed on after their recuperation.

The discovery of silver, gold, copper, iron, lead, and zinc in the mountains southwest of Socorro already had attracted miners who set up rudimentary camps near their claims. In 1871, Silver City was established and soon became a place where rowdy miners swapped stories, ordered supplies, and enjoyed an occasional home-cooked meal. With the arrival of a spur that linked the mining camp to the Deming station, miners no longer had to travel as far to haul in supplies and ship valuable ores. Speculators and businessmen of a type not inclined to endure dusty, bumpy stagecoach rides now began crowding onto trains headed to the fledgling mining towns. Farmers and ranchers took a new look at the arable land along the Rio Grande, which became appealing once the threat of Apache attacks was removed. Now that passengers were protected inside rail cars, the forts were no longer needed, and they were all abandoned by the end of the century.

◆ OUTLAWS AND LAWMEN

During this era, legends were born. Billy the Kid, known as Henry McCarty to his Silver City classmates, lived in the mining district with his mother, brother, and stepfather in the early 1870s. One legend has it that he killed his first man in a barroom brawl when he was 12 years old. According to historical accounts, however, the famous outlaw had his first brush with the law at 15, when he was arrested for robbing a Chinese laundry and subsequently escaped from the Silver City jail. As a youth, McCarty was supposedly bold, daring, and reckless, but also generous, frank, and ready to offer his assistance to the town's elderly residents.

BILLY THE KID

Barefoot and bareheaded, Billy the Kid thought he was among friends in the darkened bedroom of Pete Maxwell when he asked who was sitting at the foot of his friend's bed. That hesitation, on a summer evening in 1881, cost him his life. Sheriff Pat Garrett answered the question with two bullets, the first entering just above the outlaw's heart.

The violent death of Henry Antrim, aka Henry McCarty, a.k.a. William Bonney, failed to put an end to a legend that germinated during the Lincoln County War, which broke out in 1878. The Kid's early death at 21 in a Fort Sumner bedroom merely elevated the outlaw's status to a mythical one that would continue to blossom as the years passed.

Henry McCarty, as the Kid was first known, was born in the Irish slums of Brooklyn in 1859. He made his way west with his older brother Joe and his mother, Catherine McCarty, who suffered from tuberculosis. In 1873, she married William Antrim at the First Presbyterian Church in Santa Fe, and they moved the family to Silver City, where Antrim went about seeking his elusive fortune in the silver mines.

One of Henry's school teachers there recalled him as "a scrawny little fellow with delicate hands (he supposedly loved to play the piano) and an artistic nature, always willing to help with the chores around the schoolhouse."

Catherine Antrim died when Henry was 14, and he started hanging out with George Shaffer, a young friend who liked to drink and steal. One night they made off with a bundle of clothing from a local Chinese laundry, for which Henry was caught. While in jail, he wriggled his wiry body up a chimney to freedom. At 15, he headed for Arizona where he shot his first man on record and didn't stick around to plead self-defense.

Back in New Mexico, Henry, now a seasoned outlaw, changed his name to William Bonney. His baby face and beanpole body secured him the nickname "the Kid." Wavy brown hair accented his 5-foot 7-inch, 135-pound frame. Innumerable books have been written about Billy, and while these mountains of words paint a picture of a half-crazed, ruthless, bratty teenage killer, in reality, Bonney was charming, cheerful, loyal, and generous. He didn't smoke or drink, refused to consort with prostitutes, and dressed neatly in dark colors—except for an occasional Mexican sombrero. His downfall was a hair-trigger temper that could be set off without warning.

Shortly before the outbreak of the Lincoln County War, Bonney was hired to work on a ranch owned by John Tunstall, a young Englishman who sought to undermine the economic stronghold of Lincoln's James Dolan and Lawrence Murphy.

After the murder of Tunstall set off the war, the young Bonney vowed, "I'll get some of them before I die." As a member of the Regulators, a group of men that formed to avenge Tunstall's death, he did just that. Bonney played a role in the killing of three men he believed were Tunstall's murderers, and he was blamed for shooting Sheriff William Brady, who previously had mistreated some of the outlaw's friends. It was for Brady's murder that Bonney was convicted in a rundown adobe Mesilla courtroom in April 1881, and returned to Lincoln for his hanging.

Shackled and handcuffed, Bonney awaited his fate in an upstairs room adjacent to the sheriff's office in the Lincoln County Courthouse, guarded closely by deputies Bob Olinger and James Bell. One evening while Olinger took five other prisoners across the street to eat at the Wortley Hotel, the Kid found himself alone with Bell. He asked Bell to escort him to the privy. As they returned, Bell carelessly lagged behind, which gave Bonney a chance to beat the deputy to the top of the stairs, shackles and all. Hiding behind a corner, Bonney quickly twisted his skinny hands from the handcuffs. When Bell topped the staircase, Bonney viciously swung the loose cuff across the deputy's head, cutting open two gashes across his scalp. Bleeding and slightly stunned, Bell was no match for the agile outlaw who wrestled away the deputy's holstered revolver. As Bell retreated down the stairs, Bonney shot him dead.

Next, the outlaw grabbed Olinger's loaded shotgun from his office and ran to a corner window. Olinger rushed across the street and after opening the outside gate to the courthouse looked up into the barrel of his own shotgun pointing at him from an upstairs window. Bonney didn't hesitate to fire, shredding Olinger's upper body with a heavy load of buckshot the lawman had loaded earlier in the day.

The town was terror-stricken. No one moved to approach Bonney as a friend saddled up a horse for him. According to an account from *Billy the Kid, a Short and Violent Life,* by Robert Utley, Bonney smashed Olinger's shotgun across the railing of the courthouse porch and hurled its pieces at the dead lawman who had despised and verbally abused the desperado.

His bold and fearless flight from Lincoln solidified Bonney's standing as the territory's leading fugitive. The *Las Vegas Optic,* a daily newspaper editorialized, "With a heart untouched to pity by misfortune and with a character possessing the attributes of the damned, he has reveled in brutal murder and gloried in his shame."

After his escape, Bonney was taken in by his many friends throughout the region, who fed and sheltered him. One of these was Pete Maxwell, son of Lucien

Maxwell, previous owner of the Maxwell Land Grant, who had renovated the barracks of Fort Sumner as his home. Spending the night at the old fort, Bonney was heading to Maxwell's house to cut a slab of meat for a midnight snack when he entered his friend's bedroom asking about a couple of strangers outside.

Inside was a third visitor, Sheriff Pat Garrett, who had come to inquire about the Kid's whereabouts and by chance found his prey.

William H. Bonney, otherwise known as Billy the Kid. (Museum of New Mexico)

The arrival of the railroad didn't eliminate the need for lawmen, and Socorro had one of the flashiest in Elfego Baca. In 1884 at the age of 19, Baca traveled 137 miles from his home in Socorro to Frisco (now Reserve) to stump for a sheriff's candidate. While Baca was trying to win votes for his friend, an inebriated Texas cowboy began shooting up the town and harassing residents. Since Baca was the closest thing to a lawman the town had at that moment, he appointed himself deputy sheriff. His first act was to arrest the perpetrator. Baca quickly found himself surrounded by 80 agitated cowboys who demanded he release their friend. He refused and barricaded himself inside a low-slung *jacal,* a small hut constructed of poles spaced at least two inches apart and connected by mud plaster. During the next 36 hours, more than 4,000 shots were fired at the jacal. A total of 367 bullets riddled the small front door, hitting nearly everything inside, including silverware and a plaster-of-paris reproduction of a saint, known as Nuestra Señora Santa Ana, which Baca slyly used as a decoy. The self-appointed sheriff was untouched, though he killed four of the Texans. Baca gave up the fight when a deputy arrived from Socorro. He was subsequently tried and acquitted.

Baca eventually served as mayor of Socorro, deputy U.S. marshal, county clerk, and school superintendent. He earned a law degree and in 1919 became the no-nonsense sheriff of Socorro County. Once, instead of having his deputies arrest suspects indicted by a grand jury, he sent the suspects a letter that read, "I have a warrant here for your arrest. Please come in by March 15 and give yourself up. If you don't I'll know that you intend to resist arrest, and I will feel justified in shooting you on sight when I come after you." The Socorro native's life has been immortalized on screen by Walt Disney in a 1958 movie entitled, *The Nine Lives of Elfego Baca.* His survival skills are also remembered every June on the final day of the Hilton Open, a Socorro Pro-Am golf tournament. The Elfego Baca Shoot challenges golfers to tee off atop 7,500-foot Socorro Peak, then scramble down the mountain after their balls, until they arrive at the golf course at the New Mexico Institute of Mining and Technology. About 15 shots usually win the hole. *For information, call the First State Bank; 505-835-1550.*

♦ DAMS AND ONIONS

By the early 1900s, farmers along the Rio Grande were beginning to tire of the muddy waterway's irregular behavior. One year, the river would flood its banks, only to dry up the next. Wanting reliability, they actively encouraged construction of a dam that would store water from the wet years and release it during the dry ones. Surveys started in 1903, followed by construction in 1911; Elephant Butte Dam was completed in 1916. The lake that formed behind it would be an oasis for recreational boaters, fishermen, and anyone else seeking relief from the relentless summer sun. A second lake was formed when Caballo Dam was completed in 1938 as a secondary storage reservoir 11 miles south.

The already fertile farmland downstream became even more abundant, its fields soon brimming with white cotton bolls, green and red chile peppers, and shady pecan orchards. Today, US 85 passes through the hamlets of Arrey, Hatch, and Radium Springs, beside which neat rows of crops spread to the river and nearby hills. You can tell the season by the smell that greets your nostrils: if it's the sharp aroma of ripe onions, it must be summer. The unmistakable strong odor of chiles means it's fall, and when tufts of wayward cotton bolls stick to roadside signs and litter the highway, winter is nigh.

■ SOCORRO   *map page 179, B-4*

Socorro, which means help or aid in Spanish, was named by Juan de Oñate, New Mexico's first governor, in appreciation for the food and water Indians provided his entourage there one desperate afternoon in 1598. He had just led the first expedition across the Jornada del Muerto, or Dead Man's Journey, a 90-mile expanse of near waterless desert.

◆ SOCORRO WALKING TOUR

The best way to see this quiet town is on foot. To guide walkers through the small historic district, the Socorro Chamber of Commerce has published a map. *101 Plaza; 505-835-0424.*

Kittrel Park

The self-guided tour begins at the tree-shaded plaza, unromantically named Kittrel Park in memory of the dentist who first planted trees and grass there in the 1880s. There is a gazebo in the center of this peaceful park, and black cast-iron benches where you can relax and listen to the songs of robins and finches.

Hilton Block

The brick-solid Hilton Block, anchored by the Hilton Drugstore, founded by a relative of Conrad Hilton. (Nobody seems to know which one.)

Val Verde Hotel

The hotel was built in 1919 to serve passengers on the Santa Fe Railroad. Abandoned in the 1960s, it reopened in the late

1980s, its rooms rented exclusively to students at the New Mexico Institute of Mining and Technology. The main floor is open to the public and contains the Val Verde Steak House *(see page 302)* and the Dana Bookstore (which has a respectable collection of Southwest titles).

J. N. Garcia Opera House

No operas ever have been performed here, but the recently renovated 1886 building has been the site of concerts, masked balls, school programs, and college basketball games. *110 Abeyta Ave.*

San Miguel Mission

Unlike most Spanish communities in New Mexico, Socorro's church was not built on the plaza. Rather, San Miguel Mission was erected three blocks north on the site of the original 17th-century mission, which was destroyed during the Pueblo Revolt of 1680. Underneath the present church, built between 1819 and 1821, are four sub-floors beneath which lie the remains of once prominent residents, including Gen. Manuel Armijo, the last Mexican governor of the state. *403 El Camino Real.*

The walking tour proves there is more to this dusty town than California Avenue, where businesses, motels, and restaurants line up in a mass of concrete.

Tall trees shade the green lawns on the campus of the **New Mexico Institute of Mining and Technology,** founded in 1946 to train mining engineers. The school has since branched out to include research projects in petroleum mining and explosives technology. Its mountain-top laboratory is the only one in the country dedicated to studying the physical dynamics of thunderclouds.

Rockhounds might enjoy a stop at the institute's **Mineral Museum,** which boasts a collection of more than 10,000 specimens, including bison vertebrae, giant ground sloth fossils, turquoise, quartz, and lesser-known gems such as yellow zippeite and charcoal gray goethite. Although the exhibit is mostly geared toward aficionados, giant mammoth fossils and a case of fluorescent minerals from around the world are interesting even to regular folk. Some specimens are for sale. *505-835-5420.*

♦ **VERY LARGE ARRAY**   *map page 179, B-3*

West of Socorro, US 60 traverses the windswept Plains of San Agustin. Past the old shipping center of Magdalena, giant white satellite dishes mysteriously sprout from the horizon, part of a 27-antenna network that makes up the **Very Large Array,** the world's most powerful radio telescope. Each 94-foot antenna weighs 235 tons and moves about on railroad tracks. A visitor center is open daily, displaying photos of Neptune taken by Voyager 2 in 1989. A self-guided tour also takes visitors past exhibits that illustrate how radios and the telescope work, and how they came to be. If you continue the tour outside, you can walk past one of the giant dishes. *www.aoc.nrao.edu, From US 60, turn south on NM 52, then west on the VLA access road.*

♦ SOUTH OF SOCORRO   *map page 179, B & C-4*

The sleepy community of **San Antonio** sits on a drainage ditch along the Rio Grande. This is where young Conrad Hilton worked as a bellboy in his father's hotel, but travelers should know it for the **Owl Bar,** reputed to serve the finest green chile cheeseburger hereabouts. Sandhill cranes, pure white snow geese, and ducks fly overhead along NM 1, which winds south past fields of wheat, corn, and millet—a lavish dinner table for the birds who spend their winters at the nearby **Bosque del Apache National Wildlife Refuge.** The refuge was established

The dish-shaped antennas which make up the Very Large Array are laid out in the shape of a **Y** *and are connected to form a radio telescope. (Paul Chesley)*

in 1939 to provide a winter home for the graceful whooping crane, then threatened with extinction. A handful of the rare white birds winter at the refuge. While birdwatching is best at dawn and dusk from October to February, in the summer, more than 3,000 ducks, hundreds of Canada geese, and scores of wading birds such as herons and egrets take over the wetlands. *505-835-1828.*

■ TRUTH OR CONSEQUENCES   *map page 179, D-4*

In 1950, when Ralph Edwards put out the word he was looking for a town willing to name itself after his off-beat radio show, cattleman Burton Roach took up the challenge. As a state senator and president of the Hot Springs Chamber of Commerce, Roach thought this might be a way to distinguish his hot springs from all the other hot springs and get some free advertising in the bargain.

The town's citizens voted on the idea, and Hot Springs was transformed into Truth or Consequences, the name of a variety show that reunited long-lost relatives or flew servicemen overseas to see their mothers. Sometimes questions were asked of audience members who were penalized in silly ways if they failed to respond with the correct answer. As promised, Edwards brought his Hollywood production staff and show crew to New Mexico for the first live, coast-to-coast broadcast from its new namesake. It was no joke that the show was aired on April 1, 1950. In fact, since that first year, Edwards has returned every May to emcee the Ralph Edwards Fiesta, accompanied by a handful of his Hollywood cronies. During the first fiesta, 10,000 people lined a two-mile parade route, and Edwards honored the occasion by breaking a bottle of mineral water over the head of Roach. Edwards also has his own room at the **Geronimo Springs Museum** where photos and show memorabilia line the walls. *211 Main Street; 505-894-6600.*

Perhaps it was this brilliant marketing strategy, or more likely the hot mineral springs beneath the town and the oases in nearby **Elephant Butte** and **Caballo reservoirs,** but T or C, as the town is called, has become a haven for retirees. Some call themselves "snowbirds" because they return every winter for the mild days, for trophy fishing at the nearby reservoirs, and for the soothing waters of six mineral baths that line up on or near Broadway at the southern end of town. Downtown sits atop a supply of steaming underground mineral water. Long before the town was established, Indians soaked aching muscles in the soothing waters after a long days' ride. Most of the bathhouses that survive were built in the 1930s to go along with tourist court motels. Each retains a rustic charm and personality of its own.

In the early 1980s it occurred to entrepreneurial landowners outside T or C that the moderate, dry climate might be perfect for wine grapes. They weren't the first to think of the idea. In 1662, a century before the first grapes were planted in California, Franciscan priests were producing naturally fermenting wine for their masses from mission grapes grown in southern New Mexico. If you want to sample local cabernets and chardonnays drive 30 minutes east of town to the abandoned rail shipping point of Engle, where you'll find Chateau Sassenage vineyard. *505-894-7244.*

◆ NEARBY GHOST TOWNS   *map page 179, C & D-3*

Several once-thriving mining and commercial centers are scattered in the vicinity of Truth or Consequences, their busy streets now deserted, their bustling mercantile stores now reduced to wooden skeletons. Northwest of town, NM 52 passes through **Cuchillo**, a Hispanic hamlet tucked into an abrupt outcropping. During the 1860 gold rush days, prospectors and suppliers changed horses here, and stagecoaches let their passengers off to stretch their legs. Cans of soup and small jars of spices line the walls of the general store, which has doubled as a bar since opening its doors in 1850.

Stagecoach leaving Silver City for Georgetown, 1885. (Museum of New Mexico)

Gently rising hillsides dotted with piñon pines give way to a broad meadow of pale green and yellow grasses amid which the mining district of **Winston** sits. Silver was the lure in the 1880s, attracting prospectors to try their luck in the nearby hills. Today, cattle graze in the valley, and tall weeds and grass are what prosper, jutting up between the false-fronted and mostly abandoned wooden buildings. Beyond this almost non-existent town, the road turns gravel, ending two miles closer to the looming mountains at **Chloride**. In 1879, Henry Pye, a muleskinner and prospector, discovered veins of silver chloride in a nearby rock outcropping. He established a claim, but a few months later, before he could enjoy the wealth he had envisioned, he was killed in an Apache raid. The boom that followed attracted hundreds of miners who built a picturesque settlement of adobe and wooden homes in the range's wrinkled foothills. Today, many original buildings remain, most of them abandoned. A few hardy residents have restored some of the structures and built new ones. Even though they live at the end of a gravel road, 42 miles from T or C, they hold yard sales.

At the southern end of the Black Range and southwest of T or C, NM 152 crosses rugged mountains, winding among steep, pine-covered slopes. But first, it

SOUTHWESTERN
NEW MEXICO

(above) Pioneer home near Mora.
(opposite) Panning for gold remains one of the quixotic hobbies of the Southwest. (Paul Chesley)

bisects the old mining district of **Hillsboro,** its tin roofs hidden underneath giant cottonwoods. Once a gold- and silver-mining boom town and Sierra County seat, Hillsboro turned into a ranching center after the minerals were depleted. Today, a collection of novelty shops, art galleries, and antique stores line the main street. Eccentric artists, solitary writers, and slow-moving retirees share star-filled evenings and quiet days with rough-riding ranchers and diehard miners.

Every Labor Day weekend, the village comes alive during the Hillsboro Apple Festival. People gather in the streets and along sidewalks lined with arts and crafts booths, food stalls, and apples harvested from nearby orchards. *505-895-5686.*

Nine miles farther into the mountains, **Kingston** is the last stop before NM 152 climbs over 8,228-foot Emory Pass on its way to the Mimbres Valley. In its heyday that began in 1880, 7,500 fortune hunters flocked to Kingston's pine-covered slopes, which surrendered more than $10 million worth of silver in less than 15 years. For a short time the town boomed. Twenty-two saloons lined the broad sidewalk on the main street, and Lillian Russell performed at the town's theater. Kingston had no church until a hat was passed in the saloons one night to raise money for one. Today, 30 resourceful people live in this mountain town, writers and retirees joining long-time residents who continue to hold regular meetings of the Spit and Whittle Club. They say they love the clean air and sweet smell of burning piñon on cold days.

■ LAS CRUCES   *map page 179, E/F-4/5*

Framed by the lush banks of the Rio Grande and the dry, rugged Organ Mountains (named for their resemblance to pipe organs), Las Cruces sits in the heart of the Mesilla Valley. When New Mexico was being settled, the wagons of Spanish colonists that passed this way were frequently ambushed by Apaches. In 1787, the bodies of several oxcart caravan drivers were found and crosses were erected atop their graves. Forty-three years later, a party of 30 travelers from Taos met the same fate and more crosses were raised. What began as an eerie graveyard known as La Placita de las Cruces, "The Place of the Crosses," has grown to become the second largest city in New Mexico.

In the mid-1800s, colonists began putting down roots, cultivating corn, beans, and pumpkins along the banks of the Rio Grande. They lived in jacales, created by placing poles vertically in a ground trench. The poles were lashed together and coated with mud plaster, forming walls that could be whitewashed. Vigas and latillas supported dirt roofs. Adobe bricks were used in later homes, brick copings

DRIPPING SPRINGS

At first glance, the jagged Organ Mountains outside Las Cruces appear as dry as the desert around them. And for the most part, they are, except at Dripping Springs. There, a trickle of water seeps from the volcanic rock, forming a few refreshing pools. During and after a rainstorm, the drip becomes a waterfall, sending a roaring river through nearby Ice Canyon.

Until 1988, this desert oasis was known primarily by Las Cruces residents who enjoyed hiking in the mountain foothills, poking around the ruins of an abandoned resort, and soaking in the cool pools. The spring itself was part of a cattle ranch owned by the A. B. Cox family, which generously permitted public use of the property.

In late 1988, the family sold the 2,852-acre spread of cactus-laden foothills and rugged rock outcroppings to the Nature Conservancy, which then transferred title to the Bureau of Land Management. In exchange, the Nature Conservancy, an international non-profit organization committed to protecting significant natural areas, received other blm lands that it could still sell to cover the cost of purchase.

Now that it's in the public domain, the main ranch house has been turned into a visitor center, and maintained trails wend through ocotillo, cholla, and prickly-pear cactus. A 1.5-mile uphill path leads to the spring and ruins of past resorts, the original one built in the 1870s by Col. Eugene Van Patten, who called the place Van Patten's Mountain Camp. At that time, the retreat consisted of a 16-room building that included a dining hall and large ballroom. By the turn of the century, it was known as Dripping Springs Resort and attracted such notables as Pat Garrett and Pancho Villa. Van Patten was married to a local Indian woman, and as a result, a number of Indians lived and worked at the resort, hand-carrying water from the nearby spring to the rooms.

In 1917, Van Patten went bankrupt, and Dripping Springs was sold to Dr. Nathan Boyd, who had homesteaded on a tract of land adjacent to the resort. Dr. Boyd's wife had contracted tuberculosis, which prompted him to turn the resort into a sanatorium. New buildings were constructed in the canyon, including a cabin for the Boyds, and a stilt house used as a dining hall. Dr. Boyd eventually sold the place to another physician, Dr. Sexton of Las Cruces, who continued to operate it as a sanatorium until the early 1940s. In the following years, the buildings deteriorated after local citizens rejected attempts to purchase and preserve the resort. Today, all that remains are two rooms of the main lodge, the tin-roofed stilt house, and Dr. Boyd's stone cabin.

*Short-horned
lizard, com-
mon to the
deserts of the
Southwest.
(Paul Chesley)*

The present-day visitor center was built by the next owner, Franklin Hayner, who operated a Las Cruces lumber yard and traveled the bumpy 10-mile gravel road to the former resort only on weekends. In 1958, the Cox family bought the place and turned it into a cattle ranch.

In addition to the spring and ruins, a second trail leads from the visitor center to La Cueva, a volcanic rock outcropping named for a 10-foot-tall cave at its southeastern end. Excavations of La Cueva have revealed that it was inhabited as long ago as 5000 B.C.E., probably as a shelter for early hunters in pursuit of rabbit, antelope, deer, and bighorn sheep. Later, members of the Jornada branch of the Mogollon culture sought the protection of the cave during storms.

In the late 1860s, an eccentric hermit, Giovanni Maria Agostini, moved into the cave. As the story goes, Agostini had been born of noble parents in Italy, but chose to spend most of his life traipsing around Europe and South and North America. Before arriving at La Cueva, he spent four years living atop a mountain near Las Vegas, New Mexico. The mountain retains the name honoring him, Hermit's Peak. In 1869, the 66-year-old man announced his plans to live in the Organ Mountains, despite warnings that Indians were roaming the area. His body was found in the cave later that year, apparently the victim of Apaches.

Today, a picnic area has been installed near La Cueva, along with a few tables near the resort ruins. But even though the ranch is now open to the public seven days a week, preservation of the fragile environment remains of primary concern to the Bureau of Land Management.

Of nine threatened and endangered plant species located on the ranch, five are endemic to the Organ Mountains. In addition, seven endangered birds and two mammals live on the ranch along with two extremely rare mollusks, the earred terrestrial snail and Organ Mountain snail. BLM employees are adamant that visitors take care not to disturb the ecosystem. Employees will lead interpretive tours with advance notice. They also request that groups of more than 10 people take guided tours.

To reach the ranch, take University Boulevard east off I-25, heading toward the mountains. When the pavement ends, you are on Dripping Springs Road. Most of the 10-mile trip is on gravel, and it takes about 30 minutes. *505-525-4300.*

The yucca is New Mexico's state flower. (Paul Chesley)

topped parapets, and square wooden columns supported porches. Many of these houses are still visible in the **Mesquite Street** area, east of downtown, Las Cruces's oldest neighborhood. Homes are stuccoed in pastel pink, green, blue, and shades of brown that range from tawny to deep chocolate. An occasional shrine graces a front yard.

After the Santa Fe Railroad reached Las Cruces in 1881, farmlands between the Mesquite district and the depot were transformed into homes that reflected the styles of the town's new residents who came from the East Coast. Architectural designs include Hip Box, Queen Anne, and Bungalow, along with some patterned after the traditional adobe style. A few pre-railroad farm houses survive in the **Alameda-Depot Historic District,** which is worth exploring on foot.

South of town, the College of Las Cruces opened in 1880 and within a decade had grown into the New Mexico College of Agriculture and Mechanic Arts, which later would become **New Mexico State University.** The second largest university in the state, it is noted for its agricultural research, especially the cultivation of chile. Thirty of the 200 known varieties of chile peppers are grown and studied in fields irrigated by the Rio Grande. Researchers continually work to develop milder hybrids so people with sensitive palates, most of whom seem to reside east of the Mississippi River, can enjoy its unique spiciness. The grassy campus, with its red-tiled roofs atop tan stucco buildings, stretches across 6,250 acres that include grazing pastures, one of the largest computer centers in the Southwest, and one of three full-time planetary observatories in the country. Clyde Tombaugh, discoverer of the planet Pluto, was professor emeritus at NMSU until his death in 1997.

The University's museum has exhibits on Southwest archeology and history. *505-646-3739.*

In 1998, the New Mexico Farm and Ranch Heritage Museum opened on 47 acres east of the university. A working ranch and farm, complete with sheep, bunnies and cows, help tell the 3,000-year story of New Mexico agriculture.

The city's major employer is White Sands Missile Range, a 4,000-square-mile (10,360 sq-km) expanse of lonely desert that follows the eastern edge of the Organ and San Andres mountain ranges. Nearly 9,000 residents cross San Agustin Pass every day to punch timeclocks on a tree-shaded campus at its base. In 1942, the U.S. military designated White Sands Proving Grounds to test weapons. Three years later, the world's first atomic bomb was detonated at its northern end. After the Germans destroyed parts of London with their V-2 rockets in the war, the

United States decided to improve upon its own missile capability and began by enlarging the test area to include 2.7 million acres of tall grassland, displacing hundreds of ranchers and their families. Its new name, White Sands Missile Range, reflects an expanded mission: testing rockets, missiles, and payloads for the space shuttle program. To protect travelers from wayward rockets along US 70-82, which cuts through the missile range, roadblocks are erected during firings. *For a recording of scheduled road closures call 505-443-7199.*

■ MESILLA   *map page 179, F 4/5*

Although Mesilla lost out, in population and prestige, to Las Cruces in the great railroad rush of the 1880s, the sleepy town has succeeded in retaining its 19th-century character. From miles away, the white crosses atop two steeples of the **San Albino Church** can be seen towering above the tree-shaded town. This block-long brick church anchors the northern end of a quiet central plaza, with a white-washed gazebo in its center. Black wrought-iron benches with wooden seats are a perfect place to watch the afternoon sun transform the mud-brown walls of shops and galleries into hues of soft yellow and rose red. Sit back and muse about the days when the plaza bustled with stagecoaches in for repair at the Butterfield station and when, over shots of whiskey, cowboys impressed each other with tales of herding cattle on the untamed range. The Confederate flag flapped above the plaza for a year between 1861 and 1862, and 20 years later in a stuffy courtroom, a shackled Billy the Kid was sentenced to die for the murder of Lincoln County Sheriff William Brady. And don't forget: for a time Mesilla was the capital of the Territory of Arizona.

Today, the blacksmith shop, saddle shop, and horse stables of the Butterfield station have been turned into the dining rooms of **La Posta,** a superb Mexican restaurant. Across the street, the **William Bonney Gallery,** once the jail that housed Billy the Kid, sells Frederic Remington bronze sculptures and vases painted by R.C. Gorman. Next to the courthouse you'll find Navajo kachinas along with a large selection of Hopi, Zuni, and Navajo jewelry in the **Corn Maiden Gallery.** On the west side of the plaza is **Mesilla Book Center**—an excellent source for books on the Southwest's history, geology, anthropology, and culture.

Away from the plaza on Mesilla's narrow back streets, residents still live in 100-year-old adobe homes, some displaying brightly painted wooden window casings and

SOUTHWESTERN
NEW MEXICO

others crumbling to the ground. It's easy to imagine horses plodding along, neighbors sharing news in rapid Spanish, Mariachi music wafting from doorways, and the delightfully greasy smell of *chicharrones* (crispy fried pork skin) cooking in oil.

◆ THE VALLEY   *map page 179, F-5*

South of Mesilla, with the jagged peaks of the Organ Mountains a distant backdrop, NM 28 follows the bends of the Rio Grande, passing beneath a three-mile-long canopy created by thick groves of pecan trees. This extensive pecan orchard, whose 3,850 acres of trees make it one of the largest in the world, is owned by the Stahmann family. Deep-dug irrigation ditches filled with swiftly flowing water feed wide expanses of deep-green chile fields, white-tufted cotton plants, and pale green heads of lettuce. Mixed in with these lush crops, clusters of grapes grow along vines that surround a tasting room at **La Viña Winery.** Stop in for a glass of chardonnay or zinfandel. *420 S. Highway 28; 505-882-7632*

Farmers who tend these fields live in small hamlets with names like San Miguel, Chamberino, and La Mesa. They meet to share a beer and discuss local politics at **Chope's Bar and Cafe** in La Mesa. As the conversation heats up, so does the green chile that smothers plates of enchiladas and burritos served here. This chile is for palates accustomed to fire. If yours isn't, expect to leave with a runny nose and perspiring brow. *On NM 28 in La Mesa.*

■ DEMING   *map page 179, E/F-3*

Deming is a railroad town named after the daughter of an Indiana sawmill owner. Mary Ann Deming also happened to be married to Charles Crocker, a California silver baron and one of the promoters of the Southern Pacific Railroad, which in 1881 met the Atchison, Topeka & Santa Fe Railroad among creosote bush and cholla cactus north of the Little Florida Mountains. He named the resulting ramshackle gathering of tents and shanties after his wife.

She'd probably be pleased to know that the boisterous railroad camp that bore her name grew into a quiet, tidy, tree-lined town that boasts clean air and pure water. The water comes from the Mimbres River, which passes underground through town; the clear skies remain unsullied by heavy industry or auto traffic. Most Deming residents walk around their town—to work, the beauty shop, or the post office. Rarely do they lock their doors behind them. In the evening, they sit

Tom Day on the Culberson Ranch displays the tails of 110 rattlesnakes found on the ranch during a 12-month period. (Paul Chesley)

on their porches, taking in the last rays of a golden sun, or they go for a stroll through their neighborhoods. Daytime finds cows and steers outside of town, chewing on patches of desert grass that have sprouted up between mesquite trees and yuccas. Fields of waving milo and the white pods of cotton plants flourish in the intense sun.

◆ DEMING DUCK RACE

According to some people, the best thing about Deming is the Deming Duck Race. It all started on a slow day in 1980 when realtor Steve Marlowe and his friend, Harold Cousland, editor of the *Deming Headlight,* were bemoaning the tedium of small-town life over coffee. Marlowe asked Cousland whether he thought duck races might liven things up. He knew full well there weren't any ducks flying around their hot, dry, landlocked hometown, but that was no obstacle. Marlowe had heard that such races took place at the Long Branch Saloon in North Las Vegas, Nevada.

Cousland considered Marlowe's idea daffy, but liked it because it lent itself to endless puns, a newspaper man's dream. A week later, Marlowe scheduled a meeting to plan the first Great American Duck Race. A Saturday night Duck Ball, during which a Duck Queen would be crowned, would open the late-August weekend festivities, followed the next day by the races. Marlowe, already calling himself the event's "chief quacker," had sent away to Las Vegas for official rules. The entry fee would be $5 and ducks would be vying for a $1,000 purse. Billing itself as "The World's Richest Duck Race," the event drew 184 downy competitors and 5,000 spectators.

Through the years, the wacky races have gone from a joke to the town's most popular annual attraction, typically drawing up to 25,000 spectators on the fourth weekend in August. More than 500 webbed entrants compete for the top prize, about $4,000 in prize money.

The 16-foot-long, eight-lane course is erected at Deming Duck Downs, at Southwestern New Mexico State Fairgrounds. The lanes are separated by "duck wire," otherwise known as chicken wire. A carpeted Duck Deck atop each lane serves as a platform upon which the trainer crawls, hollers, and threatens— whatever it takes, short of touching his protegé, to instill a winning spirit. Throughout the weekend, ducks run in elimination heats until the final round on Sunday afternoon. "Be a winner, or be dinner," is a common phrase trainers impart to their contestants.

The raid on Columbus by Pancho Villa in 1916 was the only land invasion of the U.S. in the 20th century. (Museum of New Mexico)

Competitors come from across the country, some renting trucks big enough to hold portable wading pools to keep ducks content before their races. Prior to the 1981 event, Marlowe received a call from a Utah duck trainer whose entrant was so fast that it had suffered burned breast feathers and blistered feet during practice runs. The trainer wondered if he could use a drag chute on his duck to stop it at the end of the race. Permission was granted, but the braggart never showed up. *888-345-1125.*

Deming's main link to the past is the **Deming Luna Mimbres Museum,** located in the old National Guard Armory. One room is dedicated to the display of more than 500 lovingly costumed dolls; another holds a collection of intricately stitched quilts dating back to 1847. A chuckwagon conjures up the traveling kitchens of roundup days, and Mimbres pottery, arrowheads, and baskets represent the tribes that once roamed the region. *301 South Silver; 505-546-2382.*

Southeast of town, the relentless sun beats down on the Little Florida Mountains, reflecting specimens of cloudy agate, blood-red jasper, shiny black perlite, and smoky quartz. Here among the granite and volcanic breccia outcroppings of **Rock Hound State Park,** people wander through the spiny thorns of yuccas, beavertail, and barrel cacti, searching for precious geodes. In an unusual twist, visitors are encouraged to take their favorite finds home. *NM 497; 505-546-6182.*

■ COLUMBUS   *map page 179, F/G-3*

This sleepy border town hasn't been the same since the early morning hours of March 9, 1916. That morning, as the townsfolk lay sleeping, Pancho Villa led a band of Mexican revolutionaries in an attack on the quiet village and burned most of it to the ground. Eighteen Americans were killed—some residents, and other soldiers stationed at Camp Furlong. The following day, U.S. Army Gen. John J. Pershing headed across the border into Mexico, leading 10,000 soldiers through a

SOUTHWESTERN
NEW MEXICO

desolate desert covered with thorny cactus and parched mountains. Trucks and motorcycles provided support for soldiers on horseback, and eight cloth-covered Curtis JN-3 biplanes, known as Jennys, of the First Aero Squadron took to the sky. This punitive expedition marked the introduction to warfare of motorized vehicles and aircraft. Unfortunately, the deep sand and mud in the roadless expanse of northern Mexico proved too much for the vehicles. The biplanes, worn out from long use as trainers, suffered engine breakdowns. And when running, they didn't have enough power to clear Mexico's 12,000-foot mountains. The planes did prove useful in speeding messages between units. Pershing spent most of a year vainly chasing Villa through Mexico. He returned to Columbus on February 5, 1917.

Despite the devastation wrought by Villa, the citizens of Columbus have named a state park after him. Apparently, they figured Pershing State Park wouldn't draw as many visitors as **Pancho Villa State Park** and they could be right because the

Pancho Villa at his headquarters in Ciudad Juárez just before his advance on Torreón in 1914. (Museum of New Mexico)

Motor trucks delivering supplies to the U.S. Army in Mexico; Pershing Punitive Expedition, 1916. (Museum of New Mexico)

park, dedicated in 1961 alongside the ruins of Camp Furlong, is the community's main attraction. Campsites are carved out of a dense mass of orange-tipped ocotillo, knee-high beavertails, century plants, mesquite bushes, yuccas, and yellow-budded cholla. Five thousand varieties of cactus and wildflowers are crowded into this botanical paradise. *505-531-2711.*

Columbus has remained a small, slow-moving community. Gaunt dogs unhurriedly cross wide dirt streets. The entire town has been designated a National Historic Landmark, as it is the only place in the United States ever invaded by a foreign army. There aren't many architectural examples, but each one is interesting, from the wrought-iron lettering on the white-washed post office to the two-story yellow clapboard Southern Pacific Railroad depot, which has been restored as the **Columbus Historical Society Museum.** *505-531-2620.*

◆ A Stroll to Old Mexico   *map page 179, G-3*

As one of only two official ports of entry into Mexico from New Mexico, people stroll across the border to the town of **Palomas** to buy liquor, sample the fresh fruit sold from a pushcart, or visit the beautiful stone **Parroquia Guadalupe Catholic Church.** If you're looking for great bargains on a wide selection of Mexican goods, you'll have to go elsewhere in Mexico, but Palomas does offer visitors a wonderful taste of the country. Few people in town speak English, but they are more than willing to communicate through a friendly exchange of hand gestures. From a distance, Palomas looks to the eye to be about the size of Columbus, yet there are 500 residents in Columbus and 12,000 in Palomas.

■ LORDSBURG   *map page 179, E-1*

Named for a Southern Pacific engineer, Lordsburg is mainly a gas-up and stretch stop, but three miles southwest of town a collection of tin-roofed adobe buildings is worth a longer look. Hidden among a group of small hills covered in mesquite, yucca, greasewood, and beavertail cactus, the old townsite of **Shakespeare** has gone through numerous incarnations: first as a watering hole for Apache Indians, then as a stop on the Butterfield Trail, then as a boisterous mining boomtown. In 1935, it was purchased by the Hill family.

Shakespeare's status grew from a stopover into a destination point in 1870 after W. D. Brown, a dropout from a government survey party, discovered some promising-looking ore in the nearby Pyramid Mountains. Overnight, tents and adobe shacks shot up across the stark brown landscape. After the silver boom died down, reports drifted across the country of a diamond strike in an undisclosed location outside of town. After showing off a bag of uncut stones to California banker William Ralston, two scruffy miners convinced him to pay them $600,000 for their claim in the Pyramid Mountains. Within a few weeks, more than 3,000 prospectors converged on Shakespeare. More tents and buildings went up until the main street was lined with seven saloons, stores, a barber shop, assay office, Chinese laundry, restaurants, and boarding houses. Nobody was finding any diamonds, but nobody seemed to care. There was no church, no newspaper, and no law. Free-for-all fights and murder were commonplace. Within months, the diamond strike was determined to be a swindle: the mountainside purported to contain the rich deposit had actually been salted with a few appropriately placed diamonds and the now-wealthy miners were nowhere to be found. Within a few days, Shakespeare was nearly empty.

A bumpy dirt road cuts through greasewood and yuccas to the few remaining buildings of Shakespeare. In April 1997, the town suffered a desvastating fire that destroyed a number of buildings, most notably the old general store, which doubled as a museum. A hay barn, blacksmith shop, and general store have been rebuilt. Tours are offered on the second weekend of each month or by appointment. Janaloo Hill lives with her husband Manny Hough on site. *Write to P.O. Box 253, Lordsburg, NM 88045 or call 505-542-9034..*

Straddling the Continental Divide in New Mexico's boot heel, the tall grass-lands of the **Gray Ranch** were preserved by the Nature Conservancy, which in 1990 purchased the richly endowed 500-square-mile spread. In 1994, the private Animas Foundation bought the ranch and continues to carry out the Nature Conservancy's preservation work. Although the ranch is not open to the public, its reputation as one of the nation's most significant biological areas is far-reaching and it continues to be studied to death. The ranch, once owned by California mining and livestock baron George Hearst, father of publishing magnate William Randolph Hearst, is home to nearly 100 rare and endangered plant and animal species, including the ridgenosed rattlesnake, Sanborn's long-nosed bat, the white-sided jackrabbit, and night-blooming cereus, a spiny-stemmed bush with delicate white blooms that come out at night.

■ SILVER CITY   *map page 179, D/E-2*

One prospector who traveled to Shakespeare to check out its famous silver strike took a quick look at the distinct ore, scratched his head, and headed back home north to Pinos Altos, a gold-mining burg in the foothills of what today is the Gila National Forest. John Bullard knew where there was plenty more of the valuable silver: right outside his home. Soon the pine-covered hills were covered with makeshift tents and shacks, which became known as Silver City. Banks, saloons, restaurants, billiard halls, and meat markets popped up on the dirt streets, along with the offices of doctors, lawyers, dressmakers, and tailors. Smooth-talking gamblers in wide-rimmed black hats warmed seats in gambling houses. Bow-legged cowboys swaggered up to bars, demanding shots of mescal. All of these people apparently were eager to know of the larger world, for by the end of 1882, six newspapers were being published in the mining district.

Prior to the arrival of the railroad, which reached Silver City in 1881, 12- and 14-horse teams hauled ore from the Mogollon Mountains to town, where it was shipped off by stagecoach and wagon train. Stacks of gold and silver bricks stood outside freight offices. Incredibly, the temptation to pinch one or two proved even stronger than the threat of the noose: public hangings were frequent.

Unlike civic officials in most of the boomtowns of the day, Silver City's lawmakers had the foresight to prohibit frame buildings within the town's limits, hoping to prevent widespread destruction from fires. As a result, most of the original townsite has survived. Brick and adobe buildings, which mix Victorian architecture with the flat-roofed vernacular style, line almost every street.

A white picket fence surrounds the two-story H.B. Ailman House at 312 West Broadway. Now the Silver City Museum, this is a good place to start a stroll. Stop inside for a historical walking tout brochure. *505-538-5921.*

An example of the town's resourcefulness is **Big Ditch Park,** a 55-foot-deep trench that once was Main Street. As miners sought their fortunes, they loosened the soil of Silver City's hills, which, along with heavy rains, caused massive flooding between 1895 and 1903. Walls of water as high as 12 feet, raged through town, gutting Main Street to the bedrock. In 1980, it became a city park.

Silver City, like so many other cities in New Mexico, lays claim to Billy the Kid. As a child known as Henry McCarty, the outlaw attended school and worked as a waiter at the Star Hotel. He moved there with his mother and stepfather, who had a burning desire to strike it rich in the silver mines. You can follow the outlaw's brief presence in the mining district by wandering past the site of his boyhood home (since torn down), the Star Hotel, his mother's grave, and the site of the jail from which he made his first escape.

◆ OUTSIDE SILVER CITY   *map page 179, D/E-2*

Santa Rita Pit

Unlike many early mining districts that fizzled after the ore played out, Silver City's mines are still producing, though copper has replaced silver as the primary metal extracted from the rich earth. Thirteen miles (21 km) east of Silver City, the village of Santa Rita has been swallowed up by a massive **open-pit copper operation.** From an observation deck, you can peer into the 1,000-foot-deep mine that stretches more than a mile across. Trucks appear small as they drive along the terraced red-brown earth.

City of Rocks

Southeast of Silver City off NM 61 is an island of house-size boulders rising from the burnt-sienna prairie. This jumble of Tertiary tuff that flowed from an erupting volcano a million years ago has been turned into **City of Rocks State Park,** where picnic tables and campsites are wedged among the boulders. The only sound in this wide plain comes from the wind, which regularly whistles through ocotillo, cholla, and yucca cacti. Slate-blue mountain ranges line the horizon in every direction. *505-536-2800.*

Bear Mountain Guest Ranch

Three miles north of Silver City amid a flat expanse of piñons and junipers sits a commanding two-story Pueblo Revival bed-and-breakfast inn that caters to naturalists. The Bear Mountain Guest Ranch is the vision of naturalist Myra McCormick, who in 1959, began welcoming visitors to the inn she built with her husband. Upon her death in 1999, the 160-acre guest ranch that backs up to the Gila Wilderness became the property of the Nature Conservancy of New Mexico, which began an extensive renovation to turn it into a deluxe destination. When it reopens in Spring 2001, McCormick's bird feeders will still be welcoming birds and naturalists will lead tours to nearby conservancy preserves. *See page 301.*

Pinos Altos

The old gold mining district of **Pinos Altos** seven miles (11 km) north of town hasn't fared as well as Silver City. But the cozy hamlet, named for the surrounding tall pines, has done well at preserving its frontier past. A walk along the dirt streets of town takes you past the Pinos Altos Ice Cream Parlor, housed in the old Norton Store. The creaky wooden floors of the Buckhorn Saloon don't seem to bother Indian Joe, a life-sized doll who sits at one end of the bar—day and night. He's the only one who gets to drink Buckhorn Beer. At an adjacent brick-walled dining room, some of the best steaks in these parts are served atop red checkered tablecloths. Around a bend and up a hill, the Gold Avenue Methodist Episcopal Church houses an art gallery which is open seasonally. The adobe building, with its stained glass windows and steeply pitched roof, was built in 1898 with the financial assistance of Phoebe Hearst, mother of California newspaper publisher William Randolph Hearst. Her late-husband, George Hearst, had fared well in the Pinos Altos mines. Another western celebrity with an interest in Pinos Altos was Roy Bean who, with his brother Sam, operated a store here before the Civil War. Roy went on to become a famous frontier judge in West Texas.

■ GILA NATIONAL FOREST   *map page 179, C & D-2 & 3*

◆ GILA CLIFF DWELLINGS   *map page 179, C-2*

Heading north from Pinos Altos, NM 15 enters the the 2.7-million-acre Gila National Forest and, within it, the 438,360-acre **Gila Wilderness,** which was promoted by conservationist Aldo Leopold and established in 1924 as the first in the country. After crossing the Gila River and Gila Hot Springs the road ends at the **Gila Cliff Dwellings National Monument.** A one-mile (1.6 km) loop trail takes you up and through 42 rock-walled rooms built into the side of a volcanic cliff. You can climb ladders to explore the dark interiors. The well-protected dwellings look pretty much like they did when the Mogollon Indians lived in them from the 1280s into the 1300s. During the day, these people cultivated squash, corn, beans, and tobacco on nearby mesas and along the West Fork of the Gila River. They also hunted deer and gathered wild berries and nuts in the nearby forest. For generations their voices and children's laughter echoed throughout the steep-walled canyon. By the early 1300s, the only sounds remaining came from birds and the gurgling river. No one knows why they left, but many think they joined other Pueblo Indians to the north and south. *505-536-9461*

◆ GLENWOOD   *map page 179, C-1*

Northwest of Silver City, US 180 passes through a few small ranching communities. **Glenwood** has the most to offer—a few motels, a bar, and the Catwalk, a two-and-a-half-mile steel walkway anchored to a rock wall above the rushing waters of Whitewater Creek. Before gold and silver were discovered in the Mogollon Mountains above the creek, the box canyon served as a hideout for the likes of Geronimo and Butch Cassidy, who carefully picked a path along the creekbed. In the 1880s, a group of miners looking for an easier way to do things built a wooden pipeline along the wall to carry water to a millsite and mining camp at the mouth of the canyon. The pipeline, installed three miles upstream where water was always plentiful, was needed because the creek often dried up by the time it reached the settlement. While this water supply worked just fine, the pipeline did need repairs, which in places could be done only by walking on the dangling tube, thus the name "catwalk." After the mill closed in 1913 (followed by the mines in 1942), a trail was completed on the same route in 1936. The steel catwalk came later, in 1962. Today, this steel pathway passes alongside hybrid oaks, sycamores, and alders. Golden lichen cover boulders, and farther upstream the trail meets up with others that weave through the Gila National Forest where Rocky Mountain bighorn sheep and mule deer roam the slopes.

◆ MOGOLLON   *map page 179, C-1*

A few miles past Glenwood is the turnoff to **Mogollon**, an old mining town wedged into a narrow canyon. In 1890, it was a bustling mining camp that boasted 20 saloons and 2,000 residents, including Ben Lilly, one of the West's most adept mountain lion hunters. Lilly charged ranchers $50 for each dead mountain lion he brought them. He bagged 110 during his career. Silver and gold ore was processed at nearby mills, which produced 18 million ounces of silver before the mines closed at the outbreak of World War II.

The Mogollon Indian ruins at Gila Cliff Dwellings National Monument. (Kerrick James)

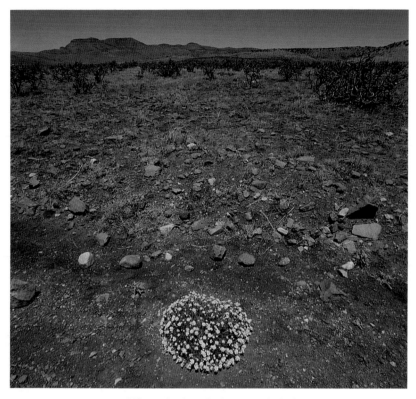

Wildflowers brighten the desert. (Paul Chesley)

A walk through town takes you past a clock that reads 4 o'clock, the time the last shift ended in the mines. Today a handful of hardy people live year-round in the weather-beaten hamlet along Silver Creek. They are joined in the summer by about 31 others, mostly shopkeepers, who cater to vacationers heading into the Gila Wilderness. The road leading to this rustic village is only nine miles long, but it takes a good 30 minutes to negotiate its steep incline and sharp curves. Past Mogollon, NM 78 becomes gravel and penetrates the wilderness.

Further up US 180, NM 12 turns off toward the ranching centers of Reserve, Aragon, and Horse Springs, you're passing through the ancient home of the Mimbres Indians. These people lived throughout the Gila National Forest, down into the Mimbres Valley southeast of Silver City. What distinguished them from their

Mogollon relatives was their pottery decorated in geometric designs and surreal animal figures. Many of these pots, typically found at gravesites, have been dug up on ranches throughout the Tularosa Mountains near Reserve and Aragon. The Mimbreños abandoned their homes in the twelfth century, long before their distant Mogollon relatives left the Gila River. As you drive through this grassy mountain valley, you won't see any remains of Mimbres dwellings because none have been preserved. You can only imagine the hours of painstaking work that went into the unspoiled quality of their designs. (The nation's largest permanent exhibit of Mimbres pottery is on display at the Western New Mexico University Museum on Tenth Street in Silver City. *505-538-6386.*)

■ THE LIGHTNING FIELD   *map page 179, A-1*

In the middle of a high-desert sagebrush plain 30 miles northeast of Quemado, a grid of 400 stainless steel poles rises to the sky, looking like a giant bed of nails. In this unlikely array of metal, the poles are spaced 220 feet apart in rows that measure one-mile by one-kilometer. This is the precisely calculated statement of Walter De Maria, an internationally known artist who spent five years searching for just this spot.

No cattle roam this 3,400-acre plateau that stands at an elevation of 7,200 feet, and not many people either. Between the months of May and October, six people at a time are permitted to visit The Lightning Field. Each pays a mini-

The Lightning Field—400 poles of an extraordinary landscape sculpture. (Paul Chesley) mum of $85 to spend the night in a renovated homesteader's cabin on the land and share a hot meal.

Most importantly, they share the experience that De Maria envisioned when he conceived the field in the early 1970s. For five years, the artist combed remote areas in California, Nevada, Utah, Arizona, and Texas before deciding on a site in western New Mexico 11.5 miles east of the Continental Divide. He considered the land a major part of the work, and his priorities included isolation, flat terrain, and high lightning activity. It was also important that only a few people at a time visit the site, so they could easily lose each other when walking among the 20-foot-tall poles.

Completed in 1977, the project was commissioned and is maintained by the DIA Art Foundation, a New York-based non-profit organization that promotes large-scale art projects. The foundation has since established a Quemado branch, which houses a few of De Maria's smaller works. The doors usually are locked, but if you'd like to ask a few questions, try Jonay's Bar a few doors down.

Despite the esoteric nature of this place, the experience is in demand. About 300 people visit the field each year, making advance reservations a must. Walk-ins typically are turned away. Those who do have reservations are picked up at 2:30 P.M. in front of a two-story white building. A caretaker drives them for a 45-minute ride over gravel roads to a weathered cabin where he helps unload luggage, then leaves. He returns at 11 A.M. the following day. The interval in between is completely unstructured, allowing plenty of time to walk around the field, breathe in the fresh sage, marvel at the immense sky, and wait for it to rain.

During thunderstorms, which occur most often in July and August, the poles become lightning rods and perform spectacular light shows. But most of the time the pointed steel shafts stand silent. That fits with De Maria's vision: that the light be as important as the lightning. Early in the morning and at sunset, light transforms the poles into radiant rods as they reflect the soft rays of the sun. When the sun is overhead, that dimension is lost as they seem to fade from sight.

Comments from visitors vary. Some claim a visit to the Lightning Field is a religious experience, while others say it's a total waste of time. But both agree it is an experience not soon forgotten.

The Lightning Field, P.O. Box 2993, Corrales, NM 87048, www.diacenter.org; 505-898-3335.

A Form of Paradise

*B*rightest New Mexico. In that vivid light each rock and tree and cloud and mountain existed with a kind of force and clarity that seemed not natural but supernatural. Yet it also felt as familiar as home, the country of dreams, the land I had known from the beginning.

We were riding north from El Paso in my grandfather's pickup truck, bound for the village of Baker and the old man's ranch. This was in early June: the glare of the desert sun, glancing off the steel hood of the truck, stung my eyes with such intensity that I had to close them now and then for relief. And I could almost feel the fierce dry heat, like that of an oven, drawing the moisture from my body; I thought with longing of the cool water bag that hung from the hood latch over the grille in front, inaccessible. I wished that Grandfather would stop for a minute and give us time for a drink, but I was too proud and foolish to ask him; twelve years old, I thought it important to appear tougher than I really was.

When my eyes stopped aching I could open them again, raise my head and watch the highway and fence and telephone line, all geometrically straight and parallel, rolling forever toward us. Heat waves shimmered over the asphalt, giving the road far ahead a transparent, liquid look, an illusion which receded before us as fast as we approached.

Staring ahead, I saw a vulture rise from the flattened carcass of a rabbit on the pavement and hover nearby while we passed over his lunch. Beyond the black bird with his white-trimmed wings soared the western sky, the immense and violet sky flowing over alkali flats and dunes of sand and gypsum toward the mountains that stood like chains of islands, like a convoy of purple ships, along the horizon.

Those mountains—they seemed at once both close by and impossibly remote, an easy walk away and yet beyond the limits of the imagination. Between us lay the clear and empty wilderness of scattered mesquite trees and creosote shrubs and streambeds where water ran as seldom as the rain came down. Each summer for three years I had come to New Mexico; each time I gazed upon the moon-dead landscape and asked myself: what is out there? And each time I concluded: *something* is out there— maybe everything. To me the desert looked like a form of Paradise. And it always will.

—Edward Abbey
Fire on the Mountain, 1962

S O U T H E A S T E R N
N E W M E X I C O

SOUTHEASTERN NEW MEXICO SEEMS TO STRETCH ON FOREVER, its vast plains pulling spacious skies down upon an endless horizon. A few lofty mountain ranges interrupt occasionally monotonous emptiness, across which notable and notorious figures have sallied forth, the most famous being the desperado Billy the Kid. The baby-faced outlaw roamed the region's piñon-covered hills, grama-grass plains, and heavily forested mountains, charming women and pulling his sharpshooter on others until he himself was shot with his boots off. Later notables include Smokey Bear, a tiny black bear cub who became the nation's symbol of the fight of forest fires; Peter Hurd, who captured on canvas the people, orchards, and fields of the pastoral Hondo Valley; and Norman Petty, who launched the careers of many rock-and -rollers in his Clovis music studio.

On the eastern plains, the state's border seems fused with its influential neighbor, though New Mexicans there bristle when their area is referred to as "Little Texas." But Texas-type, stretched-out terrain and the long lazy drawl that goes with it carry across the state line into the feedlots at Clovis and the oil wells at Hobbs. Sleek black pumpjacks rhythmically bob up and down beside sheep and cattle who nonchalantly munch on grass. A strong wind sweeps across boundless fields of peanuts, white bolls of cotton, tall corn stalks, and sweet-smelling onions. Between this high tableland and the mountains that rise grandly from the cactus plains, the Pecos River flows.

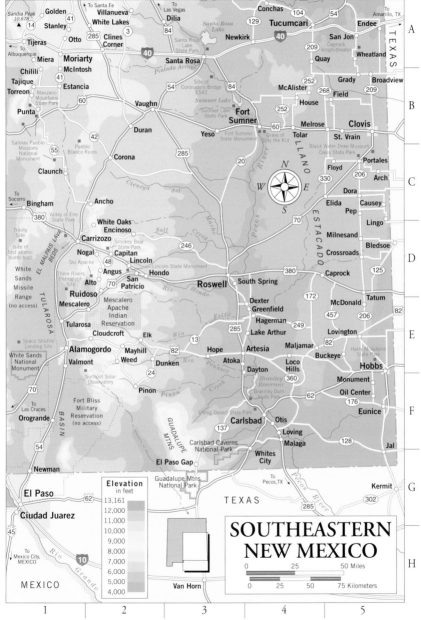

SOUTHEASTERN
NEW MEXICO

Elevation
in feet

13,161
12,000
11,000
10,000
9,000
8,000
7,000
6,000
5,000
4,000

0   25   50 Miles

0   25   50   75 Kilometers

The cool pine-scented mountains of the Lincoln National Forest run the length of the region. From them rises solitary Sierra Blanca—at an altitude of 12,000 feet, the tallest peak in the range. At the southern end, Carlsbad Caverns extends more than 800 feet below a cactus-covered ridge, revealing an underground world of skyscraper-tall limestone sculptures.

On the western fringes of the mountains, the Tularosa Basin—a vast expanse of harsh Chihuahuan desert—stretches between the rugged San Andres and Organ mountains to the west, and the Sacramento Mountains to the east. Within this flat-bottomed bowl is the world's largest surface deposit of fine gypsum granules, partially preserved as White Sands National Monument. These windswept dunes escaped the federal government's grasp in the 1940s when the military appropriated much of the surrounding range to develop weapons. The atomic bomb was first tested here, and today 2.7 million acres of this spiny cactus desert make up the top-secret defense installation of White Sands Missile Range.

■ HISTORY

Cool wetlands and forests covered much of southeastern New Mexico when the state's first inhabitants arrived from the north, pursuing mammoth and mastodon. By about 12,000 years ago, the Clovis culture was stalking now-extinct forms of antelope, dire-wolves, and bison through the grasslands, eating the meat and crafting warm clothing from the hides.

Mescalero Apaches arrived in the region sometime after A.D. 1200, hunting deer and bison and harvesting berries, roots, seeds, and cacti in the forests and on the plains east of the Pecos River and west of the Rio Grande. A favorite treat was mescal, the heart of the agave cactus, which they roasted and ate. Women wove its fibers into baskets.

These roving Indians did not welcome the arrival of European settlers in the 19th century, who began raising sheep and growing corn and beans on Mescalero hunting lands. Comanche and Kiowa Indians came to the region and, like the Apaches, they frequently stole cattle and sheep, raided settlers' food supplies, and sometimes took captives. After the Civil War, government officials turned their attention to the problem and assigned Brig. Gen. James Carlton to put a halt to the attacks. In 1862, his men rounded up 400 Mescalero Apaches and confined them at the Bosque Redondo Reservation that had been carved out alongside the Pecos River. Two years later, famed Indian scout Kit Carson burned the fields and homes of Navajo Indians in eastern Arizona and western New Mexico, forcing their surrender. Gaunt and humbled, 8,500 Navajos then embarked on the "Long

Walk," a forced march more than 300 miles long across cactus plains, rivers, and hardened lava flows to the reservation, where Fort Sumner had been built. There they lived unhappily alongside their traditional enemies, the Apaches.

Carlton, military commander in New Mexico at the time, set out to make farmers of these nomadic tribesmen. Confined on a reservation, the Indians were miserable from the outset, and Carlton's plan was a fiasco. Parasites ravaged the crops and alkaline water infected the Indians with dysentery. The general finally admitted defeat, and in 1868 the Navajos were given 3.5 million acres straddling the Arizona-New Mexico border. Additional acquisitions increased their holdings to 17 million acres, making their reservation the largest in the United States.

Today, Navajos continue their rural lifestyle—many raise sheep and plant small gardens atop red clay soil under which lie vast deposits of oil, gas, and coal. In 1873, the Mescaleros received 460,177 acres of timbered slopes and pastures in the Sacramento Mountains. (They have since turned into astute businesspeople, successfully operating a first-class resort, Inn of the Mountain Gods, and a ski area, Ski Apache on the flanks of Sierra Blanca.) In 1874, the Comanches made their peace with the military.

Once the free-roaming Indians were confined to reservations, more settlers moved into the region and established large sheep and cattle operations. In the late 1800s, the Santa Fe Railroad stretched across the region, passing through the Estancia Valley. Construction camps were erected in Willard and Encino, and Clovis on the far eastern plains. Three more lines entered the state from the south. In the early 1900s, a steady stream of homesteaders settled on the eastern plains, intending to farm 160-acre plots. In Roosevelt County, the population more than tripled between 1904 and 1910.

During World War II, New Mexico began its close relationship with the U.S. military as numerous Air Force bases were established across the creosote desert. In 1942, bases were opened at Clovis, Alamogordo, and Roswell—small towns that had plenty of room between them, where men could test out new aircraft under the wide azure skies. Only one is now closed: Walker Air Force Base at Roswell.

As weapons became more sophisticated, federal officials sought a safe place to test new rockets. In 1942, ranches in the Tularosa Basin were turned into White Sands Proving Ground. In the early hours of July 16, 1945, an atomic bomb was detonated here for the first time, melting the earth upon which it sat, and launching the world into the atomic age. Today, rockets regularly shoot skyward at what has become White Sands Missile Range, and sleek Stealth fighters swoop across the cholla and yucca-filled desert.

■ TULAROSA BASIN   *map page 219, E & F-1*

This 100-mile desert valley flanked by two mountain ranges has been home to
Mogollon Indians, Spanish colonists, and railroad and ranch families. Today,
much of the area is controlled by the military—at the top-secret White Sands Missile Range, Holloman Air Force Base, and McGregor Range.

◆ WHITE SANDS   *map page 219, E/F-1*

In order to create these extensive military installations, begun as weapons testing
grounds during World War II, ranchers patriotically agreed to leave their land. At
White Sands, 150 families were displaced.

   One place that escaped the military's condemnation was a span of glimmering
white desert dunes created by erosion of the Permian rocks that form the San Andres Mountains. **White Sands National Monument** spreads across 230 square
miles of windswept dunes that look like ocean sand, but actually are fine granules
of gypsum. Only one-half of the extensive rolling hills are included in the monument. The sweet fresh smell of gypsum permeates the air, and the fine-grained
sand swirls about picnic shelters. The undulating expanse of white is interrupted
only by an occasional yucca cactus shooting skyward. At the edge of the 50-foot-
tall dunes, animal species have taken on the protective shade of gypsum: there are
white mice, white lizards, and light-colored insects. This soft, silent, ghostly world
of grit seems like an oasis in the surrounding harsh desert of sharp cactus and
cracked earth. On nights when the moon is full, the glistening sands reflect an
eerie glow and the effect is unearthly. From May to September, the dunes are open
until midnight on full-moon nights. Guided walks and talks are offered daily.
*White Sands National Monument Headquarters, 15 miles southwest of Alamogordo on
US 70; 505-479-6124.*

   White Sands Missile Range is off-limits to the public, but a major highway, US
70-82, runs through it, connecting Alamogordo and Las Cruces. Travelers on this
road often find themselves peripherally involved in the range's activities when they
are stopped at one of the regular roadblocks erected during missile firings. In
1982, another group of bystanders witnessed the graceful landing of the Space
Shuttle Columbia when it descended onto the missile range's hard-packed sand at
Northrop Strip.

   But very few people were on hand in the early morning hours of July 16, 1945,
when the first atomic bomb was detonated near the upper edge of this sparsely

Brilliant gypsum sands at White Sands National Monument.
(Kerrick James)

populated rangeland just west of the Oscura Mountains. The explosion vaporized everything in its path and created a blinding flash of light, followed by a shock wave that shattered windows 120 miles away in Silver City. Even early-rising Albuquerque residents noticed a flash on the southern horizon and felt the shock waves. The massive nuclear explosion left a crater 400 yards in diameter and eight feet deep, and intense heat fused sand in the crater into a glasslike solid the color of jade. This substance was called Trinitite after the code name of the top-secret project, Trinity.

Until 1953, Trinity Site was off-limits due to dangerously high levels of radiation left behind by the blast. A lava-rock obelisk now stands at the site, which is open to visitors two days a year: the first Saturdays of April and October.

On the opposite side of the Oscura Mountains, another spectacular eruption that preceded the atomic bomb by nearly a thousand years left behind a 44-mile-long lava flow that in some places is five miles wide and 70 feet deep. Indian legends tell of a volcanic eruption that caused a valley of fire five miles west of present-day Carrizozo. Because the cracked black rock carpet isn't much good as rangeland or farmland, the state made it into a state park and appropriately called it **Valley of the Fires.** Remarkably, cholla, sotol, prickly pear, and gray-green saltbush sprout from between the dark rocks. *Valley of the Fires National Recreation Area, US 380 west of Carrizozo; 505-648-2241.*

♦ ALAMOGORDO AND VICINITY   *map page 219, E-1*

In 1897, Charles Eddy, a rancher who became a major railroad developer, coaxed a group of Eastern investors to tour the Tularosa Basin. They traveled the region in horse-drawn coaches, slept in bedrolls, and ate from a chuck wagon. Eddy wanted them to see the gold, cattle, and timber that could fill rail cars. Before a month had gone by, Eddy received financing for the El Paso and Northeastern Railroad, which was to run from El Paso to Tucumcari, passing along the edge of the Sacramento Mountains. Within a year, he had purchased Alamo Ranch from Oliver Lee. The ranch served as a division point on the rail line and later grew into Alamogordo, which means "Fat Cottonwood." For years, the settlement was a trading center for ranchers, farmers, and the lumber industry. Later, Alamogordo became home to one of New Mexico's favorite writers, Eugene Manlove Rhodes, and to a major branch of New Mexico State University.

But it wasn't until World War II brought the atomic bomb to the cattle country that the town began to establish its modern-day identity as a major military training and testing center. Nearby, missiles are launched and payload experiments for the space shuttle are conducted at White Sands Missile Range; pilots learn to fly Stealth jets at Holloman Air Force Base just outside of town.

In 1954, a Holloman flight surgeon became the fastest man in the world when he tested a rocket sled that blasted across the desert at 632 m.p.h. Colonel John Stapp strapped himself into the one-ton contraption, powered by nine rockets with a total thrust of 40,000 pounds. Stapp suffered two black eyes, burns from the straps, and bruises from bits of sand that whipped into his body. The sled today is on display at the **International Space Hall of Fame**, a $2 million mirrored, four-story gold cube set against the dry foothills of the Sacramento Mountains. Inside, try your hand at the controls of Space Station 2001, learn how an RL-10 rocket engine works, or check out the lunar rover and envision yourself behind its controls as you gather moon rocks. *In downtown Alamogordo, on NM 2001; 505-437-2840 or 877-333-6589.*

Down the hill is a theater named after astronomer Clyde W. Tombaugh, who discovered Pluto in 1930. The Omnimax theater shows regularly changing films on a four-story, wrap-around screen that gives you the feeling you're an astronaut on a space shuttle mission, or a passenger aboard a raft crashing through roiling rapids in the Grand Canyon. When movies aren't showing, a special projector can recreate the heavens from any vantage point on Earth on any night of the year. And there are laser shows in which brightly colored lights are choreographed to the rhythm and mood of music. Lest you lose your head in the clouds of progress, the annual **Rattlesnake Round-up** in April will remind you to watch where you walk. Local wranglers typically trap up to 1,500 pounds of rattlers from the nearby desert to be sold for meat to a Colorado restaurant. But before they are turned into wallets and boots, the snakes are displayed at the gathering. One teenager even willingly crawls into a sleeping bag with about 50 rattlers.

About 10 miles south of Alamogordo, just before the mountains give way once and for all to dry, cracked, cactus-covered earth, is **Oliver Lee Memorial State Park,** a 180-acre oasis tucked away in Dog Canyon at the base of the Sacramento Mountains. Long ago, Apaches lived here, enjoying the seeps and springs of the lush canyon and the protection of its steep rock walls. They also lured soldiers up the dead-end gully only to ambush them. The canyon got its name in 1850, when a group of settlers pursued raiding Indians up the box canyon only to find a lone dog at the end. *505-437-8284.*

In the mid-1880s, a Frenchman by the name of Francois-Jean Rochas built himself a rock house in the canyon and raised cattle and cultivated grapes, olives, and figs. Because the canyon contained the only year-round water source in the area, "Frenchy" was constantly harassed by his jealous neighbors. In 1894, his body was found in the cabin, pierced by three bullets. His death was ruled a suicide, but most folks agreed he was killed for his water. Meanwhile, a quarter mile south of Frenchy's cabin, cattleman Oliver Lee built his ranch headquarters. Today, the building serves as the Oliver Lee Park Museum. You can still see the remains of Frenchy's place and hike up the canyon on the old Indian trail, which climbs 3,000 feet as it follows a steep bluff, here and there draped with green moss.

South of the park the desert sprawls out and once again becomes the property of the U.S. government. **McGregor Range**, yet another missile testing ground, stretches for 1,000 square miles to Fort Bliss, an army base in El Paso, Texas. Like its neighbor White Sands Missile Range, McGregor Range displaced about 200 ranchers when it was created in 1954. Except for one crusty character, that is, who continued to resist attempts by the government, both peaceful and otherwise, to remove him from his home. "I am not afraid of missiles," 82-year-old John Prather said. "I've raised mules all my life." By 1957, the Army admitted defeat and permitted the stubborn rancher to live out his life at his home in the middle of the missile range. He was buried there in 1965. Prather's principles inspired Edward Abbey's 1962 novel *Fire on the Mountain.*

♦ CLOUDCROFT   *map page 219, E-1/2*

Cloudcroft was founded after the El Paso and Northeastern Railroad Company ran out of timber for cross ties during construction of a rail route connecting El Paso with Tucumcari. The only logical solution was to build a spur into the Sacramento Mountains where wood was plentiful. This steep, winding route, known as the Cloud Climbing Railroad, rose 6,000 feet in 27 miles and passed through all of the world's life zones, from the Sonoran Desert to the Hudson Bay region of Canada. Today, a twisting road climbs the mountain.

In 1899, the year before the rail line was completed, a Victorian log lodge was constructed at the 9,200-foot summit, but it was destroyed by fire in 1909. Two years later, a spectacular inn replaced it, this one built of stucco and in a Renaissance Revival style. Pancho Villa, Clark Gable, and Judy Garland slept here. Today, visitors seeking relief from sizzling El Paso summers are treated to a first-class experience in the cool of the Lodge, a year-round resort that features one of the highest golf courses in the world. The fairways are well-maintained and the setting is bucolic—although occasionally a bear will lope across a green just as you are trying to concentrate on your stroke. Inside, guests can belly up to a massive bullet-ridden mahogany bar that was shipped to Cloudcroft from one of Al Capone's haunts in Cicero, Illinois. The inn's restaurant is named after a resident ghost—redheaded Rebecca, a flirtatious chambermaid who was killed by a jealous lover in the 1930s. Borrow the brass skeleton key from the desk and climb a stairway to the copper-domed observatory for a panoramic view of shimmering White Sands National Monument. At night, the four-story tower is a great place to gaze at a dark sky brilliant with stars. *Lodge at Cloudcroft, see page 288.*

Speaking of star-gazing, the **National Solar Observatory at Sacramento Peak**, one of the world's largest solar observatories, is about 20 miles south of town on NM 6563 at Sunspot. Open to the public from May to October, it offers self-guided tours daily, and guided tours on Saturdays. The observatory's sophisticated telescopes, one of which rises 13 stories, enable scientists to study the sun's gaseous outer envelope and sunspots. Down the road, amateur astronomer Alan Hale first caught a glimpse of what became the 20th century's brightest celestial show, Hale-Bopp Comet. *505-434-7000.*

The friendly, rustic village of Cloudcroft, which means "Cloud in a Field," caters to tourists. In the summer, something is going on nearly every weekend, from arts and crafts fairs to music festivals. But the natural beauty of 215,000 acres of national forest is enough to make a visit worthwhile: spectacular views of the white swath of gypsum sands laid out below in the Tularosa Basin, along with the fresh smell of tall pines and a profound quiet.

Southeast of Cloudcroft the Lincoln National Forest continues along a ribbon of mountains that eventually provides Texas with Guadalupe Peak, its highest at an altitude of 8,749 feet. The Guadalupe Mountains also provide a break in an otherwise monotonous horizon. In New Mexico, the rugged range is home to 80-foot-high Sitting Bull Falls, west of Carlsbad. Across the border in Texas, the mountains are part of Guadalupe Mountains National Park, which includes desert lowlands, lush canyons, and forested hillsides.

◆ TULAROSA   *map page 219, E-1*

A welcome break in the dry basin is found at Tularosa, a peaceful, tree-shaded hamlet of simple well-tended adobe homes—some of which date from 1863. In that year, about 100 Hispanic farming families from the Mesilla Valley, which had been washed out by floods along the Rio Grande, decided to move just south of the Rio Tularosa. Here they put in orchards and planted corn, cotton, and alfalfa.

Buildings on many of the original 49 blocks of the townsite have been restored or are undergoing renovation, and reveal finely crafted ornate facades, intricate wood carving, and pressed-tin trim. There is a calming ambiance to this pleasant town which, like its neighbor to the north, was named for a reed—this time a reddish one that grows on the banks of the Rio Tularosa. Irrigation ditches that were dug when the village was settled continue to carry water to tall cottonwoods and orchards of pecan, apple, quince, peach, and cherry trees.

But Tularosa is best known as the "City of Roses." Here people take their rose bushes seriously, and they have their opinions—about when and how to prune, what fertilizer is best, which blooms are more beautiful, and which are most fragrant. Every year during the first weekend of May as red, pink, yellow, and white roses bloom throughout town, its residents celebrate the annual Rose Festival. A queen is crowned and rides in state, surrounded by roses in the Rose Festival parade.

Off US 54 in Three Rivers Canyon is the **Three Rivers Petroglyph Site**, where more than 5,000 carvings have been preserved on an assortment of rock outcroppings along a ridge overlooking the Tularosa Basin. A 1,400-yard winding path leads past etchings of stylized bighorn sheep, lizards, birds, and trees, along with handprints, sunbursts, and a variety of geometric designs. Archaeologists have determined that the Jornada branch of the Mogollon culture was responsible for the artwork. The artists, possibly sitting at this site while serving as lookouts, lived in several villages along the Three Rivers drainage about 1,100 years ago. By 1400, the culture had moved north, probably due to drought. One of these abandoned villages has been partially excavated and reconstructed. *505-525-4300.*

◆ CARRIZOZO   *map page 219, D-1/2*

At the intersection of US 380 and US 54 is the friendly community of Carrizozo. Folks here can be thankful for the high land prices in the nearby gold-mining boomtown of White Oaks at the time the El Paso and Northeastern Railroad was looking for a terminal point. In 1899, since land was less expensive at this tree-shaded spot at the base of the Sacramento Mountains, the terminal was built here instead. Carrizozo, which grew up beside it, took its name from *carrizo,* a reed native to the surrounding plain and nearby foothills. Rumor has it that a ranch foreman embellished the name with an extra "zo"—a misspelling of the Spanish suffix *so,* which indicates abundance. Carrizozo prospered, but booming White Oaks, which produced about $3.1 million in gold between 1879 and 1940, is now a ghost town.

As the popularity of rail travel diminished, so did the economic life of Carrizozo, but it continues to carry on as the Lincoln County seat. Residents have opened up a gift shop in hopes that tourists heading up to the mountains will stop to enjoy the peace and pace of this little New Mexico town.

◆ SMOKEY BEAR   *map page 219, D-2*

Further east on US 380 is **Capitan,** a village that didn't have much to brag about, especially after a devastating forest fire destroyed 17,000 acres in the Capitan Mountains in 1950. But in its smoky aftermath, firefighters discovered a badly singed black bear cub clinging to the side of a charred pine tree. The frightened cub was given the name "Hotfoot," because of his severely burned feet. His burns were treated at the nearby Flatley Ranch, then Game Warden Ray Bell flew the cub to a veterinary hospital in Santa Fe. Hotfoot soon became Smokey. Bell later kept the bear in his home, where the cub ran roughshod over the family's other household pets. Once healed, Smokey was flown to Washington, D.C. where he lived out his life at the National Zoo. The fire proved fortunate for the U.S. Forest Service, which had invented Smokey Bear six years earlier as its fire prevention symbol. The charred bear cub brought life to this campaign. When Smokey died in 1976, he was replaced by Smokey II, who also came from the Capitan

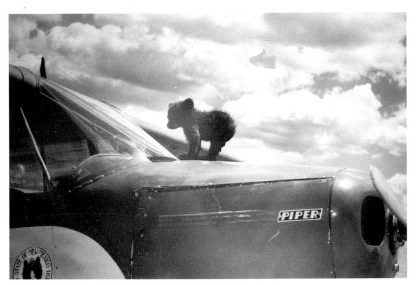

The original Smokey Bear, a cub found after a forest fire. (U.S. Forest Service)

Mountains. Capitan's townsfolk have built a log museum that houses scrapbooks documenting Smokey's discovery and subsequent celebrity. *Smokey Bear Museum, 102 Smokey Bear Blvd.; 505-354-2298.* Inside the nearby Smokey Bear Historical State Park, films of the famous bear are shown. Outside, a trail leads to Smokey's grave. Down the street there's the Smokey Bear Motel, which houses the Smokey Bear Restaurant, which features the Smokey Bear Burger. *Smokey Bear State Historical Park, 118 Smokey Bear Blvd.; 505-354-2748.*

◆ RUIDOSO   *map page 219, E-2*

Ruidoso is a popular destination for Texans hoping to cool off in the hot summer months or to ski the slopes of Sierra Blanca in the winter. Originally named for Capt. Paul Dowlin of the New Mexico Volunteers, a Union regiment, in 1885 Dowlin's Mill was changed to **Ruidoso,** which means "noisy," for the babbling river that runs through it. Dowlin's actual mill still stands and is a favorite tourist stop. It houses a gift and book shop, and the mill itself, which is still operable. Present-day owner, Carmen Phillips, grinds natural flours for sale to locals and tourists.

By the turn of the century, cabins had cozied up to the banks of the Rio Ruidoso, concealed among the tall pines of the White Mountains. The town had become, and continues to be, a summer resort for flatlanders seeking relief from the sweltering heat of southern New Mexico and West Texas. These visitors fish for trout in nearby streams, hike mountain trails, and savor the pine-scented air. When they tire of relaxing, they browse in tourist shops that line the main street, or amble down the road to the racetrack at Ruidoso Downs and raise their blood pressure betting on the quarterhorses. Every Labor Day, the horses compete for $2 million in the All American Futurity, the world's richest quarterhorse race. Or you can walk a mile to the **Hubbard Museum of the West,** where you'll see a Pony Express saddle, carriages, and wagons and the 10,000-piece collection of Anne Stradling, who began collecting horse paraphernalia when she a girl of seven. *841 NM 70 W,. in Ruidoso Downs; 505-378-4142.*

◆ MESCALERO APACHES   *map page 219, E-2*

Next door to Ruidoso is the **Mescalero Apache Reservation.** The Mescaleros didn't take well to their incarceration at Bosque Redondo in 1862, but they have adjusted quite well to the tenets of capitalism. One of the most financially successful tribes in the country, the Mescaleros operate **Ski Apache** on the flanks of

Apache dancers.

SOUTHEASTERN NEW MEXICO

the 12,000-foot Sierra Blanca. With a vertical drop of 1,800 feet, the resort has seven chairlifts and a gondola to whisk skiers up the mountain *(see page 304.)*. In the massive peak's shadows, the tribe's flagship enterprise, Inn of the Mountain Gods, sits alongside Lake Mescalero. Golf, tennis, and hrseback riding programs are available. *(See page 296.)* Also located on the reservation are a casino, and a fish hatchery that supplies the trout in a number of pueblo lakes. The tribe runs a timber operation as well.

Who exactly are your hosts? Here's what Oliver La Farge had to say about the Apaches in 1952: "In the Southwest, at least, it is the common observation that Indians have a delightful sense of humor, and of all the tribes, the Apaches have the keenest and quickest... It is a sense of the ridiculous, kidding which is never malicious, a constant, pleased awareness that the funny side of life is also always with us and a readiness to indicate it by a quick, unexpected phrase."

Back up on US 380 is **Fort Stanton**, built in 1855 to protect settlers from the Mescalero Apaches. By 1896, the fort was deactivated by the military, and two years later it was turned into a U.S. Marine Hospital for tuberculosis patients. From 1966 to 1995, the white-washed buildings served as a state-run school for the mentally disabled.

◆ LINCOLN   *map page 219, D-2*

Along the Rio Bonito, in a narrow valley at the edge of the Capitan Mountains, is the town of Lincoln, settled in 1849 by a small group of Hispanic farmers. Mescalero Apaches chased them out three times, but the feisty settlers kept return-ing. The village was known as Las Placitas del Rio Bonito until 1869, when the townsfolk renamed it after Abraham Lincoln.

Prime cattle country surrounded the town, and it became an important ranch-ing center. As Lincoln prospered, more people wanted a piece of the business it generated, and they were willing to fight for it. One struggle escalated into a noto-rious period of violence, the Lincoln County War, which began in 1878.

It all started after Alexander McSween and John Tunstall opened a store to com-pete with already established shopkeeper Lawrence Murphy. Murphy, who didn't much appreciate the spirit of competition, attempted to crush McSween and Tun-stall by filing a lawsuit against McSween pertaining to an insurance affair the pre-vious year. A month after a guilty verdict was handed down, Tunstall, the financial backer of McSween's mercantile store, was shot to death on the road to his ranch.

Tunstall store in Lincoln was part of the controversy that set off the Lincoln County War.

The same gunmen who killed Tunstall then were deputized by Sheriff William Brady and sent to search for Tunstall's killers, whom they obviously had no intention of finding.

Meanwhile, Tunstall's friends, some of whom witnessed his murder and were outraged by the lack of justice, formed a faction to avenge his death. They called themselves the "Regulators." It wasn't long before they'd shot and killed Sheriff Brady and three of Tunstall's murderers. Pretty soon, everyone in town had taken sides. You were either a McSween man or a Murphy man. More gunfights followed, culminating in the Five Day Battle of July 1878. As McSween's men holed up inside his home, one of Murphy's supporters set the house on fire. McSween was shot and killed as he was trying to surrender. After McSween's death, the Regulators fled, but they rode around the countryside terrorizing Murphy loyalists for a few more years.

One of the McSween men was an affable, wavy-haired 19-year-old ranch hand named William Bonney (a.k.a. Henry McCarty), reckless of spirit and quick with a gun. He'd been inside the McSween house at the time it was set on fire, but escaped with the remaining Regulators. Bonney was nicknamed Billy—Billy the Kid.

Today, the tree-shaded street that cuts through Lincoln isn't much different than it was 100 years ago when Billy galloped down it. The biggest change is that it has been paved and displays a sign that reads US 380. A sleepy hamlet, Lincoln is linked to its violent past through legends. The entire town has been preserved as a state monument and is listed on the National Historic Register. A walking tour takes you past and through impeccably restored buildings, including places like the Tunstall Store, the two-story Lincoln County Courthouse (which earlier had served as the Murphy mercantile), San Juan Church, and several private homes. The Wortley Hotel, which burned down in 1936, has been rebuilt on its original foundation, and it's a rare evening's entertainment that surpasses sitting in a rocking chair on the hotel's front porch, watching the waning sunlight on nearby piñon and juniper-covered hillsides, and listening to the nighttime quiet fall upon the town.

Once a year, residents honor Billy the Kid in a folk pageant that dramatizes his last escape from the Lincoln County Courthouse. Old Lincoln Days is usually held the first weekend of August, and features a fiddler's contest, arts and crafts fair, and a 42-mile Pony Express race that begins at the ghost town of White Oaks and ends at Lincoln. *(See page 309.)*

East of Lincoln, bushy piñon and junipers give way to the orchards of the **Hondo Valley** as the Rio Bonito joins the Rio Ruidoso to become the Rio Hondo. The tiny communities of San Patricio, Hondo, Tinnie, and Picacho hide among corn and bean fields that mix with cherry and apple orchards across this narrow, fertile valley. Polo is a popular pastime.

The well-known landscape painter and portraitist, Peter Hurd, born in Roswell in 1904, brought his wife, Henriette Wyeth of the Pennsylvania artist family, to live alongside the murmuring Rio Hondo in an adobe hacienda, where they both painted. Their work reflects their pastoral surroundings, capturing the simple rural life in stylized landscapes and portraits of the valley's residents.

■ PECOS RIVER VALLEY

The Pecos River Valley was a favorite stopover for early Texas cattlemen driving their livestock north on the Goodnight-Loving Trail. Here there was plenty of grama grass and water enough for a thousand head at the confluence of the Rio Hondo and Pecos River. One of these Texans, John Chisum, liked the area so much he built a ranch six miles south of present-day Roswell. He then drove his cattle west across what came to be known as the Chisum Trail.

◆ ROSWELL   *map page 219, D-3*

A primitive trading post was established in the valley in the 1860s. In 1869, a professional gambler by the name of Van Smith bought an interest in a rustic adobe hotel built nearby. Soon a town was in the making, and Van Smith decided to name it after his father, Roswell. The accidental discovery in 1891 of an artesian water source outside of town spurred irrigation efforts, which resulted in large crops of cotton, alfalfa, apples, corn, and pecans. Soon after the water was discovered, the New Mexico Military Institute, a combination high school and junior college, was established. In the 1930s, humorist Will Rogers paid a visit to the growing town and called it "the prettiest little town in the West."

The tree-lined town has become surprisingly sophisticated, while still serving as a major shipping and trading center for ranchers. An extensive permanent collection of the works of Peter Hurd and his wife, Henriette Wyeth, hang in the **Roswell Museum and Art Center,** an eclectic museum with a collection that also includes paintings by Georgia O'Keeffe, Marsden Hartley, and Stuart Davis.

Not content with art alone, the museum also has re-created the Roswell workshop of Dr. Robert Goddard, a rocket pioneer who spent 11 years in Roswell perfecting his liquid propulsion system and almost single-handedly advancing the science of rocketry through experiments conducted in a rancher's field. *Located at 11th and Main Sts.; 505-624-6744.*

At 1400 North Main, the **International UFO Museum and Research Center** is dedicated to UFO phenomena, in particular a mysterious 1947 crash on a ranch northwest of Roswell. Early reports of the crash, known as the Roswell Incident, told of a spaceship and three alien bodies. Military personnel quickly stepped in to describe the wreckage as a crashed weather balloon with no passengers. In recent years, Roswell has gained international status for its role in UFO history. To commemorate the crash, in early July, the UFO Extravaganza attracts aliens from all corners of the earth to participate in an Alien Parade, buy out-of-this-world geegaws, and discuss the latest UFO theories. *505-625-9495.*

On the town's outskirts, sailboats and windsurfers share the cool azure waters at **Bottomless Lakes State Park** *(505-624-6058).* Canada geese, sandhill cranes, ducks, and herons rest up at **Bitter Lake National Wildlife Refuge.** *505-622-6755.*

◆ ARTESIA AND VICINITY   *map page 219, E-3*

Eight miles north of Artesia, in a cotton belt unimpressive in natural beauty, is the hamlet of Lake Arthur. The town enjoyed a glimmer of heavenly fame in 1977 when an image of Jesus Christ appeared on a flour tortilla made by Maria Rubio as she was preparing burritos for her husband's lunch. The tortilla never was eaten. Instead, it is honored inside a shrine in the Rubio backyard, and thousands of visitors come to view the miracle.

Heading south, the smell of petroleum will probably greet your nostrils. This is an unmistakable indication you have arrived at Artesia, a small town most noted for its rich underground oil and natural gas reserves. The odor is coming from the Navajo Refining Company, the town's largest employer. Black pumpjacks, and lots of them, line the level horizon. Oil well rockers gently sway back and forth and could easily mesmerize you if you gazed at them too long. Natural gas wells are marked by an intricate arrangement of pipes, valves, and gauges called "Christmas trees." Residents say if you live here long enough, it gets so you don't even smell the oil.

Artesia has gone through numerous incarnations: it began as a homestead in the 1890s along the Chisum Trail when a Union soldier, John Truitt, settled near a spring three blocks from the heart of modern-day Artesia. It turned out there was lots of water below the parched surface and that it was easily tapped by drilling artesian wells. In the early 1900s, farmers flocked to the town, now named Artesia, where crops could survive droughts because of the bountiful water supply. The year 1923 brought yet another discovery: oil and gas. Today, there are 4,222 natural gas wells in the Permian Basin, which includes the southeast corner of New Mexico. And even though there is more natural gas under the surface than oil, black crude is still king with 20,019 operating wells. Artesia is now also the site of a training college for the Federal Law Enforcement Training Center.

◆ CARLSBAD CAVERNS   *map page 219, F-4*

One of the largest cave systems in the world, Carlsbad Caverns comprises a three-mile maze of concert-hall rooms whose floors and ceilings are blanketed with house-size stalagmite statues and stalagtite icicles. Filling these massive vaults are grandiose obelisks and pagodas laced with delicate tracery. A paved winding path descends through a black opening in a limestone ridge into the eerily lit bowels of the earth, leading you past dripping pale green limestone walls and into rooms that seem like they belong in a science-fiction movie, or on another planet. The names of the most spectacular formations bear witness to the lifelike shapes created by the limestone deposits: Whale's Mouth, King's Palace, Hall of Giants, Queen's Chamber Draperies. The Big Room, aptly if unimaginatively named for an expanse that could hold 14 Astrodomes, makes you feel as insignificant as an ant on a sidewalk. Its ceiling curves 256 feet above the damp floor. The temperature of 56 degrees F never varies here.

The sound of slowly dripping water is never far away and neither are the thousands of Mexican free-tail bats that spend their days clinging to the moist pale-green ceiling. Fortunately for visitors, the 300,000-member colony bunches together in an area away from the tour route. There are two ways to enter the chilly underground grotto: on a high-speed elevator or along a paved path through the gaping hole, also a bat route. Between May and November, a thick black cloud of them swirls up from the cool of the cave every evening at dusk at a rate of 5,000 to 10,000 a minute. Then they're on to a summertime night of feasting on flying insects.

The concealed cave remained unnoticed until 1901, when a young cowboy, James White, spotted what looked like a cloud of smoke spiraling upward near the foothills of the Guadalupe Mountains. The cloud turned out to be thousands of bats heading off to a night of hunting. Using a rope ladder, White descended into the damp cave and saw for the first time what thousands of people now see each year. By 1930 his discovery had become a national park.

If you're yearning for an adventure similar to White's, you can visit Slaughter Canyon, opened in 1973 for guided flashlight tours. While you don't need a rope ladder, you will need sturdy shoes and endurance in order to hike the strenuous one-mile uphill trail to the cave's entrance. Imagine you are the first person to enter the dark interior. Flashlight beams illuminate spectacular mystical sculptures such as Christmas tree stalagmites draped in smooth limestone deposits. *505-785-2232. Reservations are required for guided tours; call 800-967-2283.*

SOUTHEASTERN
NEW MEXICO

*(following pages) Carlesbad Caverns is the largest cave complex
in the United States. (Kerrick James)*

Each August, Carlsbad hosts its annual Bat Flight Breakfast, during which visitors eat scrambled eggs and sausage just as the world's only flying mammal, satiated after a night of hunting, swoops into its daytime haven of dark.

At the northwest end of town, a preserve for plants and animals native to the Chihuahuan Desert is a great alternative for people who prefer not to set foot inside a dank, dark cave. **Living Desert State Park** is laid out among a carpet of prickly pear, yucca, cholla, sotol, and agave cactus plants in the Ocotillo Hills overlooking Carlsbad. Here caged mountain lions pace back and forth among boulders; Mexican hawks perch atop branches; badgers and prairie dogs burrow into, and rattlesnakes slither across, the dry soil. All of these animals have been brought here because of injuries or illness. At the park, they are treated and returned to the wild. If their injuries are too extensive, they become permanent residents of the park. *505-887-5516.*

A self-guided trail leads past the animals' temporary homes among gypsum hills, dusty arroyos, sand dunes, and pine trees. Every year for four days in May, park personnel re-create a Mescalero Apache tradition: a mescal roast at which the heart of a flowering agave or century plant is cooked in a special midden ring at the park and served to visitors. The taste is close to that of a sweet potato with a smoky molasses flavor.

South of town, **salt beds** litter the landscape. These beds are mined for their salt, which produces potash, an ingredient of fertilizer. At one mine, what goes into the underground chambers is more important than the extracted potash. This is the Waste Isolation Pilot Plant (WIPP), a $1 billion federal facility built to house low-level nuclear waste generated by government nuclear weapons operations. Opened in 1999, WIPP was the first permanent repository for such wastes.

The citizens in and around Carlsbad also continue ranching, the economic base upon which the town was founded in 1888 by cattle baron Charles Eddy. The Pecos River, which runs along the edge of town, enables farmers to grow cotton and alfalfa, the area's two major crops. The river is also the source of warm-water, man-made lakes filled with white bass and catfish and a perfect temperature for waterskiing.

■ LLANO ESTACADO

It's been said land doesn't get much flatter than New Mexico's eastern flank. And it's true. The Llano Estacado, or Staked Plain, is an extension of the Great Plains that stretches from Canada into Texas. In New Mexico, the grassland received its name for one of four reasons, nobody's too sure which one. It could be the multitude of tall yucca plants that sprout up from the high plateau, or the stakes early Spanish explorers pounded into the ground to tie up their horses. It could also refer to the stakes that had to be driven into the ground to give travelers a sense of direction as they traversed the vast expanse. Finally, there is the suggestion that because the literal translation of *llano estacado* is "stockaded plain," early Spanish explorers were referring to protruding mesas that rise at the northwestern edge of the plains, which they thought resembled stockades. Take your pick.

◆ HOBBS   *map page 219, E/F-5*

A chance meeting between two covered wagons on the *Llano* in 1907 resulted in the settlement of **Hobbs.** After being told by the oncoming party of the hardships ahead at his destination of Alpine, Texas, James Hobbs backtracked and put down his roots just inside what today is the New Mexico border. The area full of desert grasses, mesquite, and jackrabbits proved to be suited for raising cattle and growing cotton. In 1928, discovery of a major oil reserve brought an onslaught of fortune hunters, and the scrubland was transformed into a shanty town of crude shacks, metal buildings, and tents. Overnight, Hobbs became a raucous community of oil drillers. Taverns sprung up, which served as rollerskating rinks by day and dance halls by night. The town continues to be a center for the oil industry, but it has calmed down into a peaceful family community that boasts two colleges.

Ranches still endure among the desert scrub; to celebrate those who eek their living from the sandy soil, the **Lea County Cowboy Hall of Fame** at New Mexico Junior College reflects the history of the area. In addition to artifacts, from cookware to buggies, memorabilia of those inducted into the hall of fame are on display. *NM 18; 505-392-5518.*

Because of its light winds and clear days, Hobbs attracts sailplane pilots who glide their lightweight aircraft through spacious skies. In 1983, the World Soaring Championships were held here, which spurred the creation of the Hobbs Soaring Society. *505-392-1077.*

◆ CLOVIS AND ENVIRONS   *map page 219, B-5*

Although this area remained unsettled until the 1880s, prehistoric hunters were roaming the region 11,000 years ago. One of their more successful hunting spots was a large pond fed by the headwaters of the Brazos River, near present-day Portales. Archaeologists believe woolly mammoths, sabertooth tigers, camels, and bison used the pond as a watering hole, thus providing the hunters a perfect place to trap and butcher them. All of this finally came to light in 1932, when a highway worker discovered spearpoints and mammoth bones uncovered by gusty winds that whipped across the plains during the years of the Great Drought. The lake had dried up, leaving behind a gravel pit that proved to be rich in ancient artifacts intermingled with fossils. Modern-day man named it Blackwater Draw, and the prehistoric hunter was called Clovis, after the nearby town. Today, Blackwater Draw Museum, located on US 70 between Portales and Clovis, contains many of the archaeological discoveries found at the site. *505-562-2202.*

The Athabascans probably passed through the area during their 14th-century migrations from Canada. In the 1700s, Comanche and Kiowa Indians roamed across the vast grasslands, hunting buffalo but leaving no evidence of any permanent settlements.

It was another watering hole that attracted early European immigrants—Portales Springs, a series of cave openings through which gushed streams of fresh water. Spanish explorers thought the caves resembled *portales,* the porches of Spanish adobe homes. The first settler in Portales was Doak Good, a cattleman looking for a place to call his own in 1880.

It took the railroad to bring some definition to this endless horizon, and people as well. In the early 1900s, the town of Portales was established as a construction camp for workers on the Pecos Valley and Northern Railroad. It was followed by its close neighbor to the north, Clovis, which, until 1907, was known as Riley's

Wagons on their way to market and loaded with broom corn in Clovis, 1905. (Museum of New Mexico)

Switch on the Santa Fe line. When rail officials chose the site as a division point for the Belen cut-off, they decided to make it a proper town. A daughter of a Santa Fe Railroad official was given the honor of finding a name. She had been studying French history at the time and was taken by Clovis, King of the Franks, who converted to Christianity in 486.

The railroad helped populate the area, but the discovery years later of the massive Ogallala aquifer turned it into one of the state's premier agricultural belts. This plentiful underground water source transformed the sweeping grasslands into vast fields of alfalfa, cotton, corn, wheat, and potatoes. In Clovis, cattle are fattened at some of the largest feedlots in the Southwest; at weekly livestock auctions these healthy bovines are sold to the highest bidder.

Clovis residents like to kick up their heels to the twangs of country and western music, but back in the 1950s, one lonely musician took a detour from that genre. Norman Petty built a recording studio inside an ordinary-looking building at 1313 West Seventh Street. Instead of country singers, he encouraged rock-and-roll musicians to drop by and try their luck. His biggest catch was a young band leader from Lubbock, Texas, who wore dark-rimmed glasses, played an energetic piano,

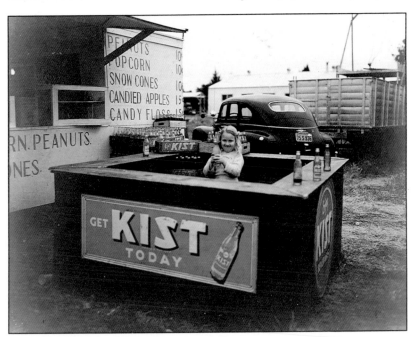

Young entrepreneur at Clovis Rodeo, circa 1940. (Museum of New Mexico)

and sang in an exuberant voice. Between 1957 and his untimely death two years later, Buddy Holly recorded most of his greatest hit records at the Clovis studio, some with his band, the Crickets, and some on his own. "That'll Be the Day," was his first hit, followed by "Peggy Sue," "Every Day," and "Maybe Baby."

Following Holly's death, Petty continued to work with local musicians, the most notable being Jimmy Gilmer and the Fireballs, who enjoyed a short-lived celebrity with their hits, "Sugar Shack" and "Bottle of Wine." Another popular 1950s musician Petty discovered was Buddy Knox ("Party Doll"). Roy Orbison, best known for "Pretty Woman," started with Petty, but left before recording any of his well-known hits. Petty died in 1984, but his inspiration is celebrated once a year in June at the **Clovis Music Festival,** when his widow, Vi, opens up the original Norman Petty Studio for tours. This six-day event attracts Buddy Holly fans, 1950s music stars, and rock-and-rollers of all ages. *505-762-0515.*

◆ PORTALES   *map page 219, C-5*

Down the road, Portales is nutty for peanuts, growing 30 million pounds of the Valencia variety every year. For three days in October, the nutty legume is honored at the Peanut Valley Festival, home of the "Peanut Olympics." Peanuts also are roasted, eaten, and displayed. At **Eastern New Mexico University,** the Jack Williamson Science Fiction Library honors the Portales author with 7,000 volumes, including the original manuscripts of most of Williamson's more than 45 novels and 150 short stories.

One Portales man, Bill Dalley, has taken the windmill off the prairie and erected 60 of the spinning antique apparati in his front yard. "A lot of old ranchers tell me that if a man wants a peaceful state of mind after a hard day of roping cattle, there's nothing better than riding up to the old windmill and listening to the groan of a wheel. It's like watching fish breathe. It's all slow motion—so slow, yet powerful," he once told a writer.

◆ FORT SUMNER AND OLD FORT DAYS   *map page 219, B-3*

Upriver from Roswell are the crumbling ruins of **Fort Sumner,** site of the unsuccessful incarceration of Mescalero Apaches and Navajos. The fort closed in 1868 after the military admitted defeat in its plan to make farmers and friends of the two nomadic tribes who weren't fond of each other. Some of the civilians who had moved to the area to furnish food for the fort stayed and continued to grow vegetables and raise cattle in the fertile river valley.

In 1881, Billy the Kid, by then the state's most notorious outlaw, high-tailed it to Fort Sumner after his escape from the Lincoln County Jail. By coincidence, Sheriff Pat Garrett was at Fort Sumner as well. He'd dropped by the home of Pete Maxwell, one of Billy's old friends, to check on the outlaw's whereabouts. Maxwell had turned the fort's old officer's quarters into a spacious home. As Garrett sat at the foot of Maxwell's bed in his darkened bedroom, in walked the baby-faced outlaw, looking for some food. Garrett shot the bullet that felled the fugitive. Billy the Kid was buried in the Fort Sumner military cemetery alongside two of his recalcitrant desperado friends, Tom O'Folliard and Charlie Bowdre. His tombstone reads: "The Boy Bandit King—He Died as He Had Lived."

Since that day, folks in Fort Sumner have erected a museum in the outlaw's honor and formed a historical society dedicated to their folk hero. *1601 E. Sumner; 505-355-2380.*

Because people keep trying to steal Billy's tombstone, a chainlink fence now surrounds his grave marker. These attempts have inspired the Billy the Kid Tombstone Race, one of the reasons people come to Old Fort Days, Fort Sumner's annual celebration of its past held each June.

Another attraction is the Cow Plop, in which a very regular bovine is let loose to stroll in a squared-off fenced field behind a hardware store. White paint divides 425 squares, which cost $5 each. Those who contributed watch anxiously, hoping the cow will heed nature's call on their square. This giant outdoor bingo game nets the winner $500 and raises money for the Chamber of Commerce.

A third reason to attend Old Fort Days is the rodeo. Professionals and amateurs deftly urge their horses to lope after a calf, stop abruptly, and stand still while the rider lassos the scared calf, then dismounts and lashes its legs together. Bull riders have the toughest job: they gingerly climb on the back of a 2,000-pound brahma bull that isn't used to carrying around anything bigger than a horsefly. It's not easy to stay atop a heaving bull and many cowboys don't last long. The voice that booms out in between events loves to comment on the misadventures of the ring's performers. Usually, the announcer is as entertaining as the rodeo clowns whose job it is to divert an angry bull bent on giving a discarded cowboy a skyward toss. In barrel racing, the only women's event, riders run the length of the dirt arena, circle a barrel, then race back and out the chute, all in the blink of an eye. *Old Fort Days; 505-355-7705.*

The eastern third of New Mexico's landscape is typical of high plains country. (Paul Chesley)

N O R T H E A S T E R N
N   E   W   M   E   X   I   C   O

■ HIGHLIGHTS   *page*

Food & Lodgings begin on page 280.

A WHIPPING WIND WHISTLES THROUGH TALL GRAMA GRASSLANDS. Brown specks on the otherwise pale-green landscape materialize, upon closer view, into cattle. The Canadian and Cimarron rivers, and a section of the Pecos, are the largest and longest of the few waterways that intersect the sprawling plains of northeastern New Mexico. Simple ranch houses, whirring windmills, and the remains of long-extinct volcanoes line the horizon. Hundreds of dinosaur footprints mark the landscape near Clayton.

Chipped stone points used by Folsom Man 10,000 years ago lie protected inside Folsom Museum. In a strong wind, you can almost hear the creaking wheels of heavily loaded wagons laboring toward Santa Fe over the Santa Fe Trail, or the shrill cries of Comanche raiding parties. For 59 years during the 1800s, cumbersome caravans linked the Spanish outpost of Santa Fe with the eastern United States. These wagon trains carried cloth and tools to the New Mexico frontier and brought back beaver pelts, silver, and gold.

In northeastern New Mexico the hunting grounds of the Apaches met those of the Comanches, and fertile plains meet the Sangre de Cristo Mountains. Here also mountain man Lucien Maxwell became the largest single landholder in the Western Hemisphere when he inherited from his father-in-law a 1.7-million-acre land grant that included mountains and valuable rangeland stretching into present-day

NORTHEASTERN NEW MEXICO

0   10   20   30   40   50
Miles

To La Junta, CO

Model

Kim

Tobe

Elevation in feet

13,161
12,000
11,000
10,000
9,000
8,000
7,000
6,000
5,000
4,000

A

Trinidad

COLORADO

389

Branson

B

Sugarite Canyon State Park

Cimarron   456   River   Gravel   Kenton

OKLAHOMA

Raton

Folsom   406

Capulin Volcano National Monument   325   Des Moines

Capulin   N Corrumpa   Creek   Moses

C

25   87   Clayton Lake State Park   370   Seneca

Elizabethtown (ghost town)   Grenville   Kiowa National Grasslands   56

38   64

Eagle Nest   Cimarron Canyon State Park   Maxwell National Wildlife Refuge   Mt. Dora

Ute Park   Cimarron   Maxwell   Carrizo   Clayton   87   Texline

Angel Fire Ski Area   21   58   Dorsey Mansion   D

Angel Fire   Philmont Scout Ranch   Springer   Creek

To Taos   Rayado   Miami   Taylor   Gladstone   56

Black Lake   Kit Carson Museum   Santa Fe Trail Museum   Jaritas   402

434   Ocate   Ocate   Creek   Kiowa National Grasslands   Sedan

Guadalupita   Coyote Creek State Park   120   Ute   E

Ojo Feliz   Mills Canyon Hotel   Yates

Mora   442   Mills   39   Gravel   102

La Cueva   Loma Parda (ghost town)   Wagon Mound   Chicosa Lake State Park   Bueyeros

Ledoux   Fort Union National Monument   120   Roy   Creek   Amistad

161   Valmora   Mora   Solano   420

Sapello   Watrous   River

25   Sabinoso   Mosquero   Nara Visa

Montezuma   Storrie Lake State Park   N   54

Las Vegas   104   419   W   E   Conchas   39

To Santa Fe   Romeroville   Fuerte Ruins   Trujillo   S   F

Los Montoyas   Conchas   Lake   Ute Lake State Park

Chapelle   Apache Springs   Aurupa Ruins   River   Conchas Lake State Park   Canadian   Logan

El Cerrito   Variadero   Conchas   River

Anton Chico   Dilia   Ruins of Old Fort Bascom   To Amarillo, TX

Dahlia   129   104   G

84   Colonias   Tucumcari   Glenrio

To Albuquerque   Santa Rosa Lake   40   San Jon   93

40   Newkirk   Montoya   469

Milagro   Santa Rosa   Cuervo   209   Caprock Amphitheater

219   Santa Rosa Lake State Park   Quay   Wheatland   H

Pastura   54   Puerto de Luna   84   To Fort Sumner   Ragland   209   Grady

Gravel   Pintada   Arroyo   River   156   Forrest

1   2   3   4   5

Colorado. It is among these tall ponderosa pine trees and this wide open prairie that the Marlboro Man (before he died of lung cancer) stood tall in the saddle for cigarette advertisements.

The secluded canyons of the Sangre de Cristos proved perfect hideouts for gunfighter Clay Allison and train robber Thomas "Black Jack" Ketchum. In the late 1800s, nearly everybody who was anybody in the Wild West stayed at the St. James Hotel in the foothill town of Cimarron when passing through. Wyatt Earp, Pat Garrett, Doc Holliday, and Jesse James were frequent guests. Oklahoma oilman Waite Phillips donated 127,395 acres of these forested slopes to the Boy Scouts of America, who turned the cattle ranch into Philmont Scout Ranch, where the organization trains its young members in camping and leadership skills.

Cattle outnumber people on this vast prairie, where people take pride in all the region has to offer: from a scuba diver's oasis in the desert at Santa Rosa's Blue Hole and the carefully preserved Victorian homes of Las Vegas to the 6,000 statuesque elk roaming the forests of Vermejo Park—once the largest privately owned ranch in the United States and now an exclusive hunting and fishing preserve.

■ HISTORY

About 100 million years ago, when the waters of an inland sea gently lapped at what today is the northeast corner of New Mexico, scores of duck-billed dinosaurs milled about near the shoreline gorging on whatever delectable plants they could find. These 10- to 15-feet-long prehistoric creatures left behind 800 footprints that escaped the path of oozing lava spewed from a series of fiery volcanic explosions 10,000 years ago. Today, the footprints are embedded in sandstone 12 miles north of Clayton. Also surviving these earth-shattering eruptions were prehistoric hunters, now referred to as Folsom Man, who stalked mastodons, woolly mammoths, bison, and antelope. Later, in the 13th century, scattered communities of Anasazi Indians grew squash, beans, and corn along the banks of the region's waterways.

By the time the Spanish explorer Francisco Vásquez de Coronado traipsed across the plains in 1541, these prehistoric Indians were gone. Coronado was en route to Quivira, where he was promised golden riches by an Indian guide. At his destination outside of Lyons, Kansas, the explorer found only the grass huts of the Wichita Indians. Greatly disappointed, he returned empty-handed to New Mexico and later to Mexico.

By 1700, the Jicarilla Apaches began pursuing buffalo and antelope through the region's grasslands and secluded canyons. In the 1700s, Comanches moved into this area, and the two tribes battled each other, along with a few pockets of hardy Spanish settlers, for regional control. These settlers, who lived in small communities, had received land grants from the government of Spain; the colonists had only to farm the land for four years and then they could call it their own. After Mexico gained its independence from Spain in 1821, the new government continued the practice.

◆ MAXWELL LAND GRANT

The largest of these land grants was the Maxwell Land Grant, which Gov. Manuel Armijo issued in 1841 to Charles Beaubien, a French trapper, and Guadalupe Miranda of Taos, a government official. The 1.7-million-acre grant, which included present-day Eagle Nest, Springer, and Raton and spread into southern Colorado, was three times the size of Rhode Island. It takes its name from Lucien Maxwell, a hunter and trapper who married Beaubien's daughter, Luz. After Beaubien's death in 1864, Maxwell inherited the massive landholding that included acres of minerals, timber, and some of the best pasture land in the region, upon which he administered numerous cattle and sheep ranches and even introduced beet cultivation. Although he seemed to prefer gambling and the acquisition of elaborate furnishings for the mansion he built in Cimarron, Maxwell still worked hard at developing his assets, and encouraged ranchers to lease portions of his hold-ings. On a handshake basis, the land baron outfitted settlers with cattle, acreage, and seed to improve upon the lush grama grass that covered the lava-rock land.

In 1870, the sale of the Maxwell grant (by then known to contain gold de-posits) to a group of British and Dutch investors set off more than a decade of fighting between settlers and the foreigners, who demanded that all squatters ei-ther buy their holdings, pay rent, or move out. During the controversy, known as the Colfax County War, farmers, ranchers, miners, and shopkeepers who had been indulged by Maxwell now claimed ownership to the land upon which they had for years carved out livings. The settlers resisted court rulings that favored the new owners, and blood occasionally was shed until 1887, when the U.S. Supreme Court once and for all confirmed the legality of the Maxwell Land Grant. Having acquired the British assets, the Dutch investors emerged as sole owners.

In 1841, the same year Beaubien and Miranda received the land grant, the town of Cimarron sprang up along the shady banks of the blue-green Cimarron River. The sheltered settlement, which began as a principal stop on a branch of the Santa Fe Trail that ended at Taos, soon became a major gathering spot for ranchers, min-ers, and gunslingers. Later on, it was Lucien Maxwell's center of operations.

♦ THE CIVIL WAR

In the 1800s, when wagon trains rolled over the Santa Fe Trail, the Comanches turned their attention to the Anglo traders and the goods and tools they brought across the plains from Missouri. Both arms of the trade route entered New Mexico through this region: the Mountain Branch, which traversed southeastern Colorado before crossing rugged Raton Pass on its way to Santa Fe, and the Cimarron Cut-off, which made a beeline through southwestern Kansas and northeastern New Mexico on into the outpost capital.

New Mexico became a U.S. territory in 1848, a development that didn't much matter to the Apaches and Comanches, who considered the plains their own and continued to terrorize the wagon trains along the Santa Fe Trail. To protect the travelers and the area's settlers, Fort Union was built in 1851 near Watrous, where the Cimarron Cutoff and Mountain Branch joined. After the Civil War broke out in 1861, the military installation was fortified for a threatened Confederate invasion that didn't come that far north. A year later a regiment from the fort, along with the Colorado Volunteers, turned back Rebel forces at the Battle of Glorieta Pass, 25 miles southeast of Santa Fe. This decisive victory, which is re-enacted every year 15 miles south of Santa Fe at Rancho de las Golondrinas, was the turning point in the war in the West and is referred to as the "Gettysburg of the West." The battlesite is on its way to being protected as part of the national park system.

◆ SMOOTH RIDES AND ROUGH RIDERS

By the late 1870s, tracks laid by the Santa Fe Railroad were entering the region, first up and over the mountainous slopes of Raton Pass, then across the prairie through Springer, Wagon Mound, and Las Vegas. On the eastern plains, the Colorado and Southern Railroad connected the towns of Clayton, Des Moines, and Folsom to the tracks at Raton. The Phelps Dodge company built a line from Tucumcari north to the coal fields of Dawson, and on the way helped develop the towns of Mosquero and Roy. The railroad brought new settlers, cheaper goods, and rendered the Santa Fe Trail obsolete.

When Cuba went to war with Spain to gain its independence in 1898 and the United States went to the aid of its southern island neighbor, New Mexico's Gov. Miguel Otero, Jr. seized the opportunity to show the territory's loyalty to the Stars and Stripes. In response to Otero's call for volunteers, 340 qualified horsemen signed up to ride under the leadership of Lt. Col. Theodore Roosevelt. New Mexicans made up about one-third of the future president's Rough Rider unit that

Arrival of the caravan at Santa Fe, 1844. (Museum of New Mexico)

charged San Juan Hill in Cuba without their horses, left behind because of a lack of transport. Said one New Mexico Rough Rider, "I was born in a dugout right here in Las Vegas, raised a cowboy, enlisted expecting to do my fighting on horseback as all the boys, but landed in Cuba afoot; marched, sweated, and fought afoot; earned whatever fame afoot."

Despite the fact that their horses were left behind, the gallantry of New Mexico's volunteers proved they supported the U.S. and not Spain—the ancestral homeland of many of them. A year later, the Rough Riders held a reunion in Las Vegas, and once again marched behind Roosevelt—this time in a parade through town. Reunions continued into the 1960s. *Rough Riders Memorial and City Museum, 727 Grand, Las Vegas; 505-425-8726.*

■ LAS VEGAS   *map page 249, F-1*

Las Vegas, a well-preserved but gritty town with the tall pine slopes of the Sangre de Cristo Mountains to the west and a carpet of grama grasslands spreading to the east, is often confused with the well-known Nevada gambling capital. The two couldn't be more different: flashing neon signs light the way to the gambling casinos that line the strip in the Nevada town; old-fashioned streetlamps light the quiet neighborhoods of restored Victorian homes in the New Mexico version.

New Mexico's Las Vegas (The Meadows) began as a land grant in 1821, when Luis Maria Cabeza de Baca received a grant for himself and his 17 sons along the Gallinas River, a meandering stream that forms high in the mountains. According to folklore, the river originated as a teardrop from an "eye" in the rock face of a tall peak. Persistent attacks by Comanche Indians who considered the region their hunting domain prevented the family from ever settling the land.

In 1835, after wagon trains had been rolling through the townsite on the Santa Fe Trail for 14 years, a group of 34 Spanish colonists established the town of Las Vegas and quickly planted crops, mostly beans. They also grazed sheep on nearby meadows and built simple dirt-roofed homes of adobe bricks. Men and boys worked long hours tending their herds, while the women cooked, spun thread, wove cloth, sewed clothing and bedding, and fashioned beautiful lacework and embroidery. Residents purchased tools and ribbons from caravans that regularly passed through. The town also served as a major way station on the Santa Fe Railroad, which arrived in 1879.

Early on, Las Vegas residents looked to construction materials other than adobe. **Our Lady of Sorrows Church** was the largest stone structure in New Mexico when it was built, between 1862 and 1870, of randomly fit blocks of Anton Chico sandstone. But it was the wave of settlers who arrived by train that definitely scorned the indigenous adobe homes. The newcomers preferred building styles popular in the Midwest. As a result, Las Vegas is an architectural treasure trove with 900 of its structures on the National Register of Historic Buildings.

West of the Gallinas River is the original townsite, built around a traditional tree-shaded plaza with a turquoise-trimmed gazebo sitting in the center. The finely restored **Plaza Hotel,** *(see page 294)* a showpiece when it was built in 1882, anchors the northwestern corner of the block. Streets in this part of town radiate from the plaza like spokes of a wheel and they follow the rolling terrain sliced with arroyos (usually dry, water-carved streambeds). The unspoiled appearance of Old Las Vegas in 1915 attracted Tom Mix who acted in *Never Again, The Rancher's Daughter,* and *The Country Drugstore*—films that were the forerunners of a genre that later became known as Westerns.

East of the river, neighborhoods look as if they were plucked from the Midwest or New England. Here, homes display Victorian gables, Tudor half-timbers, and Italianate bay windows. Well-kept lawns complement restored turn-of-the-century multi-story homes surrounded by precisely placed trees and shrubs. The **Carnegie Library,** built in 1903 and modeled after Thomas Jefferson's home, Monticello, is the focal point of a block of shady elms and deep green grass. It's hard to believe hundreds of miles of prairie spread east of town.

◆ MONTEZUMA   *map page 249, F-1*

A winding road, NM 65, follows the Gallinas River into the mountains, entering the timbered **Pecos Wilderness** west of Las Vegas and passing by a few villages. One of these, **Montezuma,** is the location of the most spectacular late-nineteenth-century structure of the area, known today as Montezuma Castle. This massive 343-room edifice was built as a spa in 1888 by the Santa Fe Railroad to take advantage of nearby hot springs. A five-mile spur led to the multi-storied wooden building with numerous turrets and balconies. For a decade, this splendid hotel was the crown jewel of the rail line, serving customers such as Ulysses S. Grant, Rutherford Hayes, Kaiser Wilhelm, and Japanese emperor Hirohito. Guests rode horses in the nearby mountains, fished for trout in the Gallinas River, played poker in oak-paneled card rooms, and soaked in the thermal baths, which reached temperatures of 110 degrees F. In 1981, the Armand Hammer Foundation turned the 110-acre complex into the United World College of the American West, a

two-year institution for students 16 to 19 years old. *505-454-4200.*

From Montezuma, NM 65 continues on through the rugged mountains, ending at the base of the 10,000-foot **Hermit's Peak.** In 1863, Giovanni Maria Agostini, a 62-year-old Italian immigrant, moved into a cave just below the peak's eastern summit seeking solitude. Men from Las Vegas built him a small cabin, and there he carved religious emblems that he exchanged in town for cornmeal. (The hermit lived mostly on mush.) Four years later, feeling restless, the hermit moved on to southern New Mexico where he sought refuge in the Organ Mountains. There he was found dead in 1869 with a dagger in his back.

Driving north for 25 miles on NM 518, you'll come to Salman Ranch, a 19th-century homestead that today is a raspberry farm. Between August and October, you can buy fresh berries at the farm's store or cool off with a raspberry sundae.

■ NORTH OF LAS VEGAS

The pointed lettuce-green leaves of an occasional yucca cactus interrupt the undulating prairie, its grasses taking on rust-red and yellow hues as I-25 traces the path of the Santa Fe Trail. At Watrous, today a roadside hamlet with less than 100 residents, the Mountain and Cimarron branches of the Santa Fe Trail merged in the shade of leafy cottonwoods and alongside the waters of the Mora River.

◆ FORT UNION   *map page 249, E/F-1*

At the end of NM 161, the crumbling ruins of Fort Union rise like a mirage from the pastel-green prairie. These partial walls are all that remain of the largest nineteenth-century U.S. military installation in the Southwest, which once protected settlers and travelers on the Santa Fe Trail, as well as serving as a major military supply station from 1851 until 1891. Preserved as a national monument, the fort is a reminder of the days when travel wasn't particularly convenient—or safe.

A flagstone walkway passes by what once served as officers' quarters. Brick fireplaces and chimneys that tower above deteriorating walls have somehow survived the relentless wind that steadily whistles through the ruins. Press a button, and a bugle interrupts the silence of the prairie. Push another one, and an officer's wife complains to her husband about a leaky roof, or a sergeant barks out orders to his men. Close your eyes, and the fort's storehouses, offices, barracks, and corrals take shape and soldiers execute drills on the parade ground. Open them, and the soft

(opposite) The European Rococo interior of Raton's Shuler Theater features elaborate woodwork, gold-trimmed box seats, and a high ceiling painted to resemble a cloud-filled sky. (Kerrick James)

snapping of grasshoppers rubbing their legs is all that permeates the stillness. Bees rise from hives wedged inside chimneys and shallow grass-covered indentations mark the once-busy Santa Fe Trail. *505-425-8025.*

◆ LOMA PARDA   *map page 249, E-1*

Before the establishment of Fort Union, the small farming community of Loma Parda, settled in 1830 on a secluded bend in the Mora River, was known for its juicy apples, plums, and pears, and an assortment of vegetables shipped to Denver and Albuquerque. The village took on a new importance, however, when the fort was built five miles away. Prostitutes moved in, bars opened, and small orchestras, probably three-piece, played 24 hours a day in dance halls. The community became known as "Sodom on the Mora." Military commanders tried unsuccessfully to forbid their men from patronizing its haunts and even attempted to buy the town.

On one occasion, the commander sent a contingent to town to arrest a number of absentee soldiers who had left the fort without permission. Not only did the troops fail to carry out the orders, but they got sidetracked and didn't come back either. Today, all that remains of Loma Parda are wall fragments melted together from pounding rain and driving wind. Roofs are gone, and heavy *vigas* have fallen into rooms that once resounded with revelry. The commander would be satisfied.

◆ WAGON MOUND   *map page 249, E-2*

Heading north on I-25, traffic is sparse and cattle amble along their grama-grass dining table. Over a rise, a few volcanic mesas jut skyward. One, which resembles a covered wagon, was the last great landmark on the westward journey across the plains. When a ranching town was established on its flanks in 1850, it took the name Santa Clara, but changed nine years later to Wagon Mound. A drive through this sleepy hamlet provides a glimpse of simple tin-roofed adobe architecture. A dog lies sleepily in the middle of the street, expecting cars will go around him. Today, the highlight of the year for the town's 310 residents is Bean Day—known to outsiders as Labor Day. This harvest celebration began in 1910 when pinto beans were a big crop for area farmers. Even though beans aren't grown here anymore, past and present residents gather for bicycle and sack races and a parade in the morning, a free noon meal of barbecued beef, pinto beans, and coleslaw, followed by a rodeo and evening dance. *City Hall; 505-666-2408.*

◆ SPRINGER AND VICINITY   *map page 249, D & E-2 & 3*

In the late 1800s, the quiet ranching centers of Springer and Maxwell grew alongside railroad tracks and riverbanks: Springer on the Cimarron River, Maxwell on the Canadian. In Springer, the town's main attraction is the **Santa Fe Trail Museum**, housed in the old Colfax County courthouse. Artifacts range from Springer High School portraits to a Santa Fe Trail–era covered wagon. *505-483-2341.*

About 30 miles east of Springer, north of US 56, the imposing **Dorsey Mansion** sits tucked into the base of Chico Hill overlooking a sprawling grama grass plain. This odd-looking log and sandstone house with its Gothic-like turret was the creation of Stephen Dorsey, a U.S. senator from Arkansas who had an elaborate vision of a ranch house. He built his pretentious mansion in stages between 1880 and 1886 and made it the site of lavish all-night parties. Its indoor plumbing (a luxury in those days), billiard rooms, lily "pond" with three islands, well-stocked wine cellar, and purebred English bulls were the talk of the region. When no one is on duty the gate is locked, so do ahead to arrange a tour. *505-375-2222.*

Southeast of Springer, in the late 1800s, an over-achieving lawyer and rancher turned to agriculture in the bowels of the Canadian River Canyon. Melvin Mills planted 14,000 trees—apple, peach, pear, cherry, plum, walnut, almond, and chestnut—and cultivated melons, tomatoes, grapes, and cabbages along a 10-mile-long ribbon of shoreline. Unintimidated by thousand-foot-tall canyon walls and a steep gravel road leading to the braided riverbed, Mills blasted underground irrigation channels, constructed cisterns, a cider press, bunkhouses, and a stone mansion on the riverplain. He hauled his crops to Springer where they were shipped to Harvey Houses along the Santa Fe Railroad. The **Mills Canyon Hotel,** now in ruins, was a popular vacation spot and served a stagecoach line that crossed the canyon here. In 1904, Mills's efforts were washed away in a disastrous flood that sent raging waters through the canyon. All that remains are partial stone walls of the hotel and a few scraggly fruit trees.

West of Springer on NM 21, at **Philmont Scout Ranch,** mule deer, stately elk, black bear, a herd of buffalo, and more than 250 head of Hereford cattle share the pine and spruce-covered slopes with thousands of Boy Scouts who practice survival skills there every summer. NM 21 follows the Mountain Branch of the Santa Fe Trail and skirts the edge of the ranch, which through later acquisitions now encompasses 137,493 acres along the Cimarron Range of the Sangre de Cristo Mountains. A raven sits atop a fence post, scanning a grassy meadow for its next meal. Nearby, a small herd of ash-gray mule deer grazes close to the road, unperturbed at passersby.

In 1845, Kit Carson built a flat-roofed adobe house and cultivated a 15-acre garden along the banks of Rayado Creek at the ranch's southeastern boundary. Four years later, Lucien Maxwell (of the Maxwell Land Grant) joined the Indian scout along the creek. But Carson's busy schedule fighting Indians and Maxwell's desire to move into the town of Cimarron forced the men to give up the operation by 1857.

At **Rayado,** young guides dressed in 19th-century clothing lead tours at the **Kit Carson Museum,** a reconstruction of the mountain man's home, and share tales of frontier life along the Santa Fe Trail during that era. On exhibit is a bed that reportedly was too comfortable for Carson: after two nightson it, he spread his buffalo robes on a hard adobe bench in the corner and slept there instead. *505-376-2281.*

Seven miles up the road, red tin roofs top tan stucco buildings, pristine in their manicured setting of close-cropped grass and gravel roads at Philmont's headquarters. Here between 1922 and 1927, Waite Phillips built a lavish Spanish two-story Mediterranean-style home where his family spent their summers. Skins of bear and cougars draped the walls, and a custom-made piano and shower with seven

Wide-open country. (Paul Chesley)

(opposite) High-plains storm looms over an abandoned farm.

showerheads are evidence of the oilman's prosperity. Daily tours are offered throughout the summer. Across the road, the Seton Memorial Library honors Ernest Thompson Seton, an author, artist, naturalist, and the first chief scout of the Boy Scouts of America. The stucco building houses Seton's library, along with his collection of 3,000 paintings of birds, rabbits, and buffalo. Seton spent many of his years at his ranch, Seton Village, just east of Santa Fe. *Philmont Museum and Seton Memorial Library at the Philmont Scout Ranch; 505-376-2281.*

■ CIMARRON   *map page 249, D-1 &2*

The wild and woolly town of Cimarron was settled in 1841 and served as a gathering place for the area's ranchers and miners. Set amid shady cottonwood trees and fragrant piñon pines along the shallow Cimarron River, the town was also a principal stop on a branch of the Santa Fe Trail that led to Taos. After Maxwell relocated the headquarters of his immense land-grant holdings there in 1857, the town's popularity grew. It received another boost in 1864 when Maxwell completed a three-story adobe mansion that covered a city block. Inside were rooms for billiards, gambling, and dancing, as well as a rear section for prostitutes. Every night large sums of money exchanged hands during games of faro, roulette, monte, poker, and dice. It had separate women's and men's sides. Chauvinism was the order of the day!

As the years went by, Cimarron, which means "Wild" or "Untamed" in Spanish, lived up to its name. Angry gamblers who didn't like a card they were dealt often picked fights. Gunslingers who tipped one too many shots of whiskey liked to show off by shooting holes in the ceiling. Disputes were settled in the dirt streets and only the victor walked away. The *Las Vegas Gazette* once reported, "Everything is quiet in Cimarron. Nobody has been killed for three days."

Hunters, trappers, and gold prospectorsd used the town as a jumping-off point for their excursions into the nearby mountains. At Cimarron's height, 15 saloons, four hotels, a post office, and a newspaper office lined the streets. Jesse James, Thomas "Black Jack" Ketchum, and Billy the Kid were frequent visitors. One of its more notorious residents was Clay Allison, a cattle rancher who was charming when sober and an untamed wild man when not. On one occasion in 1876, Allison, angered by an editorial in the Cimarron *News and Press,* enlisted the help of some friends to knock down the door of the newspaper office, smash the printing press with a sledgehammer, and dump cases of lead type and office materials into the river. The next day, he apologized and paid the paper's owners $200 to replace the equipment.

Having weathered a turbulent past, Cimarron today remains a ranching center, but it has quieted down. A solitary cow calls out for company, a buffalo grazes in a fenced pasture, and crows caw loudly overhead. A walk through the original townsite takes in the town's first well, in which a rusty bucket hangs from an untouched new rope; the iron bars of a stone-walled jail built in the 1870s; and small adobe homes with swings and friendly dogs in the yard. The white-washed National Hotel with its sky-blue wooden trim is now called the Santa Fe Trail Inn. A four-story stone grist mill built by Maxwell in 1864 serves as a museum containing antique surgical equipment, documents of the Maxwell Land Grant, and place settings and silverware from the original St. James Hotel that has been restored across the street. *Old Mill Museum; 505-376-2281.*

As it heads west, US 64 winds through the twisting gorge of the Cimarron Canyon where sandstone faces meet the road and tall ponderosa pines line the gently flowing waters of the Cimarron River. This spectacular passage through the mountains emerges at the northern end of Eagle Nest Lake in the magnificently spacious Moreno Valley.

◆ ST. JAMES HOTEL

Here's how they tell the story:

Brushing the road dust off his clothing, a polite gentleman removes his hat and inquires about lodging at the **St. James Hotel** in Cimarron. After paying for his usual room at the end of the hall on the first floor, the man swiftly signs "R.H. Howard" in the guest book. He cleans up a bit, then saunters into the hotel saloon, which hums with cocktail chatter. A sign on the wall reads: "Gents will please leave their six-guns behind the bar while in town! This will lessen the customary collections for burials." Howard abides. If it's a good night, all patrons will pay heed to the warning and no gunfights will break out in one of the most popular gathering spots in the New Mexico Territory during the late 1800s. Howard isn't looking for any fights. On the contrary, he is hoping no one recognizes him. R. H. Howard is, in fact, Jesse James.

The St. James began as a saloon, built in 1873 by Henri Lambert, a Frenchman who had served as personal chef to President Abraham Lincoln and Gen. Ulysses S. Grant. For the rest of the century, until the Santa Fe Railroad lured travelers to

the growing metropolis of Raton, the St. James played host to some of the most ornery badmen around, the likes of Thomas "Black Jack" Ketchum and Clay Allison, not to mention the 26 unfortunate fellows who left the place feet first on their backs, the victims of gunfights. Many good guys of the Old West, including Pat Garrett and David Crockett (a nephew of the famous frontiersman), slept in the hotel's comfortable beds. It was here that Buffalo Bill Cody and Annie Oakley planned Bill's Wild West Show, Zane Grey wrote *Fighting Caravans,* and Frederic Remington stayed, sketching in the nearby piñon hills by day.

Today, a walk into the restored St. James Hotel is a walk back in time. High-backed Victorian couches and chairs enhance the lobby. Deep-brown bureaus line the walls as they did 100 years ago. Linen covers tabletops in the dining room, which was the original barroom. Despite a decor that evokes subtle elegance, a look upward reveals about 20 bullet holes in the pressed tin ceiling. The white-washed ceiling was installed in 1903 after more than 400 bullets had riddled it. Three layers of oak floor boards were laid in the room above to protect guests, who most likely were thankful, considering the additional punctures.

Red-orange carpeted hallways lead to 15 rooms furnished with antique beds,

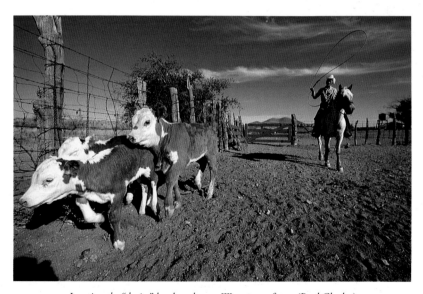

Lassoing the "dogies" has long been a Western art form. (Paul Chesley)

Cowboys Tom Day and Simon Arreola saddle up for a day on the range. (Paul Chesley)

dressers, and couches. A nameplate outside each door identifies the room with one of its famous regulars. A stairway watched over by a stuffed cougar takes guests to second-floor rooms. Near the end of the hall, a potted plant blocks the entrance to Room 18. No one sleeps here except a ghost who refuses to leave. Some claim the ghost is the restless spirit of James Wright, a gambler who was killed when trying to claim the hotel as his winnings in a poker game. They may have succeeded in carrying his body out the front door, but his spirit still stubbornly lingers.

Another ghost said to drift through the second-floor hallway is Mary Lambert, owner Henri's first wife. A rush of strong perfume is a sign she is around. Additional spirits come and go from the historic hotel, adding to the ambiance of its colorful past. *See page 288.*

■ RATON   *map page 249, B/C-2*

After the Treaty of Guadalupe-Hidalgo ended the Mexican War in 1848, a 32-year-old frontiersman began digging and blasting a well-graded wagon road across the rugged 7,622-foot Raton Pass. Once he had completed the road, "Uncle" Dick Wootton stretched a heavy chain across it and began charging travelers a toll: $1.50 for each wagon. (Indians went free.) "Whenever they (Indians) came along, the toll gate went up and any other little thing I could do to hurry them along was done promptly and cheerfully," he told a biographer in 1889.

Eight miles south of the pass, travelers stopped for water and feed at Willow Springs Ranch. In 1880, after the Santa Fe Railroad laid tracks along Wootton's path, a division point was established at the ranch, which was renamed Raton. The rail line's highest point traverses Raton Pass, and its only tunnel burrows through layers of sandstone and shale there. Within a year, the new village boasted 3,000 residents. Attracted by the area's luxuriant rangeland and rich coal deposits, folks called it the "Pittsburgh of the West." Early citizens lived in boxcars parked on sidings next to the railroad. As the years passed, brick and stone buildings were erected to house stores, restaurants, hotels, and a newspaper.

A row of fast-food restaurants and gas stations attests to the town's continued role as a major stopover for travelers crossing Raton Pass into Colorado. Downtown, however, about 70 historic buildings compactly squeezed into a five-block district beckon explorers. A variety of architectural designs is represented, ranging from the Spanish Mission–Revival style of the Santa Fe depot to the terra-cotta-trimmed windows of the Raton Realty Building and Corinthian pilasters of the

Roth Building. Most spectacular is the **Shuler Theatre,** with its European Rococo interior. When completed in 1915, the ornate building housed an opera house, fire station, and city offices. Elaborate woodwork, gold-trimmed box seats, and a high ceiling painted to resemble a cloud-filled sky decorate the 480-seat theater.

Ten miles south of downtown, the National Rifle Association operates the most comprehensive shooting facility in the United States. Located on 33,000 acres dotted with piñon and junipers, the Whittington Center contains 14 shooting ranges and hosts annual national championship events. Public tours are offered daily. *505-445-3615.*

Six miles northeast of town on NM 526, **Sugarite Canyon State Park** sits between two mesas along the banks of Chicorico Creek. Three mountain lakes are stocked with rainbow trout, and hiking trails lead onto Little Horse Mesa and among the ruins of an early twentieth-century coal mining camp. *505-445-5607.*

Forty-five miles to the west of Raton is **Vermejo Park Ranch,** a private hunting and fishing resort that sprawls across nearly 400,000 acres of pine- and aspen-covered slopes. Once part of the Maxwell Land Grant, the ranch was sold in 1926 to Harrison Chandler of the Los Angeles Times Mirror Corporation; it was Chandler who organized the Vermejo Club. The club's $5,000 initiation fee ensured a rather select membership that included Douglas Fairbanks, Herbert Hoover, F. W. Kellogg, Cecil B. DeMille, Andrew Mellon, and Mary Pickford, for whom Mary's Lake and Mary's Cabin are named. The club disbanded during the Depression, and the ranch went through a series of owners until Pennzoil purchased it in 1973. Nine years later, the oil company donated to the U.S. Forest Service 100,000 acres of towering pines, golden aspens, and grassy meadows brimming with wildflowers. Today, Vermejo Park is a working bison ranch, and this outdoor paradise accommodates fishermen in the summer who come in search of rainbow, brown, brook, and cutthroat trout in 21 of the ranch's clear blue lakes. In the fall, hunters scout for deer, elk, antelope, and bear. *505-445-3097.*

◆ CAPULIN VOLCANO   *map page 249, C-3*

Sweeping upward from a yellow-grass prairie, about 30 miles east of Raton is a gently rounded forested mound—the remains of a once-violent volcano responsible for much of the lava rock that caps the terrain in northeastern New Mexico. The last time Capulin Volcano erupted was 10,000 years ago when red-hot lava, cinders, ash, and rock debris shot skyward and fell back upon the crater, piling up to create the 1,000-foot-tall conical mound. After the eruptions ceased, grasses, juniper, mountain mahogany, and gambel oaks gained a foothold on slopes, which today are blanketed with vegetation.

The volcano is preserved as a national monument, and a paved two-mile road spirals to its summit. Two short trails begin at a parking lot: one follows the rim, providing a panorama that takes in the snowcapped peaks of the Sangre de Cristos, distant volcanic hills and mesas, and the sprawling rangeland that reaches to the horizon. The second trail descends into the center of the volcano, partially filled with pumice that has slid down its sides. Lupine, penstemon, golden pea, and bright yellow sunflowers dot the slopes, and lilting songs from grosbeaks, gold finches, and bluebirds fill the air. *On NM 325, three miles north of Capulin and US 64/87; 505-278-2201.*

One group of people who probably witnessed the fiery eruptions of Capulin Mountain was Folsom Man, who hunted bison, camels, musk oxen, and giant sloths throughout northeastern New Mexico 10,000 years ago. Long gone, their presence remained unknown until 1908, when George McJunkin, a cowboy and former slave, discovered some stone spearpoints among large bleached bones scattered in an arroyo near the tiny community of Folsom, a shipping point on the Colorado and Southern Railroad. In 1926, after years of persistent pestering, McJunkin finally convinced a group of skeptical archaeologists to inspect the site. They determined that the bones belonged to an extinct strain of giant bison and the spearpoints were those chipped by Folsom Man, one of the state's earliest inhabitants, preceded by Clovis Man and Sandia Man by about 1,000 years. Some of the spearpoints are displayed at the **Folsom Man Museum,** which is open only in the summer on Main Street in Folsom. *505-278-2122 (summer), 505-278-3616 (winter).*

■ CLAYTON AND VICINITY   *map page 249, D-5*

Two volcanic mounds, the first foothills of the Rocky Mountains, have served as a landmark since the early 1700s when Comanche Indian Chief Orejas de Conejo (Rabbit Ears) roamed the grasslands of northeastern New Mexico. After the chief was killed in battle and buried on the largest peak, the mountains were named after him. In 1717, the knobby hills north of Clayton were the site of one of the bloodiest battles of the Spanish-Comanche War, when a volunteer army of 500

Spaniards surprised the Indians, killing hundreds and taking 700 of them prisoner. In the 1800s, Rabbit Ears Mountain served as a major landmark on the Cimarron Cutoff of the Santa Fe Trail, which passed nearby. Ruts still can be seen, and six famous watering holes along the trade route can be reached within a 50-minute drive from town.

Since 1887, when the Colorado and Southern Railroad established Clayton, rail cars have been hauling fat cattle from the area's abundant grazing land to market. Named for Senator Stephen Dorsey's son, the town is mostly remembered for the celebrated hanging of Thomas "Black Jack" Ketchum in 1901.

Along with his brother, Sam, and two other partners, the Texas-born outlaw with dark, beady eyes and a habit of wearing black, murdered a few men and robbed a few trains, mostly in New Mexico. Abandoned by his gang because of his uncontrollable temper, Ketchum attempted to rob the same train he and his partners had held up three years earlier. Unfortunately for the outlaw, Conductor Frank Harrington was armed with a shotgun, which he fired into Ketchum's heart (or so he thought). The outlaw fell with a shattered arm and escaped, only to be apprehended the next day. He lived, but lost his right arm.

The next spring, after being convicted of train robbery, a crime punishable by hanging, Ketchum was prepared for his fate in Clayton, which was abuzz with newspaper reporters and spectators who bought tickets to the event. Ketchum remained calm as officers slipped the noose around his neck, but Sheriff Salome Garcia was so nervous he missed the rope with his hatchet. The second attempt was a clean cut; the trap door fell open and Ketchum fell through. His body quivered, then collapsed onto the ground. The outlaw was dead, but not by hanging: his head had been jerked off his body! A local doctor adeptly sewed it back on so Ketchum could be properly buried. No mourners accompanied the plain pine coffin to the cemetery east of town, but flowers occasionally adorn the frequently visited grave.

Few trees shade the flat streets of Clayton, which bills itself as the carbon dioxide capital of the world. Bravo Dome, the world's largest and purest carbon dioxide reserve, is embedded in sandstone 50 miles southwest of town. On the surface cows dominate, and thousands can be seen contentedly eating the grama grass. Tawny antelope and quail often share the feast.

Throughout the eastern plains, interrupted only by tiny communities with names like Bueyeros, Amistad, Mosquero, Roy, and Nara Visa, clusters of brown bovines dot the pale-green prairie that stretches to the sky in all directions. A pickup truck whizzes by and a jackrabbit hops past. One of these small towns, **Logan,** is experiencing an influx of retirees attracted to the refreshing and well-stocked waters of nearby Ute Reservoir. In town, a faded mural depicting events in the history of New Mexico graces an outside wall of the Casa Blanca Motel. Scenes on the 25-foot-long wall include Indians and conquistadors. The colorful aging work of art was painted by Manuel Acosta, a former pupil of Peter Hurd, a famous portraitist who was born in Roswell and produced most of his work at his home in the Hondo Valley.

■ TUCUMCARI   *map page 249, G-4*

Situated at the edge of the Llano Estacado, near the base of a flat-topped mountain by the same name, this tree-lined community got its start in 1901 as a construction camp on the Rock Island Railroad. Known briefly as Six-Shooter Siding, the settlement attracted homesteaders who tried for years to coax crops from the sandy soil. In 1908, when the railroad decided to turn the camp into a division point, a more respectable name was needed. The name came from the nearby mountain, which reportedly had served as a Comanche lookout in years past. Most likely, Tucumcari is a derivation from the Comanche *tukamukaru,* which means to lie in wait for someone or something to approach. The more popular meaning derives from a folktale credited to Geronimo in which Tocom, the sweetheart of an Apache Indian maiden named Kari, was slain by Tonapon, a rival. Grieving for her lover, Kari killed Tonapon and then took her own life. This action caused Kari's father, Wautonomah, to stab himself, crying out "Tocom! Kari!" as his last words. But because this was Comanche country, the first derivation is probably correct.

In the mid-1900s, Route 66 sliced through the center of town, with its tourist courts, cafés, and gift shops. Today known as Tucumcari Boulevard, this strip still boasts most of the town's 26 motels (about 2,000 rooms—billboards hundreds of miles away on I-40 claim). The **Tucumcari Historical Museum,** located in a two-story brick building, houses Folsom spearpoints, mammoth teeth, antique bottles, petrified wood, a pre-1900 windmill, a covered wagon, and old saddles. *416 S. Adams; 505-461-4201.*

During summer months, many of the cars and trucks that pass through Tucumcari are heading to **Conchas Lake,** 32 miles northwest of town. The clear, blue-green waters of this desert oasis on the Canadian River provide irrigation waters to area farmers and cool relief to swimmers. Water-skiers dip and lean as they slice through the calm water, and fishermen cast lines from boats and the rocky shoreline.

■ SANTA ROSA   *map page 249, H-2*

In 1865, when he was traveling around the state as an officer in Col. Kit Carson's First Regiment of New Mexico Volunteers, Don Celso Baca noticed a fertile plain wedged between the Pecos River and El Rito Creek. Baca set up a cattle operation that grew into one of the area's largest. He built a *hacienda* and in 1879 constructed an adobe chapel nearby to honor his mother. The tiny chapel was dedicated to Santa Rosa de Lima, the first canonized saint of the New World.

When 4,000 workers converged on the site in 1901 to build tracks that would connect the Rock Island Railroad with the Southern Pacific, the emerging town took its name from the chapel. After rail workers moved on to their next assignment, farming and ranching sustained the community until Route 66 was paved through its center.

Sleepy Santa Rosa continues to offer travelers on I-40 an assortment of cafés and motels. But it also has gained a reputation among scuba divers who travel hundreds of miles to immerse themselves into the **Blue Hole**, a 90-foot-deep artesian well carved into sharp limestone. The bell-shaped pool of crystal-clear deep-blue water is fed by a subterranean river that supplies 3,000 gallons a minute and is inhabited by goldfish, catfish, and snails that cling to the walls. The diving den maintains a constant temperature of 60 degrees F, enabling year-round use. Nine miles north of town, the still waters of Santa Rosa Lake beckon windsurfers, waterskiers, swimmers, and fishermen in search of prize walleye. *Santa Rosa Lake State Park, NM 9; 505-472-3110.*

Possibly, Francisco Vásquez de Coronado camped at Puerto de Luna as he traveled across northeastern New Mexico en route to the imaginary Quivira said to lie in Kansas. Ten miles south of Santa Rosa on NM 91, Puerto de Luna grew up on a bend of the Pecos River where his men probably built a bridge. A wonderful insight into this village and Santa Rosa is found in "Bless Me, Ultima," written by Albuquerque author Rudolfo Anaya, who grew up in the area. This tale of growing up in the 1940s on the *llano* abounds with descriptions of the river, the spring-fed lakes, and the faith by which people live.

BELL RANCH

They've never seen the Northern Lights
They've never seen a hawk on the wing
They've never seen spring hit the Great Divide
They've never heard old camp Cookie sing.

— Night Rider's Lament

Leave out the Northern Lights and the Great Divide and Jerry Jeff Walker could have been a cowboy singing about the Bell Ranch when he recorded this Michael Burton song in 1975.

Bell Ranch Country is the name used by the 16 cowboys who on horseback traverse its 300,000 acres of ankle-high grama-grass pastures. This vast ranch is one of the last places in the West where cowboys round up cattle on horseback and chuck wagons bounce and rattle en route to branding operations in its far-flung corners.

Prime cattle land, the Bell's lush meadows and vermilion rock canyons are watered by shallow streams that wind toward the Canadian River, which cuts through the sprawling ranch. In 1824 when Pablo Montoya obtained a Mexican land grant for the choice pasture land, the vast holding in northeastern New Mexico stretched across 655,000 acres located northwest of present-day Tucumcari and south of Mosquero.

Montoya had been mayor of Santa Fe, but sought a place far from the congested capital. The city was, after all, already 200 years old. Leaving behind his governmental duties in the early 1800s, Montoya became a *comanchero* who traded with Comanches throughout the northeastern plains. As he roamed the region, Montoya studied the land, searching for good grass and ample water, a place where he and his seven children could spread out and establish a ranch.

While the Bell changed hands a few times during the next 123 years, it remained intact and produced prized cattle year after year. The name comes from the bell-shaped mountain on the ranch, which also is reflected in the brand. Accompanying the rounded peak are two nearby buttes named Ding and Dong. In 1947, the ranch was divided into six sections and sold. The largest parcel was 130,000 acres and included the brand and historic headquarters with an orchard, dairy, blacksmith shop, post office, and adobe structures built by Montoya. The new owner, Harriet Ellwood Keeney, continued raising Herefords until she sold the ranch in 1970 to

William Lane. Not only did Lane promise to "keep the ranch running just like it has been in the past, a real working ranch for the production of fine cattle," but the Illinois businessman acquired 176,000 more acres from the original land grant. Lane was killed in a 1978 automobile accident, but his family continues his vision.

Cowboys still rein horses atop mesas blanketed with junipers, piñons, and thorny mesquite bushes and through canyons bursting with summer sunflowers so thick and tall the riders could hide in them. Here chaps and dusters are worn for more than their rugged good looks, and sweat stains along hat brims are hard earned.

The orchard and dairy are gone, but the original ranch house, called the White House, stands sturdy, concealed by tall, broad-leafed cottonwoods. Designated in 1970 as both National and State Historic sites, ranch headquarters are located 10 miles north of the village of Conchas. *505-868-2966.*

Cowboys take a chow break on the range of the Ladder Ranch,
circa 1940. (Museum of New Mexico)

PUEBLO POTTERY OF NEW MEXICO

PUEBLO INDIANS HAVE BEEN MAKING POTTERY for utilitarian use and for sale or barter for 1,400 years. The practice of making them for barter declined toward the middle of the 19th century, when the opening of the Santa Fe Trail flooded the region with imported goods. But with the coming of the railroad in the 1880s, and the arrival of appreciative visitors, Pueblo potters realized the commercial potential of their pottery, and entered a new period of improvement and exploration. These pots from Zuni and Laguna Pueblos were made during this period.

ZUNI POLYCHROME, 1890

Zuni Pueblo, located south of Gallup, New Mexico, near the Arizona border, was visited by conquistador Francisco de Coronado in 1540.

Laguna Pueblo is found in central New Mexico between Albuquerque and Grants and has a long pottery tradition.

LAGUNA POLYCHROME, 1910

ZUNI POLYCHROME FETISH, 1920

Ácoma pottery has long been valued by collectors. Hand-drawn, intricate, geometric designs, as the one below by S. Chino, are typical. Clays used by the different pueblos come from nearby sources, and Ácoma clay is noted for being especially white.

Ácoma Pueblo resides high on a mesa west of Albuquerque.

ÁCOMA POLYCHROME POT

Santa Clara Pueblo has produced many famous pottery families, among them the Gutierrez, Tafoya, and Naranjo. This pot by Anita Suazo is typical of Santa Clara carved pottery.

Santa Clara Pueblo is located on the road between Santa Fe and Taos.

ÁCOMA POT IN BLACK AND WHITE

SANTA CLARA POT
WITH BEAR CLAW DESIGN

SAN ILDEFONSO JAR, 1910

The polychrome pot above was typical of San Ildefonso Pueblo pottery until María and Julian Martínez began to make their famous black-on-black pottery designs. Their work is now world-famous, and it often commands more than $5,000 per piece. Many members of the extended Martínez family have also become exceedingly famous, and their work is invariably bought by collectors.

SAN ILDEFONSO POT,
MARIA MARTINEZ

The Jémez Pueblo pot to the left is typical of modern, sophisticated work found in galleries in Santa Fe.

Jémez Pueblo is located in the Jémez Mountains west of Santa Fe.

JÉMEZ POLYCHROME POT

The beautifully crafted, three-inch, black-on-red pot to the right was made by C. G. Loretto of Jémez Pueblo.

JÉMEZ PUEBLO POT

Figurines have long been a part of Cochiti Pueblo ceramics. Storyteller dolls, first made famous by Helen Cordero, are favorites. The male storyteller doll to the left was fashioned by Ada Suina, who puts coat after coat of slip on her figurines to achieve subtlety and gloss.

COCHITI PUEBLO
STORYTELLER DOLL

The figurine in the shape of a turtle at right was made by Helen Cordero. Cochiti Pueblo is located by Cochiti Lake, southwest of Santa Fe.

COCHITI TURTLE
FIGURINE

PRACTICAL INFORMATION

Listings

■ INFORMATION SOURCES

Bureau of Indian Affairs. 615 First St. NW, Albuquerque; 505-766-3754.

Bureau of Land Management, New Mexico. 505-474-9157.

Highway hotline. 800-432-4269 for road closures and conditions.

National Forest Service, Southwest Region. 517 Gold St. SW, Albuquerque; 505-842-3292.

New Mexico Art League. 3407 Juan Tabo NE, Albuquerque; 505-293-5034.

New Mexico Game & Fish Department. 505-827-7911 or 800-862-9310.

State Parks & Recreation. 505-827-7173 or 888-667-2757. Both offices: 408 Galisteo, Santa Fe.

New Mexico/Santa Fe Visitor Information. 491 Old Santa Fe Trail, Santa Fe; 800-733-6396 or 505-827-7400.

■ CLIMATE

CITY/REGION	ELEVATION	AVERAGE TEMPERATURE				TEMPERATURE EXTREMES		AVERAGE ANNUAL	
		JULY		*JANUARY*					
	(in feet)	*(Fahrenheit)*				*(Fahrenheit)*		*(in inches)*	
		MAX.	MIN.	MAX.	MIN.	HIGH	LOW	RAIN	SNOW
Albuquerque	5,311	92	65	47	24	107	-17	7.8	11
Carlsbad	3,120	96	68	59	31	115	- 7	12.4	5
Chaco Canyon	6,175	91	55	43	12	102	-38	8.5	19
Cimarron	6,540	83	55	47	19	99	-35	15.3	33
Santa Fe	7,200	85	56	42	18	99	-18	13.8	29

Sunshine spreads across New Mexico at least 75 percent of the year, which makes the state a great place to visit anytime. Because of altitudes that range from 3,000 feet to 13,000 feet, temperatures vary widely: from 98 degrees F in Deming to 70 degrees F in Chama in the summer, and 65 degrees F in Roswell, compared to 32 degrees F in Taos during the winter. Consistent dry air prevents either extreme from being too unpleasant.

Precipitation also can vary—it's not unusual for the northern mountains to get 300 inches of snow during the winter, compared to one inch annually in the southern desert. Rain usually comes in the form of afternoon thunderstorms, which unleash torrents and can cause dangerous flash floods. From mid-June through mid-September, campers should not pitch tents along streambeds and should stay on high ground until the storms have passed.

The combination of high altitude and intense sun requires use of sunscreen every day. Dressing in layers is also recommended any time of the year, and no matter where you are, casual wear is acceptable, except for dinner at a few Santa Fe resorts. *National Weather Service. 505-243-0702.*

■ TRANSPORTATION

Albuquerque International Sunport provides almost the only commercial airline access to New Mexico, which is served by 9 major carriers. Two commuter airlines serve the state: Mesa Airlines, 800-637-2247, flies from Albuquerque to the state's other cities and Rio Grande Air 505-764-3041 flies from Albuquerque to Los Alamos and Taos.

Despite the major role the railroad played in New Mexico's settlement, only two routes now pass through the state. **Amtrak trains** run once daily, east-west and west-east, between Raton and Gallup, passing through Las Vegas, Lamy (17 miles south of Santa Fe), and Albuquerque. Another route travels from El Paso through Deming and Lordsburg before exiting the state. *Amtrak; 800-872-7245.*

The **Greyhound/Trailways** bus line serves the state, connecting towns from Hobbs to Farmington. For further information, call 800-231-2222. In addition, a number of shuttle services carry people between Santa Fe and the Albuquerque International Sunport.

The best way to see New Mexico is by car, which can be rented at most of the state's small airports, as well as in Albuquerque.

FOOD & LODGING

■ FOOD & LODGING

Room Rates
per room, per night, double occupancy:
$ = under $30 $$ = $30 - 80 $$$ = over $80

Restaurant Prices
per person, excluding tax, tip, and drinks:
$ = less than $8 $$ = $8 - 16 $$$ = more than $16

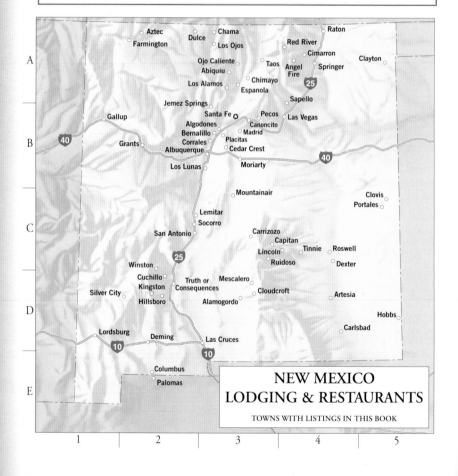

NEW MEXICO
LODGING & RESTAURANTS
TOWNS WITH LISTINGS IN THIS BOOK

Abiquiu

map page 280, A-3

⌕ **The Abiquiu Inn.** US 84;
505-685-4378 **$$**
Multi-hued pastel cliffs meet the sky and
the Chama River flows nearby this com-
fortable roadside lodging.

⌕ **Casa del Rio.** (B&B) US 84, #19946
Abiquiu 87510; 505-753-2035 or 800-
920-1495 **$$$**
An elegant guesthouse with a kiva fireplace.
On the Chama River in Georgia O'Keeffe
country

⌕ **Las Parras de Abiquiu.** (B&B) US 84,
Gate# 21341, Abiquiu 87510;
505-685-4200 or 800-817-5955 **$$$**
A luxury inn surrounded by vineyards,
alongside the Chama River. An organic
garden contributes to the morning menu.

✕ **Cafe Abiquiu at the Abiquiu Inn**.
505- 685-4378 **$$**
Owned by a nearby mosque, this comfort-
able roadside restaurant features Middle
Eastern and Mediterranean fare.

Alamogordo

map page 280, D-3

✕ **Angelina's.** 415 S. White Sands; 505-
434-1166 **$$**
The whole family is welcome to this casual
Italian restaurant that specializes in pizzas
and pasta. Salad bar is always fresh.

Albuquerque

map page 280, B-3

⌕ **Adobe & Roses.** (B&B) 1011 Ortega
NW; 505-898-0654 **$$-$$$**
Stay among lily ponds and fruit trees in bu-
colic North Valley compound.

ADOBE & ROSES

⌕ **Casas de Suenos.** 310 Rio Grande SW;
505-247-4560 or 800-242-8987 **$$$**
Flower gardens separate private casitas in
this rambling bed-and-breakfast compound
a block from Old Town. The centerpiece is
a snail-shaped main building designed by
Bart Prince, a well-known Albuquerque
architect.

⌕ **Casita Chamisa.** 850 Chamisal NW;
505-897-4644 **$$$**
This bed-and-breakfast is housed in a 150-
year-old farmhouse on cottonwood-shaded
acreage in North Valley. Site of an archaeo-
logical dig.

FOOD & LODGING

Albuquerque
continued

🛏 **El Vado Motel.** 2500 Central SW;
505-243-4594 $

Route 66 devotees will enjoy a stay in this vintage tourist court dating from the national highway's heyday. Neon sign out front. Only five blocks from Old Town.

🛏 **Hyatt Regency Hotel.** 330 Tijeras NW;
505-842-1234 or 800-233-1234 $$$

Albuquerque's newest and most luxurious downtown hotel. Swim in rooftop pool.

🛏 **La Posada de Albuquerque.**
125 Second NW; 505-242-9090 or
800-777-5732 $$$

Uniquely restored 50-year-old downtown hotel designed by New Mexico native son Conrad Hilton.

LA POSADA DE ALBUQUERQUE

🛏 **Sarabande.** (B&B) 5637 Rio Grande
NW; 505-345-4923 or 888-506-4923
$$$

Flower-filled courtyards accent this territorial-style home in pastoral North Valley. Swim in heated lap pool or explore the valley's irrigation ditches via mountain bike.

✕ **Acapulco Tacos & Burritos.** 840 San
Mateo SE; 505-268-9865 $

Painted in the bright colors of Mexico, this taco stand offers a wide variety of burritos. Either take it to go or eat out front on picnic tables.

✕ **Bangkok Cafe.** 5901 Central NE;
505-255-5036 $$

Old Route 66 storefront offers great soups and Thai curry dishes.

✕ **Barelas Coffee House.** 1502 Fourth SW;
505-843-7577 $

Bustling neighborhood landmark where politicians brainstorm and everyone else enjoys the green chile.

✕ **Double Rainbow Bakery Cafe.**
3416 Central NW; 505-255-6633;
4501 Juan Tabo NE, 505- 275-8311 $

Bustlng coffeehouses where you'll find healthy sandwiches and salads, too.

✕ **Duran Central Pharmacy.** 1815 Central
NW; 505-247-4141 $

A local favorite where you will find the most flavorful chile in town, tortillas made to order, and friendly waitresses.

The desert and plains of the West seem to provide bumper crops of abandoned automobiles.
(Paul Chesley)

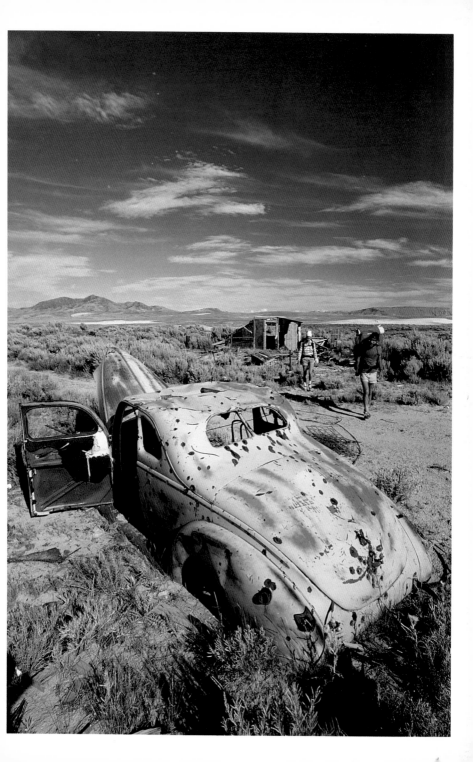

Albuquerque
continued

✕ **El Patio.** 142 Harvard SE;
505-268-4245 $
Dine inside or under a mist on the outdoor patio. Classical guitarist will accompany your evening meal. Great green chile chicken enchilada plate and sopaipillas.

✕ **Fajitaville.** 6313 Fourth NW;
505-341-9683 $
Fajitas (and accompanying salsas) have never taken so many forms, from grilled fish to heaping plates of vegetarian delights.

✕ **Frontier Restaurant.** 2400 Central SE;
505-266-0550 $
A sprawling institution where you'll find good, cheap food and a place where students and professionals gather to play chess, discuss Descartes, or plan the day's bike ride.

✕ **Gold Street Caffe.** 218 Gold SW;
505-765-1633 $
This stylish downtown cafe features creative breakfast and lunch fare, from green chile biscuits stuffed with scrambled eggs, smoked ham and marscapone cheese to a wide variety of exotic salads.

✕ **Gyros Mediterranean.** 106-A Cornell SE; 505-255-4401 $
Ordering is done at the cash register at this university-area restaurant where the gyros sandwiches, soups and vegetarian fare are wonderful.

✕ **Huong Thao.** 1016 Juan Tabo NE; 505-292-8222 $
Wonderfully creative Vietnamese cuisine.

✕ **Il Vicino.** *Two locations, both* $
3403 Central NE; 505-266-7855
11255 Montgomery NE; 505-271-0882
This trendy Nob Hill cafe serves pizza baked in a wood-fired oven. Delicious gourmet toppings; wonderful salads and calzones. The beer is brewed onsite.

✕ **India Kitchen.** 6910 Montgomery NE;
505-884-23 $$
Lengthy menu leaves out little in this cozy dining room. Many vegetarian offerings and delicious desserts complement traditional meat curries. Reservations are recommended on weekends.

✕ **Kanome.** 3128 Central SE; 505-265-7773 $-$$
You'll find Asian food with a twist at one of the city's most stylish eateries. There is nothing traditionally Asian here, except for chopsticks.

✕ **M&J Sanitary Tortilla Factory.**
403 Second SW; 505-242-4890 $
A local favorite where lawyers, students and artists mingle at lunchtime over plates of enchiladas and burritos.

✕ **Minato of Japan.** 10721 Montgomery NE; 505-293-2929 $$$
Light and airy atmosphere. Minato features excellent sushi bar and wonderful tempuras—save room for the ginger ice cream. Tatami rooms available.

✕ **New Chinatown.** 5001 Central NE; 505-265-8859 **$$**

Look for the red and green pagoda where you'll find spicy Szechuan dishes along with other traditional entrees.

✕ **Paisano's Italian Restaurant.**
1935 Eubank NE; 505-298-7541 **$$**
You'll think you've found your Italian aunt's home when you walk into this informal traditional Italian eatery. You can even order chicken tettrazini.

✕ **Sadie's Dining Room.** 6230 Fourth NW; 505-345-5339 **$**

Strong margaritas, hot and well-seasoned chile, and hefty portions combine to make this one of Albuquerque's most popular Mexican restaurants.

✕ **Salsa Fresca Burritos.** 120 Harvard SE; 505- 255-2013 **$**

This university-area cafe offers hungry-student-style burritos stuffed with beans, rice, and your choice of a variety of meats and vegetables—all accompanied by the eponymous fresh salsa.

✕ **Scalo Northern Italian Grill.** 3500 Central NE; 505-255-8781 **$$-$$$**

One of Albuquerque's most popular restaurants, this trendy spot offers exotically spiced homemade pasta dishes, along with creative meat choices and superb daily specials. Reservations are recommended.

✕ **66 Diner.** 1405 Central NE; 505-247-1421 **$**

Tetley Tea commercials are filmed here and waitresses sometimes wear saddle shoes. Art gallery of Route 66 memorabilia.

✕ **Tapas.** 3000 San Pedro NE, Suite D; 505-883-3850 **$$**

You might think you are in Spain when you walk into this airy bistro tucked into a small neighborhood shopping center. In addition to creative tapas, ranging from portobello mushrooms to tender quail, an extensive, always changing, wine list tempts the taste buds.

Albuquerque Environs
map page 280, B-3

🛏 **Apache Canyon Ranch.** (B&B) Canoncito; 505-836-7220 **$$$**

Surrounded by Indian reservations, this isolated Pueblo-style inn about 30 minutes west of Albuquerque offers 360-degree views and a putting green.

🛏 **Hacienda de Placitas.** (B&B) 491 NM 165, Placitas; 505-867-0082 **$$$**

A windmill that once serviced the Santa Fe Railroad marks the spot for this romantic inn. Gourmet breakfasts and unparalleled views of the Jemez Mountains.

🛏 **Hacienda Vargas.** (B&B) NM 1431 El Camino Real, Algodones; 505-867-9115 **$$-$$$**;

Once a stagecoach stop on the Camino Real, this horseshoe-shaped adobe inn offers rural quiet. Each room has a kiva fireplace and french doors. Relax under a 200-year-old cottonwood tree in the courtyard and visit the original chapel *(see photo on next page)*.

FOOD & LODGING

Albuquerque Environs
continued

HACIENDA VARGAS

⌂ **The Sandhill Crane.** (B&B) 389 Camino Hermosa, Corrales; 505-898-2445 or 800-375-2445 $$$

Wisteria, honeysuckle and trumpet vine drape the walls of this renovated adobe hacienda that offers views of the Sandia Mountains.

✕ **Cafe de las Placitas.** 664 NM 165; Placitas; 505-867-1610 $$$

The gourmet menu changes regularly at this refined adobe restaurant in the foothills of the Sandia Mountains.

✕ **Prairie Star.** 1000 N. Jemez Dam Rd.; Bernalillo; 505-867-3327 $$$

Enjoy a sunset view of the Sandia Mountains at this historic hacienda where Southwestern cooking takes on a contemporary flair.

✕ **The Range Café and Bakery.** 925 Camino Del Pueblo; Bernalillo; 505-867-1700 $-$$

Home-cooking has never been this good.

The biscuits and gravy are tops, as are the daily specials with a southwestern flair. Save room for dessert.

✕ **Teofilo's Restaurant.** 144 Main St., Los Lunas; 505-865-5511 $

Light and airy atmosphere where you'll find tasty traditional New Mexican fare.

Angel Fire
map page 280, A-4

⌂ **Angel Fire Resort Hotel.** 800-633-7463 $$

Modest lodging on the road to the ski area with views of the vast Moreno Valley.

✕ **Rocky Mountain BBQ and Grill.** NM 434, in the Pinewood Plaza; 505-377-2763 $

Tender to the bone is the hickory-smoked fare at this no-frills diner where you can eat in or take out.

Artesia
map page 280, D-4

⌂ **Heritage Inn.** 209 W. Main; 800-594-7392 $$

This Victorian inn, formerly an apartment building, sits above a Radio Shack. Such veneer doesn't do it justice. Continental breakfast is included in the rates.

✕ **La Fonda.** 210 W. Main; 505-746-9377 $

One of the state's finest New Mexican restaurants serves large helpings of enchiladas, chimichangas, and burritos.

Aztec
map page 280, A-2

☎ **Enchantment Lodge.** 1800 W. Aztec;
505-334-6143 **$$**
Convenient to Navajo Lake and Aztec
Ruins National Monument.

✗ **Rio Grande Coffee Company.**
122 S. Main; 505-334-0109 **$**
Try a piece of quiche with a cup of home-
made soup at this cozy breakfast-lunch
spot, which also offers fine coffees.

Carrizozo
map page 280, C-3

✗ **Outpost Bar and Grill.** 415 Central;
505-648-9994 **$**
Dine among mounted deer heads and
stuffed lizards in a local hangout known far
and wide for its delicious green chile
cheeseburger. There's even a laundry here
so you can wash your clothes while you eat.

Carlsbad
map page 280, D-5

☎ **Stevens Best Western Inn.**
1829 S. Canal; 505-887-2851 or
800-730-2851 **$$**
Outdoor pool and playground make this
centrally located lodging a good choice for
families.

✗ **The Flume Room in the Motel Stevens.**
1829 S. Canal; 505-887-2851 **$$**
Prime Rib, steaks, seafood and a plentiful
salad bar.

✗ **Lucy's.** 701 S. Canal; 505-887-7714
$-$$
Try a Gold Margarita with a plate of fajitas,
enchiladas, or chimichangas.

Chama
map page 280, A-3

☎ **Corkin's Lodge.** NM 512 on the Brazos
River; 800-548-7688 or 505-588-7261
$$$
Log-cabin luxury at this full-service wilder-
ness lodge at the foot of the Brazos Cliffs,
which rise dramatically behind.

☎ **The Lightheart Inn.** (B&B) 505-756-
2908 **$$$**
The owner is a masseuse and luxury rooms
include private jacuzzis.

☎ **The Lodge at Chama.** 16253 NM 84;
505-756-2133 **$$$**
Luxury at its finest in this elegantly rustic
hunting lodge that overlooks the Chama
Valley.

✗ **High Country Restaurant.**
NM 17 North; 505-756-2384 **$$**
Enjoy a steak sandwich, a Mexican plate or
fresh trout in this comfortably rustic dining
room.

✗ **Viva Vera's.** NM 17; 505-756-2557 **$**
Vera has been feeding the folks here since
1963 and she's still their favorite cook.
You'll long remember her hearty New Mexican dishes and sopaipillas.

Chimayó
map page 280, A-3

⏣ **Hacienda Rancho de Chimayó.** (B&B) 505-351-2222 $$-$$$
Historically restored adobe family home of Epifanio and Adelaida Jaramillo looks out onto enclosed courtyard.

✕ **Rancho de Chimayó.** 505-351-4444 $$
Tasty traditional chile dishes served in this 100-year-old adobe home or outside on a shaded terraced patio. Locally grown red chile is a favorite, as are the margaritas.

Cimarron
map page 280, A-4

⏣ **Casa de Gavilan.** (B&B) S. NM 21; 505-376-2246 $$-$$$
Turn-of-the-century adobe offers views of rolling hills and the prairie beyond.

⏣ **St. James Hotel.** NM 21, 16th St. and Collison; 505-376-2664 $$
Bed down in the room where Annie Oakley slept or Black Jack Ketchum, but stay away from the room, now blocked off, where the resident ghost lives.

ST. JAMES HOTEL

Clayton
map page 280, A-5

⏣ **Kokopelli Lodge.** 702 South First; 505-374-2589 $$
The value of this no-frills motel is its location, away from the town's feedlots. Continental breakfast included.

✕ **Eklund Dining Room.** 15 Main; 505-374-2551 $$
A stone fireplace anchors this late 19th-century hotel dining room where you can find a good steak and one of the few photos of the beheaded body of Thomas "Black Jack" Ketchum after his hanging.

Cloudcroft
map page 280, D-3

⏣ **The Lodge.** 1 Corona Place; 505-682-2566 $$-$$$
Step back into time when you enter this luxurious 19th century hotel filled with turn-of-the-19th-century furniture—but the amenities and conveniences are completely up to date. Be sure to check out the nighttime stars from the copper-domed observatory.

✕ **Rebecca's at the Lodge.** 1 Corona Place; 505-682-2566 $$-$$$
Never mind if you see a red-headed ghost floating above your head: the spirit Rebecca is probably only coveting that salmon dish you're preparing to cut into. New American cuisine among the pines.

Clovis
map page 280, C-5

✕ **Juanito's.** 1608 Mabry;. 505-762-7822 $

A local favorite for Mexican food that combines the best of New Mexico's chile with good Texas beef.

✕ **The Orient.** 116 E. 21st; 505-762-6238 $$

Cashew chicken and other similar Chinese standards.

✕ **Poor Boy's Steakhouse.** 2115 N. Prince; 505-763-5222 $$

The stockyards aren't far away, so you know where the steaks come from.

Columbus
map page 280, E-2

⌂ **Martha's Bed and Breakfast.** Main and Lima; 505-531-2467 $$

In a small town where historic buildings prevail, this new adobe inn offers an option to Pancho Villa State Park. If you're lucky, your visit will coincide with a performance of the Tumbleweed Theater, a cadre of local actors who occasionally put on musical melodramas.

✕ **Pancho Villa Restaurant.** across the border in Palomas, Mexico $

This pink building houses the best restaurant in these parts. You'll be treated to bottled water and the finest chile rellenos this side of the border. U.S. currency readily accepted.

Deming
map page 280, D-2

⌂ **Grand Motor Inn.** 1721 E. Spruce; 505-546-2631 $$

One of this town's few full-service motels, with restaurant, lounge, heated outdoor pool. You can even bring your pets.

⌂ **Wagon Wheel Motel.** 1109 W. Pine; 505-546-2681 $

Cool off in an outdoor heated pool at this small roadside lodging.

Dexter
map page 280, C-4

✕ **Ingrid's Lake Van Cafe.** 505-734-6080 $

Enjoy a plate of enchiladas that rivals anything served in northern New Mexico at this local-friendly cafe on the shores of miniscule, yet scenic, Lake Van.

✕ **Little Valley Club.** 107 S. Lincoln; 505-734-9927; $$

This is a bar where area farmers and dairymen of all ages come to eat barbecue on Saturdays and mountainous green chile cheeseburgers the rest of the week. If you listen closely, you might hear them gush about Mike Smith, a well-known jockey who grew up here.

Dulce
map page 280, A-2/3

☎ Jicarilla Inn. US 64; 505-759-3663 $$
Literally, the only lodging in town, this comfortable motel is owned by the Jicarilla Apaches and it is here they entertain all visiting dignitaries.

Espanola
map page 280, A-3

☎ Inn at the Delta. (B&B) 304 Paseo de Onate; 505-753-9466 $$$
Original artwork and southwestern furnishings adorn each over-sized room.

☎ Rancho de San Juan. US 285; 505-753-6818 or 800-726-7121 $$$
Explore the Ojo Caliente River Valley while staying at this elegant country inn.

RANCHO DE SAN JUAN

✕ Anthony's at the Delta. 304 Paseo de Onate; 505-753-4511 $$$
Once a home, this sprawling mansion with tall ceilings is known for its steaks and fresh seafood.

✕ El Paragua. 603 Santa Cruz Rd.; 505-753-6749 $$
Mexican food mixes with mesquite-grilled steaks and seafood in this elegant setting.

✕ Joann's Ranch-O-Casados. 418 N. Riverside Dr.; 505-753-2837 $
The family farm supplies much of the food served in this brightly decorated eatery on the town's main drag. As a result, everything is as fresh and tasty as it can be.

Farmington
map page 280, A-2

☎ Anasazi Inn. 903 W. Main; 505-325-4564 $$
Pastels of the desert adorn this quiet roadside motel on the western edge of town.

☎ Best Western Inn and Suites. 700 Scott; 505-327-5221 or 800-528-1234 $$
Centrally located, near restaurants and downtown shopping district.

☎ Holiday Inn. 600 E. Broadway; 505-327-9811 or 800-HOLIDAY $$
Fitness center, outdoor heated pool and sports lounge in comfortable motel.

Gallup
map page 280, B-1

☎ El Rancho Hotel. 1000 E. US 66; 505-863-9311 or 800-543-6351 $$
Stay in rooms once occupied by Hollywood stars who frequented the area when filming period Westerns. Their photos line the walls of lobby balcony. This centrally

located historic hotel retains an ambiance of yesteryear.

✗ **Dominic's.** 303 W. Coal; 505-722-0117 $$
Italian and Southwestern fare are featured in this cozy place adorned with red checkered tablecloths. Manicotti, burritos, pizza or the daily special, take your pick.

✗ **Earl's Restaurant.** 1400 E. US 66; 505-863-4201 $
A Gallup institution, this huge restaurant features American food and great people watching. Local Navajos wander about selling jewelry.

✗ **El Rancho Hotel.** 1000 E. US 66; 505-863-9311 $$
Home-cooking in a vintage dining room atmosphere, brings back memories of the hotel's heydey. Broad menu offers choices from New Mexican fare to steaks.

✗ **Genaro's.** 600 W. Hill, 505-863-6761 $$
Stuffed sopaipillas and posole are the specialties of this vinyl-boothed cafe.

Grants
map page 280, B-2

☗ **Holiday Grants.** I-40 East Interchange; 505-287-4426 $$
Quiet roadside motel east of town.

✗ **La Ventana.** 110 1/2 Geis; 505-287-9393; $$
This steakhouse is named after a giant rock arch south of town.

Hillsboro
map page 280, D-2

☗ **Enchanted Villa.** Hwy 152; 505-895-5686 $$
This adobe home was built in 1941 for Sir Vincent Sassoon, an English nobleman. Today the bed-and-breakfast is convenient to browsing the village's shops and historic landmarks.

Hobbs
map page 280, D-5

✗ **Cattle Baron.** 1930 N. Grimes; 505-393-2800 $$
Enjoy a pasta dish or extensive salad bar in this comfortably casual restaurant.

✗ **Wallace's Barbecue.** 1403 E. Broadway; 505-393-9025 $
The onion rings and barbecue in any fashion are tops at this local favorite.

Jemez Springs
map page 280, B-3

✗ **Laughing Lizard Café.** NM 4; 505-829-3108 $
Whether it's a spinach burrito with black beans, mushrooms, and cheese, or a hot shrimp pizza, there's not a bad choice at this informal restaurant.

✗ **Los Ojos Restaurant.** NM 4; 505-829-3547 $
Wood-floored tavern with big stone fireplace where you can get great green-chile cheeseburgers.

✗ San Diego Canyon Bakery. 505-829-
3956 $
Fresh baked goods served along with breakfasts and hot lunches. Menu changes often.

Kingston
map page 280, D-2

☗ Black Range Lodge. 119 Main St.;
505-895-5652 $$
At the gateway to Gila National Forest, this
mountain getaway and bed-and-breakfast
evokes Kingston's wild and wooly past with
stone walls, wood beams, and a wood-
burning stove in the kitchen. Well-behaved
pets are welcome.

Las Cruces
map page 280, D-3

☗ Las Cruces Hilton. 705 Telshor;
505-522-4300 or 800-HILTON $$
Walk to area's largest mall and enjoy views
of the city from this bluff-side motel.

☗ Meson de Mesilla. 1803 Avenida de
Mesilla, Mesilla; 505-525-2380 or
800-732-6025 $$-$$$
Southwestern colors adorn this quiet adobe
inn/bed-and-breakfast on the edge of
Mesilla. Lovely views of the Organ Mountains.

✗ Brown Bag Deli. 300 El Molino; 505-
524-2857 $
You'll find counter service at this fast-paced
eatery across the street from the university
and wonderful deli sandwiches.

✗ Dick's Cafe. 2305 S. Valley Dr.; 505-
524-1360 $
The waitresses know their business at this
local hangout where you'll find the coffee
hot and strong and the New Mexican food
hot as well.

✗ Double Eagle. 308 Calle de Guadelupe,
Mesilla Plaza; 505-523-6700 $$-$$$
Just stay away from the resident ghosts in
this elegant historic steakhouse where you
can enjoy a juicy steak or seafood.

✗ The Hacienda. 2605 Espina; 505-522-
6380 $$
A former home near the university has
been transformed into a comfortable res-
taurant with New Mexican and American
specialities.

✗ Millennium Restaurant. 1120 Com-
merce, Suite C; 505-532-9505 $$-$$$
Connie Allgood, one of Albuquerque's fa-
vorite chefs, took over the kitchen in this
gourmet restaurant at the beginning of
2000. Expect the unexpected, such as mo-
lasses-marinated filet mignon.

✗ Nellie's Café. 1226 W. Hadley; 505-
524-9982 $
A local favorite, what this small diner lacks
in atmosphere more than makes up for in
its traditional New Mexico offerings.

✗ La Posta. Mesilla. 2410 Calle de San Al-
bino; 505-524-3524 $$
You'll think you've walked into a restaurant
in Mexico with parrots in cages talking to
you and fountains gurgling instead of a refurbished stagecoach station. Excellent
New Mexican food.

Some good old boys in a good old bar in Silver City. (Paul Chesney)

✕ **Meson de Mesilla.**
1803 Avenida de Mesilla; 505-525-9212 $$$

Continental cuisine with an emphasis on seafood is featured in this romantic dining room.

✕ **Tatsu.** 930 El Paseo; 505-526-7144 $$
This is Las Cruces' only Japanese restaurant and it brims with atmosphere and delectable offerings such as sushi and sashimi.

✕ **Way Out West.** 1720 Avenida de Mesilla; 505-541-1969 $$
Tapas and nouveau Southwestern cuisine such as prickly pear salad can be found in this rustic setting, where microbrews from its own brewery are available.

Las Vegas
map page 280, D-4

⌂ **El Camino Motel.** 1152 Grand; 505-425-5994 $$
Recently remodeled in southwestern designs, this convenient motel is located in central business district.

⌂ **Inn on the Santa Fe Trail.** 1133 Grand; 505-425-6791 or 888-448-3458 $$
Pueblo style country inn furnished in handcrafted folk art; Complimentary "Sunrise coffee buffet."

⌂ **Pendaries Lodge.** 26 miles northwest of town; 505-425-6076 $$$
Isolated golf and fishing resort carved from the tall pines of the Santa Fe National Forest.

⌂ **Plaza Hotel.** 230 Old Town Plaza; 505-425-3591 or 800-328-1882 $$-$$$
The landmark 1882 Italianate hotel was tastefully restored to its original splendor with tasteful traces of modernity.

PLAZA HOTEL

✕ **El Rialto.** 141 Bridge; 505-454-0037 $$
Locals stand in line to feed their chile addiction. Walk to Old Town Plaza.

✕ **Landmark Grill.** inside the Plaza Hotel; 505-425-3591 $$
Choose from creatively prepared chicken and beef dishes and New Mexican specialties inside this historic dining room.

✕ **Spic 'n' Span Bakery and Cafe.** 715 Douglas; 505-426-1921 $
Choose from wonderful homemade sticky buns or bursting breakfast burritos. You can even buy their thick homemade tortillas by the dozen.

Lemitar
map page 280, C-2/3

✕ **Coyote Moon Cafe.** W. Frontage Rd.;
505-835-2536; $
Try a vegetarian burrito with calabasitas
(squash and corn) or a frito pie at this roadside eatery north of Socorro specializing in
home cooking.

Lincoln
map page 280, C-4

⌂ **Casa de Patron.** US 80; 505-653-4676
or 800-524-5202 $$$
Billy the Kid once napped in this 19th cen-
tury home of Juan Patron, who ran a store.
These days, the home is a bed-and-break-
fast where you might be entertained by
hostess Cleis Jordan who plays the wooden
organ there; she also makes the soap you'll
find in the bathroom.

⌂ **Wortley Hotel.** 505-653-4300 $
Rebuilt 19th century hotel where Deputy
Bob Olinger ate his last meal before being
gunned down by Billy the Kid. Brass beds
and simple adornments. Enjoy evening's
arrival in a rocking chair on the hotel's
front porch.

✕ **Wortley Hotel.** 505-653-4300 $$
You can enjoy Belgium waffles in the
morning and chicken-fried steak in the
evening, all the while imagining what it
would have been like to sup here in its heyday 100 years ago. Fresh fruit cobbler is
baked daily.

Lordsburg
map page 280, D-1

⌂ **American Inn.** 944 E. Motel Dr.;
505-542-3591 $$
Last chance to stay in New Mexico before
entering Arizona.

Los Alamos
map page 280, A-3

⌂ **Hilltop House Hotel.** 400 Trinity;
800-462-0936 or 505-662-2441 $$
Stunning views of the Jemez Mountains in
centrally located wood lodging; indoor
pool.

⌂ **Orange Street Inn.** 3496 Orange St;
505-662-2651 or 800-662-3180 $$
View the natural world from this bed-and-
breakfast situated in a forested canyon.

✕ **De Colores.** 820 Trinity Dr.;
505-662-6285 $-$$
Enjoy fare ranging from New Mexican
favorites to mesquite-grilled steak at this
popular local gathering place.

✕ **Hill Diner.** 1315 Trinity Dr.;
505-662-9745 $$
Down-home food in a down-home atmos-
phere. Great chicken-fried steak and home-
made banana cream pie.

Los Ojos
map page 280, A-3

☎ **Casa de Martinez.** US 84; 505-588-7858 **$$**
Restored 1869 Spanish adobe two-story farmhouse is now a bed-and-breakfast. Non-smoking. Near the Rio Chama.

Madrid
map page 280, B-3

✕ **Mine Shaft Tavern.** NM 14; 505-473-0743 **$$**
Steaks and burgers served alongside beers and margaritas in a wood-floored tavern.

Mescalero
map page 280, D-3

☎ **Inn of the Mountain Gods.** 505-257-5141 or 800-545-9011 **$$-$$$**
The options are endless at this Mescalero Apache-owned luxury resort alongside Mescalero Lake high in the Sacramento Mountains. You can play golf, tennis, hike and fish, and for 24 hours a day, try your luck at Casino Apache.

Mountainair
map page 280, C-3

☎ **Dripping Springs Guest Ranch and Spa.** 17 miles west of town on US 60; 505-423-3214 **$$-$$$**

Be a City Slicker with bunkhouse accommodations or a pampered guest at this working cattle ranch that offers gourmet cuisine.

✕ **Shaffer Hotel Dining Room.** Main St.; 505-847-2888
Burgers, New Mexican food and homemade desserts in a fun Pueblo Deco setting.

Ojo Caliente
map page 280, A-3

☎ **Ojo Caliente Mineral Springs.** 50 Los Banos Rd.; 505-583-2233 **$$$**
Choose from an early 20th century adobe hotel or cozy cottages at this casual, low-key spa resort.

Pecos
map page 280, B-3

☎ **Los Pinos Guest Ranch.** Cowles; 505-757-6213 **$$**
Summer-only log-cabin resort on the Pecos River that features horseback riding and hiking in adjacent national forest.

Portales
map page 280, C-5

✕ **Cattle Baron.** 1600 S. Ave. D; 505-356-5587 **$$**
Families are welcome at this come-as-you-are steakhouse where you can find some seafood selections. Full salad bar.

Raton
map page 280, A-4

⊞ **Budget Host Melody Lane Motel.**
136 Canyon; 505-445-3655 or
800-421-5210 $$
In-room steam baths and continental
breakfasts at this roadside lodging.

⊞ **Holiday Classic Motel.** 473 Clayton;
505-445-5555 or 800-255-8879 $$
Full-service motel with indoor heated pool,
game room with pool tables, dining room,
coffee shop and lounge.

⊞ **Vermejo Park Ranch.** 45 miles west of
town on NM 555; 505-445-3097 $$$
Exclusive hunting and fishing resort situat-
ed on 400,000 privately owned acres in
Sangre de Cristo Mountains.

✗ **Shang Hai.** 1156 S. Second;
505-445-2933 $
Who says there's no good Chinese food in
the desert? Come here.

Red River
map page 280, A-4

⊞ **Alpine Lodge.** 417 W. Main; 505-754-
2952 or 800-252-2333 $$
Ski to the lifts from this rustic motel situat-
ed on the Red River.

⊞ **The Lodge at Red River.** 400 E. Main;
505-754-6280 or 800-915-6343 $$
Modest full-service downtown hotel.

✗ **Brett's Homestead Steakhouse.**
W. Main; 505-754-6136 $$
Grain-fed beef or fresh rainbow trout
served in relaxed family setting.

✗ **Texas Red's Steakhouse.** Main St.;
505-754-2922 $$
The steaks are legendary at this Old West
steakhouse. Go ahead and throw your
peanut shells on the floor like everyone
else.

Roswell
map page 280, C-4

⊞ **El Rancho Palacio.** 2205 N. Main;
505-622-2721 or 800-528-1234 $$
Comfortable roadside motel near the New
Mexico Military Institute. Pool and hot tub
on the premises.

⊞ **Roswell Inn.** 1815 W. Main;
505-623-4920 or 800-323-0913 $$
Contemporary southwestern decor and col-
ors. Outdoor jacuzzi and pool.

✗ **Cattle Baron.** 1113 N. Main;
505-622-2465 $$
Extensive menu of American food, ranging
from hamburgers to steaks along with a
delightful salad bar.

✗ **Martin's Capitol Cafe.** 110 W. Fourth;
505-624-2111 $
Popular local downtown spot specializing
in homemade chile rellenos, tamales, and
platter-sized sopaipillas.

✗ **Nuthin' Fancy.** 2103 N. Main;
505-623-4098 $
The specialty is homecooking with daily
soups, cobbler and dinner specials. The
vegetables are always fresh and you can find
heart-healthy selections.

FOOD & LODGING

Roswell
continued

✕ **Pasta Café.** 4501 N. Main; 505-624-1111 $$

Traditional Italian entrees on the menu, along with steaks and seafood.

Ruidoso
map page 280, C-3

⌂ **Dan Dee Cabins.** 310 Main Rd.; 505-257-2165 or 800-345-4848 $$

Enjoy an evening fire in a fully equipped homey cabin nestled among tall pines near the Rio Ruidoso.

⌂ **Shadow Mountain Lodge.** 107 Main Rd.; 505-257-4886 $$-$$$

Fireplaces keep you warm in the winter and in the summer cool off on the veranda at this adults-only lodge where each room is equipped with a kitchenette. Outdoor hot tub and gazebo.

⌂ **Story Book Cabins.** 505-257-2115 or 888-257-2115 $$-$$$

Fully equipped cabins with rock fireplaces among the pines away from the bustle of town.

✕ **Cochera.** 1214 Mechem; 505-258-9008 $$

Mexican food is the specialty of the house in this spacious family restaurant, which also boasts 46-ounce margaritas.

It could be a long wait for a seat at the Hightower Cafe. (Paul Chesley)

✕ **La Lorraine.** 2523 Sudderth;
505-257-2954 **$$$**
Classic French cuisine, including veal and seafood in elegant setting. Patio dining during the summer.

San Antonio
map page 280, C-2/3

⊞ **Casa Blanca Guest House.**
505-835-3027 **$$**
Victorian farmhouse built in 1880 for Socorro's Territorial Sen. Eutimio Montoya. Only a few miles to the Bosque del Apache National Wildlife Refuge.

✕ **Owl Bar and Steakhouse.** Intersection of NM 1 and US 380; 505-835-9946 **$**
Green chile cheeseburgers are the specialty of this roadside landmark. Owls of all varieties adorn the walls.

Santa Fe
map page 280, B-3

⊞ **Bishop's Lodge Resort.** 3 miles north of town on Bishop's Lodge Rd.;
505- 983-6377 or 800-732-2240 **$$$**
This luxurious guest ranch was once Bishop Lamy's retreat. Today it offers tennis, horseback riding, swimming, children's programs.

⊞ **El Paradero.** 220 W. Manhattan Ave.;
505-988-1177 **$$-$$$**
One of Santa Fe's first and finest B&Bs. This 1820 adobe farmhouse offers 14 guest rooms with fireplaces and skylights, not to mention excellent breakfasts.

⊞ **Inn of the Anasazi.**
113 Washington Ave.; 505-988-3030 or 800-688-8100 **$$$**
This luxury downtown hotel is beautifully decorated with hand-crafted furniture, vigas and latillas. Health club, tennis, and pool privileges available.

⊞ **La Fonda.** 100 E. San Francisco St.;
505-982-5511 or 800-523-5002 **$$$**
A grand old hotel that can claim guests from Errol Flynn to JFK. Rooms are decorated with murals and furnishings painted by 40-year Las Fonda resident artist Ernest Martinez.

LA FONDA

⊞ **La Posada de Santa Fe.**
330 E. Palace Ave.; 505-986-0000 or 800 727-5276 **$$$**
The 119 rooms and casitas of this variously decorated (some Victorian, some Southwest) resort sprawl across six landscaped acres.

FOOD & LODGING

Santa Fe
continued

⊞ **Pueblo Bonito.** 138 Manhattan Ave.;
505- 984-8001 or 800-461-4599 $$$
Adobe arches and huge old trees shade the
grounds of this 19th-century adobe bed-
and-breakfast. Old Santa Fe-style decor is
accented with contemporary Santa Fe art-
work.

⊞ **Territorial Inn.** 215 Washington Ave.;
800-745-9910 $$$
A Philadelphia aristocrat built this Pueblo
Revival mansion around 1900. Today this
bed-and-breakfast features a lovely rose garden and a hot tub.

✕ **Anasazi Restaurant.** 113 Washington
Ave.; 505-988-3236 $$$
One of Santa Fe's premier dineries. Ancient
traditions and upscale creativity mingle in
the New Southwestern style.

✕ **Bobcat Bite.** Las Vegas Highway;
505-983-5319 $
Juicy burgers nearly too big to fit in your
mouth are the specialty of this tiny road-
side diner.

✕ **Coyote Cafe.** 132 W. Water;
505-983-1615 $$$
Southwestern cuisine reaches new heights
at this pricey, pretentious, and wonderfully
eccentric showplace. In summer, you can
enjoy an excellent margarita and more rea-
sonably priced fare at the roof-top cantina.

✕ **Dave's Not Here.** 1115 Hickox;
505-983-7060 $

No-frills American and New Mexican fare
in no-frills local cafe. Try the chocolate
cake.

✕ **French Pastry Shop in La Fonda.**
505-983-6697 $
Excellent coffees and chocolate croissants,
along with full breakfasts in a casual Euro-
pean-cafe-like atmosphere.

✕ **Harry's Roadhouse.** Old Las Vegas
Highway; 505-989-4629 $-$$
Comfort food meets new cuisine at this re-
cently renovated roadside restaurant.
Desserts are worth the anticipation.

✕ **India Palace.** 227 Don Gaspar;
505-986-5859 $$
Richly prepared southern Indian cuisine in
cozy dining room. Bottomless cups of chai
tea.

✕ **Kokoman Circus.** 301 Garfield;
505-983-7770 $-$$
Whether you need take-out food or party
platters or pastries, this gourmet deli and
package store will meet nearly any gastro-
nomic need.

✕ **La Casa Sena.** 125 E. Palace;
505-988-9232 $$$
An innovative approach to southwestern
fare can be found in what in the 1800s was
home to Jose Sena and his family. Lovely
outdoor patio and singing waiters in the
cantina.

✕ **La Choza.** 905 Alarid; 505-982-0909 $
Blue corn enchiladas are tops at this unpre-
tentious spot. Owned by the Carswells,
who also own the Shed.

✗ **Old Mexico Grill.** 2434 Cerrillos Rd.; 505-473-0338 $$-$$$
Favorites of Mexico are cooked on an open copper-roofed grill, in the best Mexican tradition. Mexican paella, fajitas, rellenos. Full bar.

✗ **Pranzo.** 540 Montezuma; 505-984-2645 $$-$$$
Northern Italian, pizza and daily grilled fish specials served by friendly wait staff in casual setting.

✗ **Santacafe.** 231 Washington; 505-984-1788 $$$
The continental menu changes seasonally in this upscale restaurant located in a 19th-century adobe home.

✗ **Saveur.** 204 Montezuma; 505-989-4200 $
Create your own sandwich or load up on baby greens and roasted eggplant at the salad bar at this gourmet deli.

✗ **The Shed.** 113 1/2 E. Palace; 505-982-9030 $-$$
A Santa Fe tradition, the red chile dishes always taste fresh. Try the corn chowder but be sure to save room for dessert. Full bar. Beautiful patio.

✗ **Shohko Cafe.** 321 Johnson; 505-983-7288 $$-$$$
Authentic Japanese cuisine, including a sushi bar, sashimi, tempura with vegetarian and seafood specials.

✗ **Tia Sophia's.** 210 W. San Francisco; 505-983-9880 $
Hearty breakfast burritos are hard to beat, as is the rest of the New Mexican fare here. Daily specials.

✗ **Zia Diner.** 326 S. Guadalupe; 505-988-7008 $-$$
Hearty choices, from pizza to meatloaf and mashed potatoes. Great homemade pie.

Silver City
map page 280, D-1/2

☗ **Bear Mountain Guest Ranch.** Bear Mountain Road; 505-538-2538 $$$
Birdwatching is the favorite activity at this newly renovated inn on the edge of the Gila National Forest.

☗ **Carter House.** 101 N. Cooper; 505-388-5485 $$
Walk to galleries and shops from this three-story 1906 mansion bed-and-breakfast in the town's historic district. Spacious front porch offers mountain view.

☗ **The Cottages.** 2037 Cottage San Rd.; 505-388-3000 or 800-938-3001 $$
Secluded cottages, each in its own private setting, all nestled in a virgin forest.

THE COTTAGES

Silver City
continued

✕ **The Red Barn.** 708 Silver Heights;
505-538-5666 $$
Friendly, family restaurant that boasts a
wonderful salad bar.

Socorro
map page 280, C-2/3

✕ **Val Verde Steak House.**
203 E. Manzanares; 505-835-3380 $$
This Spanish Mission Revival-style restaurant, once the main dining room of the Val
Verde Hotel, appears much as it did when
built in 1919.

Springer
map page 280, A-4

🛏 **Brown Hotel.** 505-483-2269 $$
Nineteenth-century boarding house still
has bathrooms down the hall, handmade
quilts on the beds, and a restaurant downstairs with in-house bakery.

Taos
map page 280, A-3

🛏 **Casa de las Chimeneas.** corner of
Los Pandos and Cordoba roads;
505-758-4777 or 877-758-4777 $$$
The eight charming rooms at this comfortably elegant B&B open onto bountiful
gardens with fountains and tall trees.

🛏 **El Pueblo Lodge.**
412 Paseo del Pueblo Norte;
505-758-8700 or 800-433-9612 $$-$$$
Walk to the Plaza from this comfortable
southwestern-style three-acre spread.

🛏 **The Historic Taos Inn.**
125 Paseo Pueblo del Norte;
505- 758-2233 or 800-862-7466 $$$
Most of the rooms in this downtown hotel
have fireplaces and there's local art on display. Although the inn opened in 1936,
parts of the building date from the 17th
century.

THE HISTORIC TAOS INN

🛏 **La Posada de Taos.** 309 Juanita Ln.;
505-758-8164 or 800-645-4803 $$$
Cozy bed-and-breakfast compound tucked
into quiet neighborhood; within walking
distance of the plaza.

✕ **Apple Tree.** 123 Bent St.; 505-758-1900
$$
Always bustling, this cozy, casual and wildly popular spot features delightfully seasoned American and vegetarian specialties,
along with fresh fish.

✕ **Bent Street Deli.** 120-M Bent St.; 505-758-5787 $

Enjoy a sandwich or a salad where service is friendly and swift. In summer months, the outside patio is great for people watching.

✕ **Doc Martin's.** 125 Paseo del Pueblo Norte in the Taos Inn; 505-758-1977 $$-$$$

Choose from innovative New Mexican fare or equally interesting fish and meat entrees in this casually chic restauarnt.

✕ **Eske's Brew Pub.** 106 Des Georges Ln.; 505-758-1517 $

Bratwursts or tabouleh are on the menu, but it's the daily changing beer selection that's worth an afternoon stop at Taos' first brew pub.

✕ **Joseph's Table.** 4167 Paseo del Pueblo Sur, Ranchos de Taos; 505-751-4512 $$

You walk through the kitchen to your table at this intimate restaurant where the innovative menu changes daily.

✕ **Lambert's.** 309 Paseo del Pueblo Sur; 505-758-1009 $$-$$$

Lamb and fresh seafood are featured in this austere setting where locals mix with visitors.

✕ **Orlando's New Mexican Cafe.** 114 Don Juan Valdez Ln.; 505- 751-1450 $

Locals line up at this festive, family-owned place that specializes in traditional New Mexican fare.

✕ **Taos Pizza Out Back.** 712 Paseo del Pueblo Norte; 505-758-3112 $

Gourmet pizzas made with organically grown flour, pastas, salads, and homemade soups. A fun spot with crayons on the tables.

Tinnie
map page 280, C-4

✕ **Tinnie's Silver Dollar.** US 70, 25 miles east of Ruidoso; 505-653-4425 $$$

Enjoy a steak in rustic elegance among the rolling hills of the Hondo Valley.

Truth or Consequences
map page 280, D-2

🛏 **Quality Inn Elephant Butte.** NM 195 in Elephant Butte; 505-744-5431 or 800-228-5151 $$

Remodeled full-service motel with views of Elephant Butte Lake; golfing, volleyball, tennis, pool

✕ **Hot Springs Bakery.** 313 Broadway; 505-894-5555 $

The homemade muffins are fabulous, but if you need more substantial fare, try an omelette at this cozy spot.

✕ **Los Arcos.** 1400 Date St.; 505-894-6200 $$

Dimly lighted informal steakhouse north of downtown.

✕ **Cuchillo Cafe.** Cuchillo (14 miles west of Truth or Consequences); 505-743-2591 $

Isolated roadside cafe en route to the Gila National Forest specializes in blue corn enchiladas and taquitos. Open Friday-Sunday only.

■ SKI AREAS

When it comes to skiing, New Mexico is unmatched in its combination of fine powder and cloudless skies. The state receives more sun during the winter than Florida! To help you take advantage of such conditions, ten downhill ski areas, two nordic centers, and countless miles of national forest terrain await. Following is a detailed list of the patroled areas. For up-to-date conditions on the slopes and nearby roads call the New Mexico Snophone. *505-984-0606*

Daily adult lift ticket prices:
$ = under $30 $$ = $30-35 $$$ = over $35

Alpine Skiing

Angel Fire Resort. P.O. Drawer B, Angel Fire, 87710; 800-633-7463 $$$
A full-service resort with comfortably wide slopes and panoramic views of the Moreno Valley. Families and beginners enjoy carpet-like, mostly intermediate slopes. There are 67 marked trails, the state's only high-speed detachable quad chairlifts, and four double chairs. Slopeside lodging is available.

Pajarito Mountain Ski Area. P.O. Box 155, Los Alamos, 87544; 505-662-5725 $$
This day area in the Jemez Mountains is privately owned by a non-profit, the Los Alamos Ski Club. To keep that status, the resort can't advertise its challenging mogul runs and smooth, wide open beginner and intermediate trails: 37 marked trails, one quad lift, a triple chair, three double chairs, and a surface lift.www.skipajarito.com.

Red River Ski Area. P.O. Box 900, Red River 87558; redriver@newmex.com; 505-754-2223 $$$
This friendly, full-service resort provides ski access to the town, runs for the expert, a ski-through "mining camp" for children, 58 marked trails, two triple chairlifts, four double chairs, and one surface lift. www. redriverskiarea.com.

Sandia Peak Ski Area. 10 Tramway Loop NE, Albuquerque, 87122; 505-242-9052 $$
Just across the mountains from Albuquerque (about 45 minutes away), this small day area caters to intermediate skiers and snow-boarders. It can also be reached by the Sandia Peak Tramway, which takes skiers to the area's summit. The area has 25 marked trails, four double chairlifts, one Pomalift, and one surface lift.

Sipapu. Route Box 29, Vadito, 87579; 505-587-2240 $
Rustic family-run ski resort tucked among two ridges in the Carson National Forest, 22 miles south of Taos. This small ski area offers short lift lines and unintimi-dating terrain. Twenty marked trails, one triple chairlift, and two surface lifts. Dormitory-style lodging and cabins. www.sipapunm.com.

Ski Apache. P.O. Box 220, Ruidoso, 88345; 505-336-4356 $$$

This sweeping day resort on the flanks of Sierra Blanca, about 16 miles northeast of Ruidoso, is owned and operated by the Mescalero Apache Tribe and boasts New Mexico's only gondola. Because of its proximity to Texas and Mexico, you'll hear many foreign accents here. The area has 55 marked trails, one four-passenger gondola, two quad chairlifts, five triple chairs, one double chair, two surface lifts.

Ski Cloudcroft. P.O. Box 1290, Cloudcroft, 88317; 505-682-2333 $

This small, village owned, day area caters to beginner and intermediate skiers. Its unintimidating atmosphere makes it a great place to learn to ski. Even innertubers have their own lift. There are 21 marked trails, one double chairlift and one surface lift.

Ski Santa Fe. 2209 Brothers Rd., Suite 220, Santa Fe, 87505; 505-982-4429 $$$

A day area that offers top-of-the-world views of the Jemez Mountains and the Santa Fe Basin, along with challenging tree skiing and confidence-building trail skiing. At 10,350 feet, its base elevation is the highest in the nation, promising excellent skiing conditions. About 16 miles east of Santa Fe, this area has 43 marked trails, one quad chairlift, one triple chair, two double chairs, and three surface lifts.

Ski Rio. P.O. Box 159, Costilla, 87524; 505-758-7707 or 800-227-5746 $$

Located 40 mi. (64 km) north of Taos. Recently reopened with the addition of snowmobiling, dogsled tours, sleigh rides, and nordic skiing. There are 64 marked trails, two triple chairlifts, one double chair, and three tows. Slopeside lodging. www.skirio.com.

Taos Ski Valley. P.O. Box 90, Taos Ski Valley, 87525; 505-776-2291 $$$

This full-service resort 19 miles northeast of Taos is New Mexico's contri-bution to world-class skiing. Conditions are consistently good, and Taos' ski school is repeatedly ranked the best in the country. The area has 72 marked trails, including a series of legendary chutes; four quad chairlifts, one triple chair, five double chairs, and one surface lift. Some lodging packages include ski school. www.skitaos.org.

Nordic Skiing

Enchanted Forest. P.O. Box 521, Red River, 87558; 505-754-2374

Skiers can kick and glide across 35 km of groomed trails that wind among tall pines and aspens and through sweeping meadows. On full-moon nights, tours are offered. Lessons and rentals; no lodging. About 3.5 miles west of Red River.

■ SPAS & HOT SPRINGS

Whole books have been dedicated to the naturally heated pockets of water that rise to the surface across New Mexico. These hot springs where temperatures can reach 130 degrees Fahrenheit are the result of a violent volcanic past. Most are located in isolated areas, often on public lands, and clothing is usually considered optional. The soothing waters are harnessed at licensed public spas in three areas: Jemez Springs, Ojo Caliente, and Truth or Consequences.

Jemez Springs

Jemez Springs Bath House. 602 Jemez Springs Plaza, NM 4; 505-829-3303
One gurgling fountain serves this quaintly refurbished 19th-century bath house on the banks of the Jemez River. Water is piped into private tubs deep enough to submerge a basketball player. Men and women are separated and bathing suits are optional. Also offered are massage, herbal wrap, fitness room and outdoor group hot tub area. Lodging is available in the village.

Ojo Caliente

Ojo Caliente Mineral Springs Spa Resort. P.O. Box 68, 87549; 505-583-2233
This turn-of-the-century spa may be the only place in the world where arsenic, iron, lithia, soda and sodium are found in the same place and each bubbles to the surface from its own spring. Men and women have separate bath houses where they can enjoy an arsenic soak and a wrap in wool blankets. Outside are soda and iron pools and an Olympic-size swimming pool. A variety of massages and skin treatments are offered. Overnight lodging is available.

Santa Fe

Ten Thousand Waves. Hyde Park Rd.; 505-982-9304
The pools here are not fed by natural springs, but the spa is wonderful anyway. It resembles a Japanese bath house, with private and public hot tubs interspersed among the pinon pines and junipers in the foothills outside of town. Massages and a variety of skin treatments are available. www.tenthousandwaves.com.

Truth or Consequences

Artesian Bath House. 312 Marr, 505-894-2684
Private tubs in private rooms in rustic 1930s bath house. Do-it-yourself wool blanket wrap. Massage available. Adjacent RV park or lodging in town.

Charles Motel and Bath House. 601 Broadway; 505-894-7154
Private tubs, men and women separated. Blanket wrap. Sauna, massage, and aerobics classes available. www.golbaldrum.net or sierranewmexico.

Hay-Yo-Kay Hot Springs. 300 Austin; 505-894-2228
Oldest bath house in town, built in the 1920s. Private tubs in private rooms. One equipped with a whirlpool. Also, massage and reflexology.

Indian Springs Hot Mineral Baths. 218 Austin; 505-894-2018
Water seeps up from a gravel bottom in this continually flowing pool encased in volcanic rock. Motel attached.

Marshall Hot Springs. 311 Marr; 505-894-9286
Gravel-bottomed tubs fed by natural flowing water.
www.marshallhotsprings.com.

Riverbend Hot Springs Hostel. 100 Austin; 505-894-6183
Connecting open-air tubs once used as fish tanks overlook the Rio Grande and Turtle Mountain beyond. Attached motel.

■ FESTIVALS & EVENTS

A small sample of what's available is listed below. For a more complete listing, contact the New Mexico Department of Tourism at 800-733-6396.

February

Chama: Chama Chile Classic. Citizen's cross-country ski race atop Cumbres Pass north of town. 505-756-2306

Grants: Mt. Taylor Winter Quadrathlon. Grueling 75-kilometer endurance race up the 11,000-foot-tall mountain and back to town. Contestants bike, run, ski and snowshoe. 800-748-2142

Angel Fire: World Shovel Race Championship. Contestants speed down a ski slope aboard a contraption built atop a snow shovel in this wacky, sometimes dangerous event. 505-377-6661

Red River: Mardi Gras in the Mountains. Red River Ski Area hosts a Mardi Gras celebration with bead throwing, daily parades, face painting and lots of parties. 505-754-2366

March

Deming: Rockhound Roundup. Field trips and shared stories of discoveries of favorite gemstones. Second weekend. Southwest New Mexico Fairgrounds. 505-546-0348

Las Cruces: Border Book Festival. Authors from Mexico and the Southwest gather. www.zianet.com/bbf; 505-524-1499

April

Alamogordo: Trinity Site Tour. Car caravan to the site of the world's first atomic bomb explosion on White Sands Missile Range. First Saturday of the month. 800-826-0294 or 505-437-6120.

Alamogordo: Rattlesnake Roundup. Scores of poisonous snakes are displayed. 505-434-0788

April *continued*

Albuquerque: Founder's Day/Fiestas de Albuquerque. A cultural and historical celebration commemorating the city's founding by Gov. Francisco Cuervo Valdes. 505-768-3483

Los Ojos: Tierra Wools Spring Harvest Festival. A community celebrates new lambs and new fleece. 505-588-7231

Taos: Taos Talking Picture Festival. Four days of film presentations, discussions and lectures. 505-758-3873

Winston: Winston Spring Fiesta. Barbecue, music and crafts in this nearly extinct community. 505-743-2701

May

Statewide: Cinco de Mayo celebrations.

Carlsbad: Mescal Roast. Traditional Mescalero Apache ceremonies including dances, craft demonstrations, blessings and mescal tasting. Third weekend. 505-887-5516

Clayton: Dinosaur Days. Booths, games and contests celebrating the region's wealth of dinosaur fossils. 505-374-9253

Farmington: Farmington Invitational Balloon Festival. Memorial Day weekend. Hot-air balloon events. 800-448-1240

Las Cruces: New Mexico Wine and Chile War Festival. Memorial Day weekend. Cookoffs and wine tastings. 505-646-4543

Santa Rosa: Santa Rosa Days. A parade, youth contests, food, entertainment and a softball tournament. 505-472-3763

Taos: Taos Art Festival. Two weeks of events celebrating the arts, from festivals to major openings. 800-732-8267

Truth or Consequences: Fiesta. Ralph Edwards' annual recognition of the town that took his radio show's name. Parades, craft booths, music, food and movie stars. 505-894-2946

Tularosa: Rose Festival. Celebrating the town's plethora of roses with a pancake breakfast, parade, arts and crafts booths. 505-585-9858

June

Aztec: Aztec Fiesta Days. Summer is welcomed with a weekend of parades, games, food, arts and crafts booths and a carnival on the first full weekend. 505-334-9551

Albuquerque: Festival Flamenco. Two weeks of flamenco including workshops, classes and concerts. 505-247-2729

Albuquerque: New Mexico Arts and Crafts Fair. Juried show. Works of 200 artists; music and food. 505-884-9043

Albuquerque: Summerfest. Every Saturday throughout summer a different nationality is celebrated on Civic Plaza. Food, entertainment, arts and crafts. 505-768-3483

Clovis: Clovis Music Festival. Concerts, car show, tours of Norman Petty Studio. 505-762-0515 or 505-763-3435.

Fort Sumner: Old Fort Days. A weekend of events including the Billy the Kid Tombstone Race and the ever-popular Cow Plop. Second weekend of the month. 505-355-7705

La Cienega: Spring Festival at El Rancho de las Golondrinas. The living history ranch holds an open house. Employees dressed in period costumes demonstrate traditional activities. First full weekend of the month. 505-471-2261

Roswell: Alien Parade. Aliens from all over the earth cather to participate. Saturday before Independence Day. 800-747-3737.

Socorro: Elfego Baca Shoot. Golfers tee off from atop Socorro Peak and drive for a hole in town. 505-835-1550.

July

Capitan: Smokey Bear Stampede. Rodeo, parade, western dances on Independence Day weekend. 505-354-2257

Chama: Chama Valley Music Festival. A different lineup entertains on every weekend of the month. 505-756-2836

Hobbs: Soaring Championship. Regional competition for ultralight aircraft. 505-392-6032.

La Cienega: Santa Fe: Santa Fe Wine Festival at El Rancho de las Golondrinas. Wine tastings, food, arts and crafts, music, entertainment. First full weekend of the month. 505-471-2261

Magdalena: Magdalena Old Timers' Reunion. Parade, food and lots of good

stories. Weekend after Independence Day. 505-854-2261

Santa Fe: Chamber Music Festival. Six weeks of concerts. 505-982-1890

Santa Fe: Santa Fe Opera. World-class productions, nightly through late August in open-air theater. 505-986-5900.

Santa Fe: Spanish Market. Artisan's woodwork, tinwork, sculpture, painting in prestigious fair on downtown Plaza. Last full weekend of the month. 505-983-4038.

August

Bernalillo: Fiesta de San Lorenzo. Parade honoring town's patron saint. Matachines dances, food, entertainment. Always on the 9th, 10th, and 11th of the month. 505-867-3311.

Carlsbad: Bat Flight Breakfast. Meet for breakfast and bat chat at Carlsbad Caverns. Second Thursday of the month. 505-785-2232

Deming: Great American Duck Race. Waddlers compete in spirited races across dryland course. Fourth weekend of the month. 888-345-1125

Farmington: Connie Mack World Series Baseball Tournament. National finals of amateur baseball teams. 800-448-1240

La Cienega: Summer Festival and Frontier Market at El Rancho de las Golondrinas. Trade goods by mountain men, Indians and traders from the Santa Fe Trail and Camino Real. 505- 471-2261.

Lincoln: Old Lincoln Days. Billy the Kid Pageant, parade, music, food and a Pony Express ride. First full weekend of the month. 505-653-4025

Santa Fe: Chamber Music Festival. Six weeks of concerts. 505-982-1890

Santa Fe: Indian Market. Largest showing of Native American artwork in the country. Traditional and contemporary arts represented. Third weekend of the month. 505-983-5220.

Santa Fe: Santa Fe Opera. World-class productions, nightly through late August in open-air theater. 505-986-5900.

September

Albuquerque: New Mexico State Fair. Two weeks of agricultural and livestock exhibits, competitions; food, midway, nightly rodeo. Starts the weekend after Labor Day. 505-265-1791.

Bernalillo: New Mexico Wine Festival. Wine tastings, ongoing entertainment, fine arts show. 505-867-3311.

Cleveland: Millfest at Cleveland Roller Mill. Folk music, historical exhibits, arts and crafts at working flour mill operation. Labor Day weekend. www.museum.net-firms.com. 505-387-2645.

Hatch: Hatch Chile Festival. Cookoffs, fiddlers' contest, chile products for sale. 505-267-5050.

Hillsboro: Hillsboro Apple Festival. Celebrating the fall harvest; food, booths and crafts. 505-895-5686

Red River: Enchanted Circle Bicycle Tour. Two-day tour takes advantage of fall colors. First weekend after Labor Day. 800-348-6444

Ruidoso Downs: All American Quarter Horse Futurity. World's richest quarter horse race. 505-378-4431

Santa Fe: Fiestas de Santa Fe. Longest running community celebration in the nation, honors the Spanish retaking of the city in 1692. Pet parade, arts and crafts fair, entertainment, burning of Zozobra. 505-988-7575

Taos: Taos Arts Festival. Two week festival showcasing town's artists. 800-732-8267

Taos: Old Taos Trade Fair. Demonstrations in traditional skills, dancing and performances at Martinez Hacienda. 505-758-0505

Velarde: Apple Festival. Celebration of the year's harvest. 505-852-2310

Wagon Mound: Bean Day. Celebrate Labor Day with a free barbecue meal and watch the parade pass twice through this tiny town. 505-666-2408

October

Albuquerque: Kodak Albuquerque International Balloon Fiesta. World's largest gathering of hot-air balloons. For 10 days, balloons take to the sky every morning in competitions. Food, music. First full weekend of the month. 888-422-7277

Las Cruces: Whole Enchilada Fiesta. Sample a piece of the world's largest enchilada, music, crafts booths. First weekend of the month. 505-524-6832

Portales: Peanut Valley Festival. Food, entertainment, crafts, and antiques. Celebrates the peanut harvest. 505-562-2631

La Cienega: Harvest Festival at El Rancho de las Golondrinas. Costumed villagers demonstrate the working farm's operation. Hand-pressed apple cider. 505-471-2261

Alamogordo: Trinity Site Tour. Car caravan to the site of the world's first atomic bomb explosion on White Sands Missile Range. First Saturday of the month. 800-826-0294 or 505-437-6120.

November

Socorro: Festival of the Cranes at Bosque del Apache National Wildlife Refuge. Goat roast, arts and crafts, birdwatching, entertainment. Third weekend. 505-835-0424

December

Statewide: Las Posadas. Re-enactment of Joseph and Mary's search for shelter in Bethlehem.

Gallup: Red Rock Balloon Rally. Hundreds of hot air balloons take to the sky. Food, entertainment. 505-722-6274

■ INDIAN EVENTS

The Indian Pueblo Cultural Center can provide information on Indian events through the state; 505-843-7270.

Pueblo and Indian Reservation Information

Indian Pueblo Cult. Ctr.	505-843-7270	Navajo Nation	520-871-6436
Acoma Pueblo	800-747-0181	Picuris Pueblo	505-587-2519
Cochiti Pueblo	505-465-2244	San Felipe Pueblo	505-867-3381
Isleta Pueblo	505-869-3111/6333	San Ildefonso Pueblo	505-455-2273
Jemez Pueblo	505-834-7359	San Juan Pueblo	505-852-4400
Jicarilla Apache Reserv.	505-759-3255	Sandia Pueblo	505-867-3317
Dulce Reservation	505-759-3242	Santa Clara Pueblo	505-753-7326
Laguna Pueblo	505-552-6651	Taos Pueblo	505-758-1028
Mescalero Apache Reserv.	505-671-4494	Zia Pueblo	505-867-3304
Nambe Pueblo	505-455-2036	Zuni Pueblo	505-782-4481

January

Most Pueblos: New Year's Day dances.

Most Pueblos: King's Day. Installation of new governors on Jan. 6. Animal dances follow, including buffalo, deer, eagle, elk.

San Ildefonso: Feast Day. Jan. 23. Dances: buffalo, deer and Comanche.

February

Santo Domingo and San Felipe pueblos: Candelaria Day dances.

March

Most Pueblos: Easter dances, including spring corn and basket dances.

Laguna Pueblo: St. Joseph Feast Day. March 19, harvest dance.

April

Albuquerque: Gathering of Nations Pow-wow. National dance competitions, arts and crafts, and Miss Indian World Contest. 505-836-2810

May

Cochiti and Taos pueblos: Santa Cruz Feast Day. May 3. Blessing of the fields and corn dance.

Gallup: Evening dances. Memorial Day through Labor Day. 505-722-2228.

San Felipe Pueblo: San Felipe Feast Day. May 1. Fiesta and spring corn dance.

Tesuque Pueblo: Blessing of the fields. May 29; corn dance.

June

Acoma, Jemez, San Felipe, Santa Ana pueblos: San Pedro Feast Day. June 29. A variety of dances and events.

Cochiti, San Juan, Taos pueblos: San Juan Feast Day. June 24; various dances.

Jemez Pueblo: Jemez Red Rocks Arts and Crafts Show. Native American crafts, food booths, traditional dances.

Sandia, Santa Clara, Taos pueblos: San Antonio Feast Day. June 13; corn dance.

July

Acoma, Jemez, Taos pueblos: Santiago Feast Day. July 25; corn dances.

Albuquerque: Native American Arts and Crafts Fair. Hundreds of arts and crafts on exhibit at Indian Pueblo Cultural Center.

Cochiti Pueblo: San Bonaventure Feast Day. July 14; dances, food.

Cochiti, San Felipe, Santo Domingo pueblos: St. James Feast Day. July 25.

Crownpoint: Eastern Navajo Fair. Pro-Indian rodeo, midway, parade, food.

Dulce: Little Beaver Roundup. Rodeo and powwow on Jicarilla Reservation; dances, food, crafts.

Laguna, Taos, Santa Ana pueblos: Feast Day. July 26; corn dances.

Mescalero: Apache girls' puberty ceremony. Powwow, rodeo.

Nambe Pueblo: Nambe Waterfall Ceremonial. Visiting tribes perform variety of dances.

Picuris Pueblo: Arts and Crafts Fair.

Eight Northern Pueblos Artist and Craftsman Show. Third weekend. 505-852-4265

Taos: Taos Pueblo Powwow. Dances, food, crafts booths. Second weekend.

Window Rock, AZ: Navajo Nation Fourth of July. Carnival, rodeo, arts and crafts, traditional Navajo song and dance.

August

Cochiti, Laguna, Picuris pueblos: San Lorenzo Feast Days.

Gallup: Inter-Tribal Indian Ceremonial. Fifty tribes from all over North America participate in rodeo, parade, arts and crafts, powwow. 505-863-3896

Jemez Pueblo: Santa Persingula Feast Day. Aug. 2; corn dance.

Laguna and Zia pueblos: Feast Day. Aug. 15; various dances.

Santa Clara: Feast Day. Aug. 12.

Santo Domingo Pueblo: Feast Day. Aug. 4; corn dance.

Zuni: Tribal Fair. Parade rodeo, midway.

September

Acoma Pueblo: San Estevan Feast Day. Sept. 2; harvest dance.

Dulce: Jicarilla Apache Gojiya Feast. Rodeo, races, powwow.

Farmington: Totah Festival. Native American juried fine arts and crafts. 800-448-1240

Laguna Pueblo: Festival of San Jose de los Lagunas. Harvest dances.

Taos Pueblo: San Geronimo Day Trade Fair. Dances, races, food.

Window Rock, AZ: Navajo Nation Fair. World's largest Indian fair, featuring rodeo, carnival, powwow, food, parade, barbecue, mud bog.

October

San Felipe Pueblo: Artist Craft Show.

Shiprock: Northern Navajo Nation Fair. Most traditional Navajo fair, features rodeo, carnival, traditional Navajo song and dances, powwow. 800-448-1240

November

Jemez Pueblo: San Diego Feast Day. Nov. 12; dances, food, arts and crafts booths.

December

Most pueblos: Christmas dances.
Zuni Pueblo: Shalako. Unique dance lasts throughout the night.

■ GLOSSARY

ACEQUIA: Irrigation ditch.

BULTO: Small wooden carved sculpture usually of a saint.

CARRETA: Rudimentary two-wheeled wooden cart hauled by oxen. They were the only vehicles used in New Mexico in the 1700s and early 1800s.

CHAMISA: Shrub with slender, flexible branches that display small yellow blooms in the fall. Also known as rabbitbrush.

FAROLITO: Small brown paper sacks in which votive candles are placed in sand. On Christmas Eve, *farolitos* line rooftops, doorways and sidewalks in celebration of Christmas.

FRIJOLES: Beans.

HORNO: Beehive-shaped outdoor oven used by rural Hispanics and Pueblo and Navajo Indians, mostly for baking bread.

KACHINA: Anthropomorphic spirit guide that manifests itself in dancers at Pueblo ceremonies. Also, small wooden figurines that resemble the costumed dancers.

KIVA: Circular or rectangular ceremonial chamber, usually subterranean, built apart from dwellings at pueblos. Off limits to visitors.

JACALES: Rudimentary buildings in which vertical poles were lashed close together and covered with mud plaster. Roofs were dirt supported by *vigas* and *latillas*.

LATILLAS: Small peeled poles used as ceiling beams, placed in between larger *vigas*. Sometimes they are arranged in herringbone patterns.

LLANO: Plains, as in Llano Estacado.

LUMINARIA: Small bonfire set ablaze on sidewalks in neighborhoods that display *farolitos* on Christmas Eve. Hands are warmed at small fires. In most parts of the state, *farolitos* are referred to as *luminarias*.

PETROGLYPH: Figure carved into rock wall by ancient Indians.

PICTOGRAPH: Figure painted on rock wall by ancient Indians.

PUEBLO: Community, village. Early Spanish explorers named the first Indians they encountered "Pueblo Indians" because their towns resembled Spanish villages.

RETABLO: Two-dimensional line painting of a saint or holy person on a flat board that is designed to hang on a wall.

REREDOS: Altar screen.

RISTRA: String of red chiles hanging from *vigas* outside homes.

SANTO: Image or statue of a holy person or saint, such as a *retablo* or *bulto*.

VIGAS: Exposed roof beams, usually made of pine, that jut from the sides of adobe buildings.

RECOMMENDED READING

Abbey, Edward. *The Brave Cowboy* and *Fire on the Mountain.* Albuquerque: University of New Mexico Press, 1956, 1962. Fiction. Both novels describe a stubborn man rooted to the state.

Anaya, Rudolfo. *Bless Me, Ultima* and *Heart of Aztlan.* Berkeley: Tonatiuh International, 1972, 1976. Mixes Hispanic folklore with fiction in two books about growing up Hispanic in New Mexico.

Bandelier, Adolf. *Delight Makers.* San Diego: Harcourt, Brace and Jovanovich, 1971. Re-creates Indian life along Bandelier National Monument's Frijoles Creek.

Bradford, Richard. *Red Sky at Morning.* Philadelphia: Lippincott, 1968. A coming-of-age story about a young boy who is shipped off to relatives in rural New Mexico when his father is called away to serve in World War II. Bunting, Bainbridge. *John Gaw Meem, Southwestern Architect.* Albuquerque: University of New Mexico Press, 1983. A look at the man behind some of the state's best examples of Spanish-Pueblo architecture.

Cheek, Larry. *Santa Fe.* Oakland, CA: Compass American Guides, 1995. Photo-illustrated travel guide to the city, this book covers history, culture, and architecture. Lots of good info on the local cuisine, too.

Chilton, Lance (et al.). *New Mexico, a New Guide to the Colorful State.* Albuquerque: University of New Mexico Press, 1984. An overall primer to the state, providing complete, up-to-date information including history, flora and fauna, architecture, and religion, organized around 18 tours.

Chronic, Halka. *Roadside Geology of New Mexico.* Missoula, Montana: Mountain Press Publishing Co., 1987. A good book to have handy when cruising the state's highways. It discusses the state's fascinating geology route-by-route.

Church, Peggy Pond. *The House at Otowi Bridge.* Albuquerque: University of New Mexico Press, 1959. Tells the story of Edith Warner, who lived alongside the Rio Grande, maintaining friendships with the San Ildefonso Indians and the scientists who were developing the world's first atomic bomb at nearby Los Alamos.

Dutton, Bertha. *American Indians of the Southwest.* Albuquerque: University of New Mexico Press, 1983. An exhaustive study of the region's Native Americans.

Hillerman, Tony. *Dance Hall of the Dead, People of Darkness, Dark Wind, Ghostway, Skinwalkers, Thief of Time,* and *Talking God.* New York: Harper & Row, 1973, 1980, 1982, 1984, 1986, 1988, 1989. Takes readers along on the fictitious crime-solving paths of Jim Chee and Joe Leaphorn, officers with the Navajo Tribal Police. His series of murder mysteries are a wonderful introduction to Navajo culture.

Horgan, Paul. *Great River: the Rio Grande in North American History.* New York: Holt, Rinehart & Winston, 1968. Deep, beautifully descriptive, and wonderful insight into the state as it matured from a primitive hunting ground to statehood.

RECOMMENDED READING

Lavender, David. *The Trail to Santa Fe.* Boston: Houghton Mifflin, 1958. A compact book that traces the birth and death of the Santa Fe Trail.

Lisle, Laurie. *Portrait of an Artist, a Biography of Georgia O'Keeffe.* New York: Washington Square Press, 1980. A well-researched biography.

Looney, Ralph. *Haunted Highways.* Albuquerque: University of New Mexico Press, 1979. Ghost towns revisited.

Nichols, John. *The Milagro Beanfield War, The Magic Journey,* and *Nirvana Blues.* New York: Holt, Rinehart & Winston, 1974, 1978, 1981. Taos resident and writer, Nichols, shares his love and reverence for New Mexico in this trilogy.

O'Keeffe Georgia. *Georgia O'Keeffe, a Studio Book.* New York: Viking Press, 1976. A full-color collection of O'Keeffe's work with accompanying text written by the artist.

Piper, Ti. *Fishing in New Mexico.* Albuquerque: University of New Mexico Press, 1989. Written for fishing fanatics. It details the state's stream and lake offerings, best bait, and best time to go.

Richter, Conrad. *Sea of Grass.* New York: Alfred Knopf, 1936. A slice of life on the eastern New Mexico plains at the turn of the 20th century

Roads of New Mexico. Fredericksburg, Texas: Shearer Publishing, 1990. Atlas with historical data, weather information, a list of movies filmed here, and incredible detail showing unnamed gravel roads, water tanks, and fence lines.

Roberts, Susan and Calvin. *New Mexico.* Albuquerque: University of New Mexico Press, 1988. A comprehensive and readable history.

Schaafsma, Polly. *Indian Rock Art of the Southwest.* Albuquerque: University of New Mexico Press, 1980. The definitive book on Indian petroglyphs and pictographs.

Simmons, Marc. *New Mexico, an Interpretive History* and *Albuquerque, a Narrative History.* Albuquerque: University of New Mexico Press, 1977, 1982. Lively and easy to read.

Spears, Beverley. *American Adobes.* Albuquerque: University of New Mexico Press, 1985. A Santa Fe architect documents New Mexico's rural indigenous architecture.

Utley, Robert. *Billy the Kid, a Short and Violent Life.* Lincoln, Nebraska: University of Nebraska Press, 1989. Among the more accurate texts on the subject.

Varney, Phillip. *New Mexico's Best Ghost Towns.* Flagstaff, Arizona: Northland Press, 1981.

Zimmerman, Nancy, and Kit Duane, eds. *American Southwest.* Oakland, California: Compass American Guides, 1995. A highly illustrated, informative guide to the American Southwest, with coverage of most of New Mexico.

I N D E X

COMPASS AMERICAN GUIDES

Critics, booksellers, and travelers all agree: you're lost without a Compass.

"This splendid series provides exactly the sort of historical and cultural detail about North American destinations that curious-minded travelers need."
—*Washington Post*

"This is a series that constantly stuns us; our whole past book reviewer experience says no guide with photos this good should have writing this good. But it does."
—*New York Daily News*

"Of the many guidebooks on the market, few are as visually stimulating, as thoroughly researched, or as lively written as the Compass American Guides series."
—*Chicago Tribune*

"Good to read ahead of time, then take along so you don't miss anything."
—*San Diego Magazine*

NEW FROM COMPASS:

Vermont
$19.95 ($27.95 Can)
0-679-00183-2

Southern New England
$19.95 ($29.95 Can)
0-679-00184-0

Georgia
$19.95 ($29.95 Can)
0-679-00245-6

Pennsylvania
$19.95 ($29.95 Can)
0-679-00182-4

Compass American Guides are available in general and travel bookstores, or may be ordered directly by calling (800) 733-3000. Please provide title and ISBN when ordering.

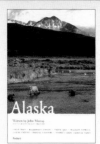

Alaska (2nd edition)
$19.95 ($27.95 Can)
0-679-00230-8

Arizona (5th edition)
$19.95 ($29.95 Can)
0-679-00432-7

Boston (2nd edition)
$19.95 ($27.95 Can)
0-679-00284-7

Chicago (2nd edition)
$18.95 ($26.50 Can)
1-878-86780-6

Coastal CA (2nd ed)
$21.00 ($32.00 Can)
0-679-00439-4

Colorado (5th edition)
$19.95 ($29.95 Can)
0-679-00435-1

Florida (1st edition)
$19.95 ($27.95 Can)
0-679-03392-0

Hawaii (4th edition)
$19.95 ($27.95 Can)
0-679-00226-X

Idaho (1st edition)
$18.95 ($26.50 Can)
1-878-86778-4

Las Vegas (6th edition)
$19.95 ($29.95 Can)
0-679-00370-3

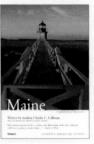

Maine (3rd edition)
$19.95 ($29.95 Can)
0-679-00436-X

Manhattan (3rd ed)
$19.95 ($29.95 Can)
0-679-00228-6

Minnesota (2nd ed)
$19.95 ($29.95 Can)
0-679-00437-8

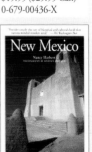

Montana (4th edition)
$19.95 ($29.95 Can)
0-679-00281-2

New Mexico (3rd ed)
$18.95 ($26.50 Can)
0-679-00031-3

New Orleans (3rd ed)
$18.95 ($26.50 Can)
0-679-03597-4

North Carolina (2nd ed)
$19.95 ($29.95 Can)
0-679-00508-0

Oregon (3rd edition)
$19.95 ($27.95 Can)
0-679-00033-X

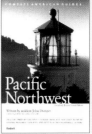
Pacific NW (2nd ed)
$19.95 ($27.95 Can)
0-679-00283-9

San Francisco (5th ed)
$19.95 ($29.95 Can)
0-679 -00229-4

Santa Fe (3rd edition)
$19.95 ($29.95 Can)
0-679-00286-3

South Carolina (3rd ed)
$19.95 ($29.95 Can)
0-679-00509-9

South Dakota (2nd ed)
$18.95 ($26.50 Can)
1-878-86747-4

Southwest (2nd ed)
$18.95 ($26.50 Can)
0-679-00035-6

Texas (2nd edition)
$18.95 ($26.50 Can)
1-878-86798-9

**Underwater Wonders of
the Nat'l Parks** $19.95
0-679-03386-6

Utah (4th edition)
$18.95 ($26.50 Can)
0-679-00030-5

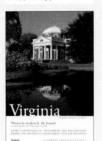
Virginia (3rd edition)
$19.95 ($29.95 Can)
0-679-00282-0

Washington (2nd ed)
$19.95 ($27.95 Can)
1-878-86799-7

Wine Country (3rd ed)
$21.00 ($32.00 Can)
0-679-00434-3

Wisconsin (2nd ed)
$18.95 ($26.50 Can)
1-878-86749-0

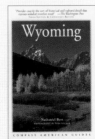
Wyoming (3rd edition)
$19.95 ($27.95 Can)
0-679-00034-8

■ ABOUT THE AUTHOR

Nancy Harbert has been a New Mexico resident since 1979, having lived in Santa Fe, Las Cruces, and Albuquerque, where she lives today. As a reporter for the *Albuquerque Journal,* she wrote extensively about the New Mexico's rural residents in towns from Reserve to Springer. She has covered the state legislature for United Press International. A free-lance writer for the past 15 years, she reports for *Time* magazine, contributes to *American Archaeology,* and writes about the outdoors for the *Albuquerque Journal.*

■ ABOUT THE PHOTOGRAPHERS

Michael Freeman is a noted photographer and writer who has traveled all over the globe for book and magazine publishers, both British and American. His work has appeared in the *Sunday Times* of London and *Smithsonian* magazine. Most recently, he did the photography for the large-picture format book *Adobe,* published by Houghton-Mifflin.

Paul Chesley has worked with the National Geographic Society since 1975 and has completed more than 35 projects throughout Asia, Europe, and North America. His photography also appears regularly in *Time, Newsweek, LIFE,* and *Fortune.* Books with his work include *24 Hours in Cyberspace, Mothers & Daughters, Golden Jubilee,* 13 *Day in the Life* books, and three other Compass guides: *Colorado, Minnesota,* and *Hawaii.*

Kerrick James is based in Mesa, Arizona, and specializes in landscapes of the Southwest and Mexico. He is a frequent contributor to *Hemispheres* and *National Geographic Traveler.* He is also the photographer for Compass American Guides' *San Francisco, Las Vegas,* and *The American Southwest,* and he is co-photographer for Compass *Nevada.*